Constructing Texts

Constructing Texts

Elements of a Theory
of Composition and Style

George L. Dillon

INDIANA UNIVERSITY PRESS

Bloomington

Manufactured in the United States of America

Library of Congress Cataloging in Publication Data

Dillon, Geoge L.   1944-
  Constructing texts.

Bibilography: p.
Includes index.
1.English language—Rhetoric—Study and teaching. 2.English
language—Style. 3.Discourse analysis. I Title.
PE1404.D5 808'.007   80-8377
ISBN 0-253-13113-8 AACR1
1 2 3 4 5 85 84 83 82 81

To the memory of my parents,
H. G. and E. N. Dillon

Contents

Acknowledgments

Several people have helped to shape and improve this book. My colleagues Frederick Kirchhoff and Jeanette Clausen have again been eager and shrewd readers. A special note must go to Avon Crismore, who thrashed through most of the main issues with me and added her experience as a teacher of writing and reading to my own. Her practical focus pulled me back many times from spinning webs of speculation. I think teachers should have some theoretical understanding of what they are doing, but theoreticians must struggle to develop points that make some difference in the classroom, writing clinic, and office. At times, it has seemed to me impossible to bridge the two domains in a way that would satisfy anyone, and often the attempt has been vexing, but I am grateful to Avon for having kept me mindful of the need to spell out practical implications.

My own students, too, have kept me in touch with the realities of freshman writing. The samples of student writing cited in this book are all drawn from papers and in-class writing submitted in 'ordinary' sections of freshman composition, which I taught at Indiana University–Purdue University at Ft. Wayne and at UCLA in 1979. They are reproduced without editing, though it should be noted that when set in print, they sometimes appear more illiterate than in the original, handwritten form.

Finally, I must acknowledge the great quantity of advice I have received concerning the handling of the third person pronoun singular and nonspecific: having tried various attacks on the problem, I finally settled on plural where possible, *he or she* sometimes, and otherwise *he* or *she* somewhat randomly. I have thus made a distinction while intending no difference, and if that practice occasionally disconcerts the reader (especially *she* meaning 'the writer' or 'the reader'), it might be a valuable experience for him, and, in a different way, for her.

Introduction

The title of this work, *Constructing Texts,* is calculatedly ambiguous, embracing the activities of reader and writer, comprehension and composition. It assumes the correctness of the view of reading that developed in literary criticism and psycholinguistics in the 1970s, namely that reading involves the construction (or reconstruction) of the text read. The meaning of the text is not on the page to be extracted by readers; rather, it is what results when they engage (e.g., scan, study, reread) texts for whatever purposes they may have and with whatever knowledge, values, and preoccupations they bring to it. Thus the written marks on the page more resemble a musical score than a computer program; they are marks cuing or prompting an enactment or realization by the reader rather than a code requiring deciphering. This view has already begun to prove fruitful both in literary criticism and in the study of reading. The prevailing understanding of composition, however, has not undergone a comparable or parallel reorientation: textbooks and teachers still speak in terms of getting the meaning down on the page, saying what one means, and so on. It seems that some of what we have learned, or at least hypothesized, about constructing texts from the reader's end ought to have implications for the way we think about and teach writing. This book will sketch some of the implications for composition of recent work in discourse grammar and processing.

The first principle to be drawn from the notion of text construction is that no stretch of writing absolutely determines what is constructed from it; it only shapes or guides the reader's construction of a meaning. Readers always go beyond what is explicitly stated, drawing inferences, enriching the text with pieces of personal knowledge, evaluating and interpreting it in terms of personal beliefs and values, interests and purposes. The trick for writers is to get these processes to go in the directions they intend, or at least ones not notably at variance with the ones they do intend.

A key notion in the control of this process is that of convention. Conventions are represented in the minds of readers as expectations about the kinds of things a writer may and should do in various types of discourses. They define the kind of experience to be shared, guiding the writer toward what needs to be said and emphasized. These conventions are complex, long in the learning, and subject to cultural variation and change. To learn them is to achieve entry into the community that employs them. Some people learn them, and wield them effortlessly, without being aware of having done so; others learn them when attention is drawn to them. The first kind of learning depends of course on substantial experience with texts employing the relevant conventions; nonreaders inevitably require more explicit instruction.

By saying that these conventions must be learned, I mean to narrow the term *convention* from its 'could be otherwise' sense to its 'not fully explicable' sense. There is a loosely shared understanding, for example, that the one who initiates a telephone call also terminates it. The callee may, of course, elect to do so, but in that case an explanation is required. Obviously this understanding is a convention in the first, broad sense ('could be otherwise'). It is relatively explicable in terms of human action and interaction ("the caller is the one who knows when his business is done"), and, indeed, the same sort of understanding applies to seeing people in their offices, so it is not a convention in the narrower sense, nor a convention special to telephone calls in any sense. The distinction is important pedagogically, for things that can be figured out from general principles of human communication do not need to be 'taught' in the same way that the less general and explicable things do. Conventions can be more or less explicable, of course: "See you later" is relatively more explicable as a parting than "Bye." What learners need to know is how far their commonsense intuitions about interactions and communication can be followed and trusted. This determination is particularly problematic in the case of college composition, because the conventionality extends beyond means to include the very ends of the discourse itself. It is not clear to many students what the purpose of their themes is, except to practice their 'writing,' which is to say that themes have no communicative purpose at all. Writers as divergent as Roger Sale and Ken Macrorie have noted the peculiar notion many freshmen have formed that an English paper is the ultimate in unnatural writing—the area where their normal intuitions and purposes, their sense of their voices, are least to be relied upon. Traditional pedagogy has tried to overcome this notion by explaining the conventions of writing and essays—i.e., to make the apparently inexplicable less so, substituting reason, or the appearance of reason, for arbitrary fiat. Some of the current interest in psycholinguistics and language processing springs from the hope that these disciplines will provide better explanations of why we value one way of saying something over another. It is very unlikely, however, that current language processing models will be able to provide explanations, or justifications, for all the conventions of essay prose. Chapter one will consider attempts to demonstrate that good writing is efficient, and the conclusion there is that it is essentially meaningless to talk about efficiency without a clearer understanding than we now have about what actually goes on in the course of reading. Later chapters explore aspects of that process (or family of processes).

Conventions define, or constitute, discourse types, and we can specify types and subtypes as narrowly as we need to in terms of the special conventions that pertain to them. Some conventions apply over many types—the paragraph indentation, for example—while others are special to subtypes such as memoranda, letters of recommendation, or expository essays. One of the points of greatest confusion in the handbooks and guidebooks of style is the range of application of the various conventions described, whether to all writing, or formal writing, or academic discourse, or college writing, or the expository essay, and so on. Often the broader terms are in fact meant more narrowly: the writer of the manual has a particular type of writing in mind, and sometimes different types at different points. For example, conventions governing variation in key terms ('elegant variation') differ markedly between learned discourse and expository essays. Any single dictum on this point is therefore misleading. Chapter two will try to specify the conventions governing the expository essay as traditionally understood. Essay writing is not a universally agreed-upon objective for freshman composition, however. It was attacked in the late 1960s for impersonality and irrelevance to the student's real needs and concerns, and it is again under attack for impracticality and irrelevance to the types of writing students will be asked to do in college (or in later life). It is not my intention to argue one position or another, though I am frankly suspicious of the tendency toward vocationalism and compartmentalism in adjunct courses and of taking academic discourse as an end rather than a means to the student's education. Rather, we can use the expository essay as a reference point for understanding and evaluating other kinds of writing courses.

The remaining chapters discuss the way the conventions of the essay function as patterns of order and expectation in constructing texts: if honored, they facilitate comprehension; if flouted, they account for much of the badness and obscurity found in composition classes and elsewhere. The model of meaning building and text construction invoked in these chapters is based on work done in the area of discourse grammar (or text grammar) by such linguists as

Dwight Bolinger, Wallace Chafe, Teun van Dijk, M. A. K. Halliday, and Susumo Kuno; on work done in discourse processing by Richard Anderson and associates, Gordon Bower, Herbert Clark and associates, Walter Kintsch, David Rumelhart, and Rand Spiro; and on the work of educators and theorists like E. D. Hirsch, Jr., James Kinneavy, James Moffett, and David Olson.

The terms *model* and *theory* as I am using them need some clarification, for readers approaching this book with expectations rooted in the sciences will not find the axiomatic and deductive articulation common in those fields, or even very many drawings with boxes and arrows. By model and theory I mean a coherent framework of ideas. There is much discussion of the adequacy of current models of discourse processing (some of which are scarcely explicit themselves) and suggestions for what more adequate models should look like, but I have not attempted to formalize these suggestions to any great degree. Thus this work is in a sense pretheoretical and prescientific, more devoted to describing and sorting out types of conventions and components of text construction. This study is concerned with questions of purpose and value, with human expression and response, as well as cognitive processing as it is currently conceived, and for these concerns, a more exploratory format seems appropriate. Also, it should be noted that in attempting to develop a theory, or coherent framework of ideas, of text construction, I am not attempting to arrive at the different and probably more ambitious theory of text production, in the sense of a theory of the writer and the process of invention. One might propose studying this question by examining the way writers size up a topic, by analysis of introspective accounts of the composing process, and by observation of classroom writing with or without special conditions or intervention along the lines sketched by Janet Emig and James Britton, but I have not tried to do that here.[1]

To say that the reader actively constructs texts is to say that the text is completed in the mind of the reader, and, since readers will differ in the actual constructions they make, there is no one fully determinate, publicly accessible text. This does not mean that it is impossible to investigate the interaction of readers and pieces of writing, but it does mean that we cannot assign a single, uniform effect to a given verbal structure. In particular, the reader's prior knowledge can increase or decrease her need for formal ordering and signals of order. A periodic construction, for example, will be more or less suspensive, depending on how predictable the final, delayed information is. In chapter three, the term *schemata* will be used to refer to prefabricated configurations of concepts that can be drawn upon in comprehending discourses, and such traditional topics as paragraph development, parallelism, punctuation, and connective words will be treated as clues to text construction—variable clues, it may be noted, to which individual writers may assign particular values.

Chapter four takes up another area of traditional handbook advice, that having to do with specificity, reference, and 'elegant' variation. Again the focus is on conventions regulating these choices and their function in actual texts. Granted that, as Richard Ohmann has recently argued,[2] specificity is not an absolute good or even the foundation of understanding, why is it so often necessary to urge greater specificity on apprentice writers? There is an implied theory in the handbooks and psycholinguistic treatments based on meeting the needs of the reader, which is that one struggles to establish coreference while avoiding boring repetition, but examination of actual texts suggests that there is more to the matter than this.

A similar treatment has been given to Topic/Comment and focusing structures, namely, that they facilitate intake of information by indicating how the incoming material fits into what has gone before, and again this account appears too simple to explain numerous uses of these structures in writing. Here, indeed, current language processing models need to be enriched to include the concepts of consciousness and perspective. This will be the work of chapter five.

Chapter six takes up the function of subordination as described in the handbooks—subordinate clauses contain less important or known information; they unclutter a string of loosely coordinated clauses—and develops the notions of perspective and topic progression introduced in chapter five to account for the stylistic intuitions found in the handbooks. Finally, chapter seven explores the role of word sense, literal and figurative, as it interacts with the construction of the whole. Words contribute their senses, but in turn are modified by their contexts, and hence exactness or choiceness of diction is not to be viewed as a hunt through the thesaurus or dictionary for the right word to plug in. There is thus a downward progression from larger to smaller elements of text construction, which reflects the general principle that parts of a text are interpreted in terms of their significance for the whole discourse and in relation to the inferred purposes and values of the writer. None of these topics can be understood as autonomous elements or aspects of style, as the standard handbook treatment suggests.

To test and exemplify many of the observations about essay style, I will cite from a corpus consisting of chunks of essays by the acclaimed masters of the essay: Samuel Johnson; Matthew Arnold;

Thomas Babington, Lord Macaulay (two chunks); Edith Hamilton; Rachel Carson; and, a personal favorite, George Miller.[3] Each chunk is about one thousand words long, giving a stretch of text long enough to study development of material and to get the flavor of the author, and each is relatively self-contained. All are examples of the expository essay as defined in chapter two. Most of them are dated in content to various degrees, which makes examination of their form easier. This corpus is rather unlike many that researchers in composition such as Francis Christensen, Kellogg Hunt, Richard Braddock, and others have employed.[4] The latter are usually weighted toward modern writers and articles published in *Harper's* and *The Atlantic Monthly*. But these passages are not intended to be a 'data base' from which rules of actual current usage are to be induced. Rather, they are an illustrative sample of what used to be considered the models of excellent, complex, literary prose, and concepts of text construction ought to apply to them as well as to simpler and more ephemeral, workaday writing. Indeed, one of the questions that will come up repeatedly is how the concept under discussion contributes to, and becomes modified by, the richness and complexity of these texts. Descriptions of function given by modern linguists are usually based on spoken and somewhat informal discourse (real or imagined), and there are numerous cases in which the function of a structure in these essays seems to break free of the function ascribed to it in speech and to develop secondary, specialized uses. The reader simply does not have the same limitations and needs as the listener. Also, treatments of given and new information seem based on face-to-face exchanges and begin to appear quite naïve when tested against texts written for 'the unknown reader.' The unsituated nature of essay writing allows the projection by the text of a Model (or Implied) Reader, and relations between real and Model readers can become quite complex. One recurrent theme of this work will be the need to supplement the purely cognitive concerns of discourse processing with a 'rhetorical' or interpersonal dimension.

The pedagogical applications of this constructivist position are limited by the nondeterministic, nonpredictive axiom. In particular, one must be very hesitant about moving from descriptions of how particular texts and structures shape particular experiences to prescriptive maxims of what the writer should or should not do. In practice, of course, such maxims are usually compensatory rather than absolute anyway—we tell one student to work toward greater syntactic complexity and another to strive for simplicity. Also, we cannot guarantee or predict that following certain formulae will

produce success or 'effectiveness.' But this is actually a valuable consequence; writing does not appear as a technology but as a challenge.
Many handbook accounts rest the point under discussion finally in
the judgment of the writer, and it is this judgment, suitably informed by an understanding of the complex interplay of language
and thought, that we should attempt to foster.

Constructing Texts

Handbooks Cited

Brooks, Cleanth, and Warren, Robert Penn. *Modern Rhetoric,* 3d ed. New York: Harcourt Brace Jovanovich, 1970.

Crews, Frederick. *The Random House Handbook,* 2d ed. New York: Random House, 1977.

Eastman, Richard M. *Style: Writing and Reading as the Discovery of Outlook,* 2d ed. New York: Oxford University Press, 1978.

Good, Donald W., and Minnick, Thomas L. *Handbook.* New York: Macmillan Publishing Company, 1979.

Hall, Donald. *Writing Well,* 3d ed. Boston: Little, Brown, 1979.

Hedges, John C., and Whitten, Mary E. *Harbrace College Handbook,* 8th ed. New York: Harcourt Brace Jovanovich, 1978.

Irmscher, William F. *The Holt Guide to English,* 2d ed. New York: Holt, Rinehart and Winston, 1976.

Leggett, Glenn A.; Mead, C. David; and Charvatt, William. *The Prentice-Hall Handbook for Writers,* 6th ed. Englewood Cliffs, N.J.: Prentice-Hall, 1974.

Stone, Wilfred, and Bell, J. G. *Prose Style: A Handbook for Writers,* 3d ed. New York: McGraw-Hill Book Company, 1977.

Strunk, William, and White, E. B. *The Elements of Style.* New York: Macmillan Company, 1959.

Winterowd, W. Ross. *The Contemporary Writer: A Practical Rhetoric.* New York: Harcourt Brace Jovanovich, 1975.

Wycoff, George S., and Shaw, Harry. *The Harper Handbook of College Composition,* 4th ed. New York: Harper and Row, Publishers, 1969.

CHAPTER ONE

Biology and Convention, Bad and Good Writing

The prestige of modern science and scientific method both attracts and bewilders humanists. Currently the field(s) of psycholinguistics and discourse processing exert a strong—and I believe sinister—appeal to teachers of composition. The general idea is that the more we know about how people read, the sounder will be our advice on how to write, and that psycholinguistics can tell us how people read. So we see English professors like E. D. Hirsch, Jr., and Joseph Williams seeking a scientific basis for rules of writing, and psycholinguists like Patricia Carpenter and Marcel Just referring to Strunk and White and Eastman.[1] But psycholinguistics currently can tell us very little about how people read real texts in real life. Psycholinguists have been just as muddled as the rest of us, and it seems that their chief contribution to thinking about reading and writing at present is their growing awareness of their principal mistakes and false starts. If science tells us anything at present, it is, "Watch out for your assumptions!" In this chapter, I will discuss four faulty assumptions that must be avoided if there is to be any fruitful contact between psycholinguistics and English composition, viz.

—that reading is like listening, and writing like speaking;
—that reading proceeds bottom-to-top;
—that each unit of discourse should be self-contained and self-explanatory;
—that reading basically extracts propositional content.

I will refer extensively to E. D. Hirsch's *The Philosophy of Composition* (hereafter cited as *Philosophy*) for several reasons: he clearly, consistently, and tenaciously embraces all four of these assumptions; he develops from them a coherent view of the teaching of 'writing'; and he makes his motives for resorting to science quite explicit, thus helping us to examine our own.

1. *Reading is like listening, and writing like speaking.*

It seems evident on the face of it that the processes involved in listening to speech and reading texts are quite different, yet the 'limitations of channel,' especially those pertaining to memory, adduced to explain facts of speech perception have been assumed to operate for reading as well. And this is but one of the ways that psycholinguistic accounts of reading have been modelled on those of listening. Speech perception, however, has many limitations to surmount that are absent in reading. It must make use of some sort of acoustic memory to retain what is heard until it is processed. It must segment the speech signal into recognizable words and larger phraseological units. It must operate at the pace set by the speaker, it cannot inspect stretches of speech before or after the small zone held in acoustic memory, and it must achieve fairly complete decoding quickly. In reading, however, the signal is presegmented into words printed in canonical recognition forms (removing word space drastically slows down reading), and punctuation supplies many signals of grammatical structure.[2] Reading is self-paced, it allows scanning ahead or checking back (regressions) in the text, and it leaves the depth and completeness of the decoding up to the reader. It is well known that when we read a passage that we feel is difficult, we slow down by increasing the number of eye fixations per line and their duration. Regressions may also increase. Duration of fixation also increases when the reader is required to take a true-false or multiple choice comprehension test and even more for a sentence completion test.[3]. These 'task-induced' increases in duration suggest that we read more quickly when reading for our own purposes and to satisfy ourselves than when we are preparing to satisfy someone else according to their definition of success. We also have the capacity to remember where information is displayed on the pages of the texts we read—a skill that seems based on a plan to look back to salient points should we desire to do so. Reading is much more private than listening, and its privacy would seem to open up a world of possible engagements with texts that listening does not allow.

Nonetheless, psycholinguists have moved freely between explanations based on channel limitation of speech perception and experiments with written sentences. Likewise, data developed from experiments based on heard phrases and sentences are held to reflect the difficulty of the *structure* of the phrase, which then is presumed to be a problem no matter whether the phrase is heard or read. E. D. Hirsch argues in this fashion several times, perhaps most extensively in his discussion of Ragnar Rommetveit's work on modification in noun phrases (*Philosophy*, pp. 115–18, 132). Although he is aware of what he is doing, which amounts to treating reading as listening, Hirsch justifies the equating by referring to the strong correlation of Fang's Ease of Listening formula and Flesch's Reading Ease (both of which are of questionable value or interest) and by one brief observation in a study by Thomas Sticht.[4] This contention is dubious and weakly argued, the more so because Hirsch's initial move to liberate writing from the 'record of speech' notion seemed to point to a much more fruitful consideration of writing on its own terms. Sticht, in fact, has begun studying ways that readers exploit the permanence of written texts and their spatial display of material when using them for problem solving or reflection—a kind of reading that he explicitly contrasts with treating print as a "second signaling system for speech."[5] Further, psycholinguists occasionally notice that their accounts of how particular structures work to ease the burdened listener do not explain the way those structures are used in some texts—this would seem to suggest that reading does not operate under the same constraints as listening, but Hirsch chooses to assume that it does. Moreover, given the general program of tailoring writing to reading, we end up assuming that writers are under the same constraints as speakers. This implication is not only wrong—it is seriously misleading as well.

There is another source of confusion in this area. Just because a study uses visually displayed texts, it does not follow that it studies reading. Many studies have used sentences displayed one word at a time (RSVP—Rapid Serial Visual Presentation) or one sentence at a time on a video screen, or by slide projector or tachistoscope. Short arrays of sentences of insipid content presented seriatim scarcely engage subjects in reading or allow them to use higher-order processing strategies (or even scanning forward and back). So in these experiments, the written 'stimuli' approximate speech, especially snatches of overheard speech, quite closely. It seems unlikely that we will learn very much about reading from studying such unnatural acts. Pysycholinguists have recently acknowledged this problem under the rubric 'ecological validity,' and experiments conducted today are generally more naturalistic in their setting and tasks.[6]

We must conclude that the assumption that the limitations of reading are the same as those of listening is unproven and unwarranted. To examine reading, we must study reading, though there are serious problems with much reading research, which we will take up below. Hirsch says that he highlights the linearity of prose (by which he means the degree to which the reader does not need to look back) by reading aloud from student papers and then testing comprehension (*Philosophy*, p. 162). Again, reading is reduced to the limitation of listening: how can one learn anything at all about reading this way, except perhaps how well the instructor reads?

Just as reading has been tied to listening, as if reading were listening with the mind's ear, so writing is sometimes viewed as a transcription (perhaps revised) of an already phonetically encoded, perhaps even subvocalized, stream of speech. Thus both reading and writing would be mediated by speech reception and production centers in the brain. We might represent this view as:

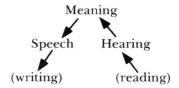

This sort of model of production seems to underlie pedagogy that stresses 'getting the voice down on the page,' whether by behavioristic conditioning or other techniques designed to reinforce the supposed linkages.[7] The well-recognized problem with this view is that students do not find it helpful and are sometimes led by it to writing an erratically edited record of conversational (or what Martin Joos calls consultative) talk.[8] Because the conventions of formal prose differ markedly from those governing talk, and most students have little experience talking like a book—indeed, they shun it—the written talk idea in fact misleads students into supposing they have a resource for writing essays which they do not. It may be that this sort of model more closely approximates the composition process of *skilled* writers, those who do know how to talk like a book or have developed a sense of a second 'voice,' which they manifest largely in writing. This would explain why so much advice to 'listen to the voice in your head' is given in vain to apprentice writers: it presupposes the skill it attempts to teach. In some treatments, it is clearly a metaphor for success, as when one speaks of 'finding (or creating) a voice on the page.' This model also appears in the traditional practice of insisting on 'good English' in classroom speech. Often misinterpreted as a matter of modelling and practicing 'standard' or 'correct' forms, it reaches far beyond these and really is something like a precondition of good essay writing if you hold this view of writing as well as reading.

I have argued that this model should not be presumed correct for reading and have listed some ways that reading may be conducted in ways partially or wholly independent of the speech reception mechanisms and their limitations. Some writers have suggested an alternative model with a verbalizing/comprehending stage, which links to speech/hearing on the one hand or reading/writing on the other:

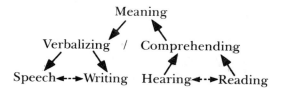

That is to say, at a certain level of abstractness, the expression system loses its specificity for mode. I suppose that most psycholinguists would endorse such a model as long as there are some interaction and parallel processing loops between the modes (indicated with dotted arrows) to allow reading and writing to make use of phonetic codings variably as need or desire dictates. So David LaBerge speculates, "It is conceivable that both the auditory and visual codes may make contact with comprehension processes, and that during reading they may make this contact in parallel, or one at a time, by fluctuating in some fashion between the two modalities."[9] Many studies indicate that there is some phonetic decoding done by readers, even skilled readers (or especially skilled readers) at certain times,[10] and writers may choose phrasing or words partly for their sounds. This matter will be taken up again in the next chapter; at present, we may note that this intermediate-stage model avoids claiming that reading is subject to the channel limitations of listening.

Although complex, such an enriched model does seem preferable to the remaining logical possibility, which is generally faulted for its lack of parsimony:

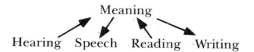

Here the various channels have nothing in common (i.e., make use of no common cognitive resources). If the intermediate-stage model has a defect, it is in the implication that reading and writing differ from hearing and speaking at some 'low' or at least identifiable 'level,' as if one were to 'verbalize' the matter and then route it either to the speech organs or the arm and fingers. What must be borne in mind is that the activity one is engaged in will affect decisions made fairly 'high up' in comprehension and verbalization as well as at the more physical levels. The nature of these differences will emerge more clearly in the next chapter when the differences between talking and writing essays are enumerated.

2. *Reading proceeds bottom-to-top.*

Bottom-to-top refers to the very widespread tendency to view reading as the recognition and retrieval of words, followed by the grouping of words into phrases, phrases into clauses, and clauses into larger units of discourse. This is what James Moffett calls the particle view of language.[11] To some degree, the tendency to think in these terms probably reflects our schooling and a kind of developmental progression that we have all undergone, with complex sentences coming after simple ones and paragraph sense coming after sentence sense. The particle or building blocks model seems to lead to the view that uncertainty at any level contributes to uncertainty of the whole. This view too is reflected in our educational system at all levels. In college, it underlies the assumption that remedial composition students must first master sentence construction, then paragraph construction, then the five-paragraph essay, and so on. It is reflected, too, in all but the most recent handbooks and guidebooks. In short, any discourse with misspelled and omitted words and obscurely indicated sentence boundaries is a discourse built on sand. What is really reflected here is the undeniable fact that a writer who makes a few spelling and punctuation errors in his opening paragraph is courting certain classification as an ignoramus whose writing is not worth the reader's close attention. The view that uncertainty at the foundation imperils the whole discourse seems to depend on the fallacious assumption that sentences are processed bottom-to-top, then the paragraph is constructed out of them, and so on. But sentences usually are not processed outside of a discourse except in psycholinguistic laboratories and English classrooms. Normally, the discourse context gives top-down guidance in the perception of sentences: it enables readers to project expectations about where the sentence is going and to look for words and phrases that refer to things under discussion and are likely to be coming next. This point is widely recognized today, though its consequences have not been fully digested.

One crippling limitation of a bottom-to-top view of processing is that things are treated as sentence-level phenomena that are essentially higher-order problems. These include ambiguous phrasing, punctuation, word order, and antecedents. We may speak of certain placements of words in sentences as making the sentences ambiguously parsable, but it does not follow from this structural property of sentences that uncertainty will arise in a reader's mind in the course of reading them. Uncertainty cannot properly be attributed to sentences (as it is by Hirsch, among others); to do so is simply a category error. Even the handbooks, or at least the more enlightened ones, do not make this mistake; rather, they warn writers about using certain constructions and forms if their use results in any uncertainty for the reader of their particular discourse. Uncertainty elimination, then, is a problem of editing, not sentence construction. Sentence punctuation itself is usually not so much a matter of sentence construction as of discourse connection: run-ons and comma splices are very often motivated by a desire to bind the second clause to the first. Similarly—and here the handbooks are not so enlightened—whether a passive sentence is warranted and whether an inversion would be effective are questions that can only be answered in terms of the discourse of which the sentence is a part. So too with problems of antecedents. It follows, then, that it is highly artificial to talk about clarity, or readability, or 'strength' of sentences as if these were properties of the sentences themselves. Obviously handbooks and textbooks are under pressure from publishers (not to mention copyright laws) to keep their citations short, but it seems advisable to abandon the handbook format entirely on most of these points in favor of intensive analysis and reanalysis of extended stretches of discourse, and this is the strategy we will follow in this book.

In general, we must be wary of enthusiasms for particular sentence types, whether they be Francis Christensen's fondness for the cumulative sentence or Joseph Williams's advocacy of an actor-action clausal style, where subjects are agents and actions/events are conveyed by verbs rather than by abstract deverbal nouns.[12] To be sure, Christensen does not base his advocacy of the cumulative sentence on ease of processing—though that can readily be done—and Williams's advice is directed primarily at the avoidance of the highly nominal embeddings characteristic of the stuffy bureaucratic style. Nonetheless, both of these proposals claim intrinsic values for their respective formulas and assert that students should be trained to use them first. Also, both assume that sentences are processed autonomously—i.e., that we build up our representation of the sentence meaning out of the clues given to us by the sentence (and then presumably plug that sentence meaning into the larger, cumulative representation of meaning)—and this is the bottom-to-top view.

It is usually possible to build a motivating context around an apparently convoluted sentence. Williams offers the first of the following two sentences as less difficult to process than the second:

The scientists analyzed what caused the genes to mutate.
The causes of the mutation of the genes received analysis from the
  scientists.

But put the second sentence at the end of this paragraph:

> From the very outset of industrial-scale production of penicillin-
> type antibiotics, a tendency of certain strains to lose potency and
> develop odd characteristics was a problem of quality control. At first,
> this 'running out' was thought to be the result of contamination, but
> it was later determined that the bad strains were in fact genuine ge-
> netic variants. It was not until 1970, however, that the causes of the
> mutation of the genes received analysis from the scientists.

One difficulty of the second version of the sentence is the long,
complex Subject (*the causes of the mutation of the genes*), which is
marked as being already in mind with the definite article. It is not
hard to understand it if we establish a context that does allow it to be
treated as 'in mind.' (We will go into these processes in more detail in
chapter four.) Reading this second sentence out of context requires
us to reconstruct such a motivating context, and that takes a little
more doing than for the first version of the sentence (there are always scientists around and they are always analyzing causes of
things).

Sometimes, however, a sentence form can be so at odds with its
content that it is hard to imagine a motivating context. This appears
to be the case with certain snippets that Williams cites from a USDA
report of an investigation of grain shipment fraud, as well as examples cited by Walker Gibson from the 1964 Surgeon General's Report and a college catalogue, by Roger Shuy and Don Larkin from
insurance policy prose, and various passages revised by Richard
Lanham.[13] Each of these snippets proves much more readable when
its complex deverbal nominals are written out as finite clauses. It
seems beyond doubt that these writers have diagnosed a tic of bureaucratic style. The nominal style is obfuscatory in all of these
passages for much the same reason: they all deal with actions and
responses on the part of individuals and institutions, and the most
direct format for dealing with past and contingent actions is the
finite clause ("if you do this, we will do that; we tried to do this, but
they prevented us").

Similarly, there may be structures that are more suitable to the
description of an essentially static situation or scene. The vast bulk of
Francis Christensen's examples of his heavily absolute, cumulative
sentence are from passages of description (or a descriptive portion
of a narrative). The sentences work by adding details to the sketch

that appears first in the sentence and seem essentially pictorial rather than linear. So the naturalness or appropriateness of a particular sentence form may depend in part on the kind of material and the way we are putting it together. I will pursue this matter further in chapter three.

Bottom-to-top thinking leads to misapplications of the notion of perceptual closure. If we assume that we assemble the text in phrasal, then clausal units, we value syntax that maximizes this local closure. But this also assumes that phrases and clauses are 'good' forms and that the larger meaning is a high-order good-form configuration of smaller closed forms. But consider the following well-known drawing:

In terms of local closure, this ought to be perceived as some sort of chalice or heavy leg of furniture. When I saw it in Peter Elbow's book *Writing Without Teachers,* however, I immediately saw it as two partial visages in face-to-face conversation. This illustrates 'set,' of course, which is another way of talking about top-down guidance. The point is that the closure involved in reading is an incrementing of the whole, not an assembling of autonomous parts. Common examples of erroneous closure that I and others have used come from the lines of Shakespeare's Sonnets 15 and 33:

> Full many a glorious morning have I seen
> Flatter the mountain tops with sovereign eye

> When I consider everything that grows
> Hold in perfection but a little moment

Here we appear to err by an autonomous closing off of the first clause. This impression is misleading, however, because there is no context in back of these lines to override or guide the syntactic closures. Syntax recedes as a basis of closure as context accumulates.

3. *Each unit of discourse should be self-contained and self-explanatory.*

The third assumption is really a consequence or application of the bottom-to-top view. Let us define a snippet as a sentence or sentences taken from a larger discourse. For a snippet to function well in a discourse, it must be easily integrable into it. This means, in practice, that it will not constitute a self-contained discourse in itself:

some of its features (word order, pronouns, connectives) will appear unmotivated. Often the act of rewriting a snippet to make it more readable (as a snippet) becomes an act of making it more self-explanatory as a discourse. This could even be called the Snippet Paradox: a readable snippet is a bad discourse chunk. The handbooks are, of course, implicated in this, but E. D. Hirsch also makes several of his examples more readable in this way. For instance, he takes the following passage from an article by J. R. Bormuth entitled "New Developments in Readability Research," published in *Elementary English* (now called *Language Arts*):

> A second question was whether or not the relationship between language variables and the difficulty of that language was linear. For example, is the difference in difficulty between two and three syllable words as great as the difficulty between seven and eight syllable words? If not, the simple correlation techniques used by early researchers yield misleading results. Bormuth (1966) found that many of the relationships showed varying degrees of curvature.

It would seem that Bormuth is involved in 'graph think' in a way that Hirsch's general readers are not and that he is indulging in the social scientists' vice of a loosely defined jargon term, *language variables*. Hirsch accordingly revises (I italicize the changes I will discuss):

> *Another unanswered* question *about readability formulas* was whether relationships such as those between reading-difficulty and word-length were constant relationships. For example, is the difference in difficulty between two and three syllable words the same as the difference in difficulty between seven and eight syllable words? If not, the simple averaging techniques of early researchers *have* yielded misguiding results. Bormuth (1966) found that the relationships between reading difficulty and the traits used in readability formulas were in fact inconstant relationships. (*Philosophy*, p. 84)

I do not question that this is a better snippet: it states its initial topic better and emphasizes its conclusion clearly. But consider the section as part of a larger stretch of text:

> *Shapes of the Relationship.* A second question was whether or not the relationship between language variables and the difficulty of that language was linear. For example, is the difference in difficulty between two and three syllable words as great as the difficulty between seven and eight syllable words? If not, the simple correlation techniques used by early researchers yield misleading results. Bormuth (1966) found that many of the relationships showed varying degrees of curvature. For example, adding another syllable to the one syllable word increases its difficulty far more than adding another syllable to

a seven syllable word. The same is true of many other features. Interestingly, it was the variables most frequently used in the old formulas that showed the greatest amounts of curvature. Hence, future readability formulas must include appropriate transformations of measurements taken of these features.[14]

In context, Bormuth can be accused neither of neglecting to signal his graph-think nor of leaving the reader unprepared for it (the previous section considers whether features influencing readability operate for good and poor reader alike), and the term *language variables* is fairly precisely defined in a way that includes word-length among others. The last sentence of Hirsch's snippet is not the conclusion of the paragraph, but a statement that immediately receives illustration. I mention three further points in passing: Hirsch substitutes *unanswered* for *second*—but Bormuth has an answer for this question, which he has previously outlined. Also, Hirsch spells out the question (about readability formulas), but this elaboration is surely unnecessary in the context of the article. Finally, he substitutes *have yielded* for Bormuth's generic *yield*—but Bormuth's point is that they will continue to yield misleading results if the error is not recognized. Virtually every point that Hirsch changes, then, is motivated in context. Hirsch's notion of readability seems to be in some difficulty, as it is susceptible of regress.

To press the paradox as hard as possible, if we rewrote discourses in Hirsch's fashion, making each sentence as self-subsistent as it could be, we would arrive at virtually unreadable discourses. Roger Shuy and Don Larkin identify just this attempt to create self-subsistent sentences as one of the primary sources of unreadability in life insurance policies. Consider their example from a revised (!) policy:

> Written notice and proof of claim must be furnished to the Home Office while the Insured is living and remains totally disabled. In event of default of payment of premiums, such notice and proof of claim must also be furnished within 12 months from the due date of the premium in default. Failure to furnish notice and proof as required above shall not of itself invalidate or diminish any claim hereunder if it is shown not to have been reasonably possible to have furnished such notice and proof and that such notice and proof were furnished as soon as was reasonably possible.[15]

Here is a revision that uses anaphoric devices and discourse connectives (italicized) to tie these sentences into a discourse:

> Written notice and proof of claim must be furnished to the Home Office while the Insured is living and remains totally disabled. If a

premium has not been paid, *this notification* must be made within the
12 months following the date *it* was due. Further, *even if this notification* is not made within *this 12 month period,* the claim will *still* be
valid provided that it can be shown that it was not reasonably possible
to have notified *the company* during *that period* and that *notification* was
made as soon as possible *thereafter.*

The connectives I have added highlight the essential point that these
are provisions governing the validity of claims made after a premium has not been paid. My revision avoids the appearance of virtual contradiction in the last sentence, which arises from the antecedent of *such notice and proof* being not simply *written notice and proof of
claim* but *such notice and proof as required above* (i.e., within twelve
months of the due date of the unpaid premium).

In general, then, authors have a right to their mode of expression,
both of terminology and even of syntax, provided that context prepares the reader for it. Snippets obscure this point. To guard against
the artificiality resulting from snippet citation, most of the passages
discussed in later chapters will be drawn from approximately 1000-
word stretches of texts, which are printed in full at the back. To be
fair to Hirsch, I should mention that in his discussion of suspensive
(periodic) syntax, he does call attention to the sanctioning effect of
context: completions may be delayed if they are relatively predictable in the context. This is a very important principle, which will be
developed in the third chapter; it is discouraging to see Hirsch make
so little application of it.

4. *Reading basically extracts propositional content.*

Much reading research is based on the notion that comprehension
is basically or essentially extraction of the propositional content (logical structure or truth conditions) of the passage read. Comprehension can thus be measured in terms of the numbers of propositions
expressed (and entailed) that subjects can recall from a text they
have read. Now it is true that we may read to extract content or
information, though this is only one of many purposes that readers
may have when they inspect a written text. Nonetheless, this purpose
is the one that experimenters focus on when they tell subjects that
they are in a memory experiment or a study of reading comprehension. But what is studied in the typical experimental situation is not
even normal information extraction, for the texts presented are
usually well below the reading level of the subjects and present material familiar to most of them, so the subjects are not actually seek-

ing information from the text, nor are they incrementing their knowledge as they read but determining which portions of what they know are in the text they are 'reading.' So the purpose of the subjects in reading the text is not really even to extract information but to score well on the tests that, in most cases, they know are coming.

This view of reading as content extraction is also reflected in the educational system, which produces students who can give at least a rough account of what is said but who cannot isolate or describe the tone. This view is deeply entrenched in most of the aptitude and achievement tests that are commonly cited as demonstrating how well students read and how adequately the schools are doing their job. Some educational testers, however, have voiced reservations about these standard procedures and interpretations, one of the more significant of which is that we should be testing what students *learn* from what they read, not how well they remember it. And, as a practical point, what readers learn from texts is heavily influenced by tone, both in terms of entry into the text (am I interested, put off, by the text?) and in terms of evaluation of the content presented (what does it mean?). Tone, like all matters of style, is generally squeezed out of the K–12 curriculum and left for 'college.' Certainly it had best not be left to the psycholinguists, who have yet to discover it as a factor in 'comprehension.'[16]

The view of reading as content-extraction has much in common with the bottom-to-top model of reading: here it is the propositional content that constitutes the bare bones or foundation of comprehension—if you don't get that, you're not to square one. Propositional content is the lowest common denominator of reading: it is what fables, arithmetic books, novels, essays, newspaper articles, and encyclopedias have in common, and the very process of abstracting and talking about reading as a skill seems to lead us in this direction. Similarly with writing—if it makes sense to abstract and generalize a skill called writing, then this skill must come down to the conveying of propositional content (thoughts).

Here we touch on one of the vulnerable points in E. D. Hirsch's treatment of relative readability. Hirsch seems to assume for the texts he considers a general intention of the writers to convey thoughts, even though he does try to build in a component of "rhetorical efficiency," which he defines as "success in affecting the implied reader in ways that transcend the mere conveying of information" (*Philosophy*, p. 75). This consideration effectively disappears, however, in his discussions of particular 'inefficient' passages that are drawn from a wide variety of discourse types (narrative, preface to public appeals, letters to the editor, a logic textbook, and Bormuth's technical article). But these passages have their rhetorical intentions too and aim as much at controlling the reader's attitude and point of view as conveying the thoughts. The particular rhetorical/semantic intentions of the passages vary greatly: about the only thing the passages do have in common is that they do convey some propositions, and so we are back at 'writing in general.'

It can certainly be argued that many of these passages as originally written are more efficient in accomplishing their ends than are Hirsch's rewrites. Consider, for example, the transitional paragraph cited by Hirsch from Cohen and Nagel's *An Introduction to Logic and Scientific Method:*

> In the previous chapters we have seen that the validity of a demonstration depends not on the truth of falsity of the premises, but upon their form or structure. We have therefore been compelled to recognize that the fundamental task of logic is the study of these objective relations between propositions which condition the inferences by which we pass from premises to conclusions. (*Philosophy*, p. 87)

The authors at this point are reviewing one of the strategies of formal logic that is most difficult for beginning students (because it is most unlike their prior understanding of logic). They use the *not A but B* presentation that Hirsch reverses in his revision (*B rather than A*), presumably because it is burdensomely suspensive. In context, however, it is not, because the positive term (B) has already been explained in previous chapters. In fact, the whole idea herein conveyed has already been explained (and so we have another snippet problem). Here is Hirsch's revision (again I italicize the changes to be discussed):

> In previous chapters we saw that valid logic depends on *the form of a demonstration rather than on the truth of its premises*. That compelled us to view the *main* task of logic as a study of the purely *formal* relations between propositions. For only these purely *formal* relations can determine the logical validity of our inferences from premises to conclusions. (*Philosophy*, p. 88)

Notice that Hirsch takes the material subordinated in the last *which* clause of the original and makes it his final main sentence. The effect is to argue the point anew and to shift the focus onto the reason rather than keeping it on the conclusion already arrived at. But Nagel and Cohen want to review and highlight this essential strategy of formal logic, not to convey it as new information or argue it again.

Hirsch's revisions of terminology also alter focus and even sense. By *fundamental,* Cohen and Nagel mean something more than *main:*

they mean that that's what logic *is.* Similarly, *truth or falsity* (which Hirsch revises to *truth*) is not just a logician's fussiness: some demonstrations appear to depend on the falsity of a premise, but this too is erroneous. Hirsch illustrates his fondness for using a tag word (*form/formal*) in his revision and does succeed in eliminating the tough phrase *objective relations* from the original but at the cost of reducing intelligibility greatly. He chooses to ignore that *these objective relations* refers to the logical connectives that combine propositions into premises of a demonstration. The validity of a demonstration is based on the form of its *premises,* not on its own form—the plural *their* was not a lapse on Cohen and Nagel's part. This alteration in sense, however, is merely a slip of Hirsch's—the point of greater concern is his overriding of the authors' focus on reviewing the difficult doctrine.

It is absolutely essential to Hirsch's approach that form and content are separable. The problematic term here is *content,* for in very many instances, a writer can scarcely be supposed to be wanting to convey the propositional content (or 'thought') of his text as information ("Four score and seven years ago . . ."). If we broadly construe *information* in these cases to include the view the author wishes us to take of the facts presented, then suddenly the opposition of form and content collapses, since this 'information' is precisely what is conveyed by the particular form selected. In many cases of bad student writing, the writer is conveying by the form chosen that he does not wish to do the assignment, come to grips with the issue, and so on—and this is why such writing makes the instructor angry.

The general point is that if we abstract 'conveying propositional content' as the common property of written discourses, we have woefully impoverished the notion of *discourse* as a human communicative act. Or, to put it another way, we have created an enormously artificial model of discourse and have obliterated from our view the elaborate sets of conventions governing particular discourse types and the ways these can be employed to signal diverse and complex intentions. This is most unfortunate, for it is just these conventions that give apprentice writers the most trouble. To cite one last revision from Hirsch's book that illustrates this point, let us consider his rewriting of the first two sentences from a letter to the editor. This time we will cite the revised version first:

Dear Sir:
Your article, published yesterday, demonstrated a strong similarity between the wording of our campaign literature and the wording of the campaign literature used by the winners of last year's election. Publication of your article now prompts us to explain why we used similar wording in our campaign. (*Philosophy,* p. 128)

Here is the original:

> Dear Sir:
> The article in yesterday's issue has prompted us to offer a clar-
> ification of our actions. We hope to eliminate any confusion which
> might have developed as a result of the strong similarity between our
> campaign literature and that used by the current administration in
> last year's election.

Hirsch again is illustrating the use of semantic tag words to keep the
essential point under discussion clearly in focus, and his revision
does relieve the reader of the need to identify their wording of their
campaign literature as the problematic 'action.' But Hirsch's revision
benefits from the snippet effect, in that it is not customary to summarize an article at the beginning of a letter to the editor written
immediately after the publication of the article. When one reads a
sentence like the first one in the actual letter, one often scans down
to the signature and with that clue brings the article to mind. The
letter as written also signals two things missing from Hirsch's rewrite: the use of *actions* signals that the group feels on the
defensive—called to account for its action—and the Washington
press secretary jargon (*clarification, eliminate any confusion which might
have developed*) attempts to strike the Olympian stance of 'it is all an
unfortunate misunderstanding.' So often in politics, conveying an
attitude is as important as or more important than revealing content.

The view of reading as extraction of propositional content is
matched by a corresponding one of writing as the encoding of propositional content into words and sentences. This view assumes that
thought and experience, at least as stored in memory, are essentially
languagelike, and that writing consists of finding the written forms
to express our thoughts. Perhaps Vygotsky's metaphor of thought as
'inner speech' has reinforced this view. Wallace Chafe argues, however, that there are good reasons not to assume that much knowledge and experience are coded in propositional form or categorized
and then stored. For one thing, we can choose different ways of
explaining the same point; verbalization involves breaking material
stored in large chunks into smaller ones that can be matched onto
the prototypes and patterns associated with language. Another consideration pointing away from exclusively propositional thought and
memory is that there are some things we think of that resist the
categorization involved in language:

> The perception of an object or event does involve individuation: the
> registering of a mental unit which is the idea of that object or event.

It does not, however, necessarily involve categorization of that idea (contrary to what seems to be implied in Pylyshyn, 1973, for example). Instead, we evidently retain enough knowledge about the peculiarities of a particular object to cause us potential trouble when we try to express that knowledge. People must be so constructed that the unique qualities of particulars are entered and retained to some degree in the mind. Otherwise codability would never be a problem.[17]

I think Chafe's cautions are well taken and point out a tendency of psycholinguists to assume that, because thought and memory can be represented in propositional form, material is stored and manipulated in this way in the mind. This view reduces verbalization to little more than the finding of proper words to put in proper places. But surely knowledge is interconnected and accessed on many planes and in various ways, which involve imagery and association as well as relations of entailment, set inclusion, and so on. The process of converting knowledge into words involves trimming and alteration and may lead to deflections, modifications, and enrichments of the original line of thought. This modification of thought by the act of expression is very interestingly described by Peter Elbow as one of his types of 'cooking' an idea.[18] The process of verbalizing is always the search for the best APPROXIMATION of one's thinking. Of course, the final selection of phrasing, as when we hesitate between *said they could go* and *permitted them to go,* can be described as a decision about how to lexicalize a particular propositional configuration, but we should not take that configuration as representing thought in the raw; Chafe's point is that such a configuration is thought *almost* converted into words: much preparatory shaping has already been done. Most of this shaping is less than fully conscious, but that does not make it any less a part of the process of verbalization. Paradoxically, most people are not aware of how they think, read, and write. But why should they be? For practical purposes, such awareness would even constitute an impediment or a distraction. But for our purposes, which require an account of how these things work, this lack of awareness is a major gap that must not be papered over with myths about how we think.[19]

It is evident that these four mistaken assumptions (speech/writing, bottom-to-top, snippets, propositional content) are closely related and often travel together. The result of holding all four of them is a theory of 'good writing,' nowhere more clearly sketched than in *The Philosophy of Composition:* good writing, or style, is viewed as a property of sentences themselves, based on human psychological mechanisms and ultimately on biology. Good writing is writing that allows

intake (extraction) of propositional content with the least effort on
the reader's part. The rules of good writing can then be viewed as
grounded in nature, and any anxiety that what the composition instructor teaches may be arbitrary and picayune, not to mention
classist and sexist, can be laid to rest. 'Writing' becomes a teachable
skill and English composition a technology.

Against this view we set as a first principle that written discourses
are governed by diverse and complex conventions, and that bad writing is a failure to meet a significant number of the reader's expectations. Like the other conventions that make up a culture, discourse
conventions may ultimately be based in some biological necessity
(say, drive reduction), but nobody, I suppose, would try to justify the
rules governing a formal dinner party as those guaranteeing the
most efficient intake of food given the relevant channel limitations.
There is an ideology that attempts to ground social conventions and
institutions, particularly existing ones, on biological realities: it is
called Social Darwinism, and its chief architect was Herbert Spenser,
the original proposer of channel limitations.

The conclusion we arrive at, therefore, is that the attempt to 'de-
duce' the rules of good writing from the channel limitations of
human processors is flawed not just in the procedures heretofore
followed but in its very conception. We must remedy more than the
procedures and assumptions outlined above: rather than obscure or
minimize the role of convention in written discourses, we must place
it at the center of our thinking. And once we understand these conventions and the role they play in reading and writing, we can teach
them, and teach them *as such,* not as the ways of thinking and writing
more naturally. In the view I will try to sustain in the chapters following, 'composition' is *not* a skill separate from personal, social, and
ethical implications, and it should not be taught as if it were.

As important as it is to stress the relative independence of many
print conventions from constraints on speech processing, we must
view them as complexly related. It is certainly necessary, for example, to integrate the material one is reading into one's larger sense of
what is going on in the discourse, and following various conventions
of formal writing such as those governing paragraph organization
and transition will facilitate this integration. Whether these conventions are the only or the most efficient ways of facilitating it,
however, is open to question and will be taken up in chapter three.
Similarly, it is plainly the case that human processors do project expectations, and writing that takes account of this and guides the
reader is better writing than that which does not. But in much writing, is there not often a game going on between writer and reader

that is a far cry from the earnest struggles to intake content depicted in the limitation model? The limitations of channel are not as great in writing as in speech, and are of a different nature, so that many speech-oriented strategies undergo a sea change, developing secondary functions and elaborations in writing that are wholly missed if we regard them as written speech.

Hirsch and the psycholinguists are not the only ones who have ignored the basis of writing rules in convention. Some handbook and guidebook writers seem to feel that the rules will be more palatable if they are presented as means of controlling the potentially lazy, inattentive, balky, or persnickety reader.[20] This is an old move, of course, and is based more on supposed limitations of attention, interest, and sympathy than of 'channel,' but it is no less disastrous for all that, and perhaps more so: the writer must believe in the reader's honest effort to catch the meaning in order to invest much of himself in the task of writing. Fred Crews very shrewdly diagnoses as a dread of rejection a writer's apparent overconfidence that he will be understood (Crews, pp. 44–45). An inattentive or overburdened Miss Fidditch is an all-too-convenient projection that no teacher should encourage.

In proposing to take *discourse* rather than *writing* as the central object of study, I am aiming at a concept much richer than 'stretch of written text or utterance': such stretches are only discourses if they are viewed as intentional communicative acts directed by one human toward others. I will use the term *discourse type* without implying the existence of a fixed, discretely partitioned set of types: a discourse type is constituted by a set of conventions governing expectations and interpretations, and the more detail we give to the descriptions of the conventions, the more numerous and narrowly defined the discourse types become. The task of the next chapter will be to give a narrow and complete account of the conventions of the expository essay, with a view toward how they may be learned and taught and how nonobservation of them produces bad texts.

One of the more damaging criticisms of Hirsch's whole project is that it does not come to grips with the more significant ways that writing goes bad—inefficiency is the least of the problems. It is not absolutely clear from the following passage that Hirsch means to equate uncertainties with badness, but that is certainly the tendency of his work: "Practical experience tells us that the main uncertainties of bad writing are small-scale, local uncertainties, persisting from word to word and sentence to sentence. These are the uncertainties that slow down the reader . . ." (p. 105). Now it is true that uncertainties of this nature do arise in student (and other) writing, and they are a nuisance. My criticism of snippets is not meant to imply that every local uncertainty finds a natural resolution in discourse context, or even any solution, for some student writers do not write very tightly structured discourses, and all writers occasionally botch things up. But many of the problems of student writing can best be understood in higher-order terms. We have not been able to see these problems in their proper perspective because we have not had a sufficiently large and rich model of discourse.

Just as Hirsch does not give us a full account of badness in writing, so he does not have an adequate theory of goodness. Neither, for that matter, will our notion of observation of conventions provide one. Nonobservation produces bad texts—but observation does not produce good ones. The terms *good* and *bad* have been the source of much confusion: not-bad writing is not necessarily good, for goodness in writing is more than the avoidance of faults. Surely everyone is aware of this, and prone to forget it. Let us provisionally define a good piece of writing as one that achieves for the reader a significant or interesting ordering of experience: the ordering may be partial and improvable, but it works. As William Irmscher suggests, this is an essentially esthetic judgment.[21] Similarly, Richard Lanham treats revision of prose as much in terms of enhancing its shapeliness and rhythm as promoting its efficiency in conveying meaning.[22] Though we will be concerned almost exclusively with badness in the next chapter, later ones will occasionally have some goodness in them. And we will try to remember the difference.

CHAPTER TWO

ᖰᖳᖰᖳᖰᖳᖰᖳᖰ

The Conventions of Text, Especially the Expository Essay

The guidebooks and handbooks used in freshman composition courses are as a rule studiedly vague about what skill they claim to impart. Many are content to say 'writing' or 'good style' or 'effective expression,' treating the expository essay as one among many kinds of writing. Some begin by focusing more narrowly on The Theme, but it is the rare one indeed that begins with a full and exact account of the special conventions and assumptions that govern what the student is expected to do in freshman composition.[1] It seems clear that this is another manifestation of the 'skill of writing' notion discussed in the previous chapter, and, as we would expect, E. D. Hirsch deplores the narrow focus of "the handbooks" on "the college essay" (*Philosophy*, p. 167). Reading the sections in the handbooks on the role of the teacher, the audience for the essay, and the relation of essay writing to other kinds of writing, one begins to suspect a real discomfort and uncertainty and perhaps even a desire to conceal from the student (and instructor?) the realities of the situation and the strangeness of the whole undertaking. But from obscurity and uncertainty on these points many errors spring; when we understand the discourse situation and the conventions that constitute it, we gain a new perspective on what needs to be taught.

The notion that education in literacy consists largely of learning a special set of conventions of expression—a *code*—has been argued by Basil Bernstein and applied to the learning of academic writing by David R. Olson.[2] Paralleling Bernstein's contrast of restricted and elaborated codes, Olson describes two extreme views and codes of discourse, which he calls Utterance and Text. He traces the evolution of Western culture as a gradual shift from the culture of Utterance to that of Text and suggests that this evolution is recapitulated in the schooling in reading that children in our culture undergo. These categories are at least as useful in thinking about the schooling in composition as the schooling in reading and, somewhat modified and amplified, give us a way of describing where the student in a freshman composition class is coming from and going toward.

To state the opposition of Utterance and Text in the starkest and most schematic terms, we can tabulate the following attributes that cluster around each pole:

Utterance	Text
1. Utterance thinks of discourse as face-to-face conversation.	1. Text thinks of discourse as face-to-page reading/writing of essays.
2. Speakers are to reproduce accepted wisdom, attitudes, and values; cogency and assent are based on conformity to received opinion and common sense; speakers and hearers enact solidarity with their social group.	2. Writers are to produce novel, even counterintuitive, facts and viewpoints; cogency and assent are based on logical consistency and evidence; writer and reader enact membership in an imagined community of inquiring minds.
3. Utterance is spontaneous.	3. Text is planned.
4. Word senses are based on conversational exchanges and shared experience and are used without redefinition.	4. Word senses are based on formal written usage as recorded in dictionaries and are subjected to scrutiny and stipulative clarification.
5. Bridging premises are based in common assumptions and stereotypes and may be largely implicit.	5. Bridging premises and logical structure are to be made explicit.
6. Speakers are expected to speak understandably.	6. Writers are to write correctly according to the rules and canons of usage given in the handbooks.
7. Utterance aims at the sharing of experience; hearer interprets speech in relation to the speaker.	7. Text aims at proving the correctness of its models of the world; reader interprets Text in terms of what is on the page.

Accepting for the moment these terms without refinement or illustration, we can see that Text embodies many of the traditional values of the liberal arts education, offering as it does the means of emancipation from the confines of received opinion and the limiting (though often sustaining) solidarity with family and peer groups. If we think of education as inducing or enabling students to move from Utterance to Text, we can see why composition teachers have traditionally viewed their work not merely as the imparting of a prerequisite for a liberal education but as the very heart of a liberal education itself. In taking the expository essay as the discourse type that most fully illustrates the conventions of Text, I am redefining it slightly to exclude the purely reportive or textbook notion of exposition, as if everyone were in training to write for the *New York Times* or the *Encyclopaedia Britannica*. This sort of writing (expository prose, if you wish) does not generally even attempt to meet the criterion of novelty. Textbook writers may content themselves largely with presenting received opinion and standard approaches, or they may attempt a new interpretation of their subject—the latter, by meeting the criterion of novelty, would qualify as a kind of extended expository essay. George Miller's *Psychology: The Science of Mental Life* illustrates this latter type of textbook-essay. The expository essay as here understood has a rhetorical purpose beyond 'conveying information': it attempts to convince the reader that its model of experience or the world is valid.[3] It does not seek to engage the reader in a course of action, however, but rather in a process of reflection, and its means of convincing are accordingly limited to the use of evidence and logical proof and the posture of open-mindedness. These methods are also associated with the liberally educated person, who is meditative, reflective, clear-headed, unbiased, always seeking to understand experience freshly and to find things of interest in the world.

Type distinctions of this sort can be carried a bit further. James Kinneavy divides the general 'expository' area into scientific, informative, and exploratory discourses, the last most directly harking back to Montaigne's and others' use of the term *essay* as a trial or attempt (Montaigne is also Olson's point of departure). A typical exploratory discourse involves the identifying and discussing of a problem (Kinneavy suggests Freud's writings as an example). We could probably further subdivide—the point to be stressed here, however, is that exposition is not merely laying out information on the page. Most of the model essays contained in commonly used 'readers' are in fact heavily evaluative in aim even when 'objective' in presentation. For some reason obscure to me, this fact is not pointed out to the students. At least one commonly used reader even sets up a section of 'evaluative' writing, as if this were a type of development like comparison and contrast, exemplification, cause and effect, and so on.

We proceed now to a point-by-point consideration of these oppositions, using them to explain many of the limitations of student writing (viewed as Text) and some of the difficulties students experience
in leaving them behind.

1. *Utterance thinks of discourse as face-to-face conversation; Text thinks of it
   as face-to-page writing/reading of essays.*

This first opposition has been central in most discussions of the
difference between spoken and written language. E. D. Hirsch describes written language as 'context free' (another common term is
'unsituated'), contrasting it to spoken language. Conversation is
situated in concrete terms: speaker and hearer are visible to each
other; speaker can monitor the impact of what he says on hearer,
and hearer can interrupt or register a vast array of other responses.
Speaker can surround his words with gestures of hand, face, and
body, and place infinite shadings of emphasis by these means as well
as intonation. Speaker and hearer share the same space and can
refer to a whole set of perceptually common experiences. In addition, they usually have personal knowledge of each other and can
take for granted many views and values they know or have reason to
expect the other to hold.

Compared to face-to-face conversation, the various types of written discourse are unsituated to various degrees. By convention, the
expository essay is unsituated to an extreme degree: the reader and
writer do not know each other, communicate only via the written
page, and are not members of any special group. This is in marked
contrast to the learned article, which assumes vast amounts of shared
information as well as common interests and outlook. Many have
observed that the less you know about whom you are communicating
with, the harder it is to communicate with them, and, of course, most
handbooks exhort the writer to imagine the audience, which is something he has never had to do before at this degree of abstractness.
This imagining has principally to do with the group of readers one
would like to have, the body of knowledge they may be assumed to
possess, how they will respond to one's words, and the interest they
may be induced to take in the essay. Many composition teachers have
found that if they specify the audience for students ("imagine your
audience is a Chinese visitor/your next-door neighbor/someone who
has read the book but not attended class") the writing brightens
considerably. Exercises of this nature would seem to be useful transitions on the road toward the abstracted audience of the expository

essay. If one aims at developing self-consciousness on this point, a possible topic would be 'Describe rearranging your bedroom to a friend who has been there and one who hasn't.'

Note that all these stipulations of audience specify both knowledge *and interest*. Without specification, students naturally and realistically take the instructor as the audience, though many are doubtful that they can assume as much interest in what they might have to say on the instructor's part as they can from a next-door neighbor. Signs of interest from the instructor, both personal and in comments on the papers, will strengthen the confidence of many students on this point. I think Peter Elbow's concern that teachers cannot be as interested in a student's essay as a real reader would be, or interested in the same way, is somewhat exaggerated.[4] Frank acknowledgments of lack of interest also seem in order. Students often do not know how to be interesting, doubt they can be, and need to be told when they have succeeded and when they have failed. Instructors who pretend they are not the audience but an over-the-shoulder 'facilitator of expression' deprive the students of anything to aim at. Writing for classmates is helpful here, both because students are somewhat more confident of being able to interest their classmates and because possible idiosyncrasies of the instructor are subjected to discussion. Further, sometimes the instructor can be too sympathetic, patient, and ingenious in reconstructing the student's meaning. But fundamentally the instructor remains the audience of record and may feel it necessary to intervene in a class discussion to compensate for limitations in the perspective of peers. One of the rare handbooks that address these realities frankly and gracefully is Crews's.[5] Other handbooks generally sidestep this question in favor of giving advice on how to imagine the 'universal audience.' Some advise the writer to project himself as the audience (Winterowd, p. 148; Irmscher, p. 13; more diffidently, Eastman, p. 52). The most extraordinary discussion of this point that I have seen is Brooks and Warren's, which begins by suggesting that the student may if necessary imagine that the ideal audience is "some particular person—the most intelligent and discriminating person that he knows."[6] Or, they suggest, the writer may attend to his own sense of fitness. Their line of thought now takes a direction that requires citation:

> The writer himself becomes the audience at which he aims. The question which he asks is not, "Have I made this convincing to Tom, or to Dick, or to Harry?" but rather, "Have I made this convincing to myself?"; or, to put the matter more succinctly still, "Have I made this convincing?"

In writing for this "ideal" reader, then, the author can transpose all problems of tone into the problem of handling the material itself. The problem of tone alters only when the writing is addressed specifically to Tom or to Dick—not to just any reader—and in proportion as Tom or Dick differs from the ideal reader.

As I understand this, the work becomes absolutely free to be, in the writer's mind, 'the essay in itself.' This is the turn of mind one associates with the New Criticism. It is interesting to note that the passage Brooks and Warren cite as absolute in tone is from T. E. Lawrence's *The Seven Pillars of Wisdom*—a personal journal or apologia. I do not want to say that this account is completely wrong—it does capture a certain subtle psychological tone—but I do think it is extremely unhelpful and perhaps even pernicious advice to give the freshman writer. Brooks and Warren have reconsidered this passage and omitted it from the fourth edition.

Returning now to the matter of the instructor as actual audience, we may note an ingenious suggestion in a recent handbook by Wilfred Stone and J. G. Bell that the freshman writer should imagine that he is writing for publication, "and that your teacher is not your audience so much as your editor, receiving and judging a manuscript you have sent him at his request" (p. 10). The teacher's personal reactions, they tell the student, should be thought of as "secondary to his views on how your imaginary audience will react, and on what revisions might make its reaction more favorable" (p. 11). I must say that I find this view a tempting one, and have sometimes thought of my work in this way, but have been unable to get my students to carry out the necessary imaginative gymnastics. Stone and Bell seem to be offering the instructor a way out of the uneasiness that many feel at being the primary reader. The uneasiness is that in so being he will exert pressure on the students (or cater to their abjectness) to echo his beliefs and values. But surely this is excessive self-doubt and scrupling: the reader that the students need most to believe in is one who tolerates honest differences of opinion, even welcomes them—and who can better model that individual than the instructor? We should bear in mind, however, that the instructor-as-reader is to be understood as a transitional stage: if the writer ever does attempt the essay in 'real life,' the audience is the imagined one of the general reader.

It may be useful to distinguish the imaginative specification of the reader and writer of the expository essay from the related imagination of narrator and audience in fictional discourse. Robert Brown and Martin Steinmann, Jr., define fictional discourse as a pretense of the author to report the utterances of a speaker to a fictional hearer, with the reader overhearing this pretended report.[7] The narrator and the audience, by the convention constituting fictional discourse, do not exist, though author and reader agree to pretend that they did/do. This sounds a bit like 'imagining your audience' but is in fact entirely distinct: the fictional/nonfictional distinction cross-classifies genre types and subtypes, so that we can speak of fictional expository essays and nonfictional sonnets as well as the reverse. Indeed, the so-often read "A Modest Proposal" and Defoe's "The Shortest Way with the Dissenters" are examples of fictional essays, though they can be and have been misinterpreted as nonfictional. Thus the alternative interpretations of these works arise not just from imagining different speakers and audiences, as E. D. Hirsch suggests, but from imagining that they are uttered *in propria persona* or 'pretend.' When Hirsch claims "In writing, it is the normal convention for the implied author and audience to be semifictional and rather vague" (*Philosophy*, p. 30), he seems to be conflating 'imagined' with 'imaginary.' The distinction is hardest to see in the case of someone like Keats, where no great interpretive reversals attend the decision to regard the "I" of many poems as John Keats or as a fictional speaker ('persona'). (Brown and Steinmann, however, argue fairly persuasively that both speaker and audience are fictional in "An Ode to Melancholy.") The stipulated audiences mentioned above ('next-door neighbor') are fictional (imaginary), but the imagined audience for an expository essay is not.

One should remember, however, that the fictional/nonfictional distinction is one about the way texts are regarded or taken, not something inherent in the text, and it is, of course, possible for a composition student to construct an imaginary persona and/or audience and thus to intend a fictional essay. It is interesting in this connection that David Siff found that his policemen students wrote far better essays when asked to adopt the point of view of their 'opposites' than they did writing *in propria persona*.[8] The fictive persona would seem to have at least two advantages for the apprentice essayist: it limits his self-exposure, and it usually is a type familiar both to reader and writer—that is, personae selected by students tend to represent stereotyped points of view, and the writer can be reasonably confident that the reader will recognize the values and outlook of the persona. Thus it can happen that essays with fictional writers and fictional audiences are easier to write than real ones.

Composition teachers often base their explanations of the need for explicitness and standard punctuation in writing in the 'deficiency' of the situation of written communication. It is useful, however, to distinguish differences of *situation*, which we have been concentrating on, from differences of *medium*. The written medium is deficient in intonational cues to the groupings of words and highlighting of material, and punctuation does to some degree supply this lack, though it introduces indicators of its own (apostrophes, shudder quotes, some commas) that do not directly correspond to anything in intonation. The need for explicitness, however, derives from the conventional assumption of the 'strangeness' of the reader of the expository essay—that the only information the writer can assume in common with the reader is the general information that can be assumed to be known by most educated persons.[9] This convention does not hold for much practical writing, as of personal letters, memos and reports within an organization, articles in special interest journals, and so on. The tendency of beginning writers to make comma splices and fragments in most cases comes from an overly simple basing of punctuation on intonation and as such reflects an incomplete transition from the medium of speech to that of writing, but the tendency to rely on relatively private word senses and implicit premises reflects an incomplete shift from the conventions of Utterance to those of Text; in most cases, in fact, inexplicitness arises from assuming a reader too much like the writer.

2. *Utterance expects speakers to reproduce accepted wisdom, attitudes, and values: cogency and assent are based on conformity to received opinion and common sense; speakers and hearers enact solidarity with their social group.*
Text expects writers to produce novel, even counterintuitive, facts and viewpoints; cogency and assent are based on logical consistency and evidence; writer and reader enact membership in an imagined community of inquiring minds.

This second polar opposition provides a way of thinking about the apparent dullness and dreary conventionality of student writing considered as Text. Utterance does not expect originality of its speakers—at least not originality of thought, though it will admire skillful expression of common, home truths and accepted wisdom. The sometime composition teacher/narrator of Robert Pirsig's *Zen and the Art of Motorcycle Maintenance* observes of a student unable to write a 500-word essay describing Bozeman, Montana (the location of her campus), that she was of course trying to repeat all the retellable things about Bozeman that she had heard—it never occurred to her to formulate observations of her own. Even in high school, most students are content to absorb and reproduce what is known and thought; classes in critical thinking are usually only for the college bound, and then they are not very common. So, many students come to college expecting to write a few more 'reports' on the Incas and laundry lists on The Causes of the American Revolution. Another way of viewing the difficulty here is to think of it as a confusion about ideas, reflecting a tendency to think of them as preformed things (like 'opinions on a subject') rather than processes or the results of processes. Students generally doubt that they could possibly have any original or novel ideas; what they need to be shown is that the way one comes at and thinks about something is just as important as the abstractable generalization that can be made about it. One obvious problem with 'retelling' assignments is that the student is being given a task in unsituated writing without the purpose of the expository essay (to construct a novel model of the world). Some teachers even tell their students simply to answer the five questions of journalism (Who? What? When? Where? Why?). 'Hot,' provocative topics like "Not All Women Want to Be Liberated" or "Organized Athletics Are a Waste of Time" do at least have the advantage of stoking the rhetorical furnace, but they are usually developed by reproducing familiar, even standard, arguments couched in the usual vocabulary and are modelled after a family free-for-all or bull session. Further, such topics can be at most only a halfway stage to Text because of the Text convention of disinterested inquiry. Invited to come out and take a stand, many student writers head for the end of a limb. Bald, clearly defined, extreme points of view are somehow easy to take (because preformed?) and easy to read. In my experience, freshman composition students have the greatest difficulty reading essays in which the writer is not taking a familiar stance or in which what he is saying is not consistent with the stance they think he is taking. I will return to this in section seven.

Even when the assignments push students in a subjective direction, they are content to apply conventional categories uncritically and, as it were, complacently. Responses I have gotten to the topic "The Type of Person I Am" are built around terms like *outgoing* or *introverted* or *athletic* or *nature-loving*. One of the more 'unconventional' was *Aquarian*. The uncritical attitude appears in two ways: some users accept the value judgments attached by their immediate culture ("I am introverted but I want to help people")—these writers delight in describing themselves as perfect examplars of a full-blown stereotype; others are puzzled by the way no category they know seems to fit over them and conclude, "I'm just a mixed-up kid, I guess." Questioning of existing categories or construction of new ones is fairly rare. This general pattern of results is doubtless familiar to many teachers. Some consider it evidence that nineteen-year-olds don't have very developed or interesting selves; others, that they lack the vocabulary to express them. But these explanations fail to account for the complacency and satisfaction of these descriptions. It is as if the assignment is taken to mean: which of the well-known boxes do you fit in? and there is satisfaction and security in fitting into one of them. Indeed, the topic is probably a loaded one, and many students would be ready to entertain and express novel views on other matters considerably before they would entertain them about themselves. Loaded as it is, the example does illustrate the appeal of reproducing received wisdom and opinions and the loss of solidarity in casting them off.

This tendency to view one's experience as an instance of common experience and to touch base via common terms probably explains the appeal of clichés for some writers—these are the ultimate in common, basic, and earthy categories. In using them, one's voice merges with that of the folk. I have noted that students who come to composition in mid-life seem to derive particular satisfaction from using them. These are students who have learned to see their lives in terms of established patterns, and for them the pithiness of a cliché seems the distillation of their experience: to make their experience public is to render it in the common tongue. Much has been written on the effect of clichés on the reader, but less on their effect on the writer. They often appear in essays at the end of a train of thought and seem to have terminated it: they are carbarns that gather the lurching and swaying argument into their comforting proverbial dark.

3. *Utterance is spontaneous; Text is planned.*

The result of the planning assumed of Text is that the discourse must be structured in a more sustained fashion than is usual in conversation. Conversations vary, of course, in the degree to which participants hold to, and hold each other to the point; not all oral discourse is "punctuated with false starts, changes of mind, changes of subject in the middle of sentences" (Hirsch, p. 152). But rarely can one expect undisputed possession of the floor for the duration of a statement as long as a four-page paper. The luxury of so much attention allows the writer to articulate his design more fully than the exigencies of Utterance situations usually permit. The convention of Text is that he will structure his discourse more than he would an impromptu speech. This convention also constitutes an obligation on the reader to attend to how the parts go together and assumes some competence in discerning these formal patterns. College students appear to differ in the degree to which they carry out ('perform') this integration into higher-order patterns. One finding of a series of reading comprehension experiments conducted by Nancy Marshall and Marvin Glock with students at Cornell University and the neighboring Auburn Community College was that the Cornell students made far greater use of the logical relations among statements in paragraphs of expository prose in recalling them than did the community college students.[10] Marshall and Glock concluded that the community college students did not seem to integrate the passages they read to the degree that the Cornell students did, and that their recalls were not truly connected discourse, but a "list of referentially linked sentences" (p. 51). We might say that the Cornell students were more privy to the convention of Text that the paragraphs may have a logical structure, more able to detect it if it was there, more able to exploit it as a way of organizing material in memory, and more ready to reproduce it on recalls of the paragraph (though in fact the evidence only *directly* supports the last). It is almost as if the community college students regarded the arrangement of sentences on the page as a matter of convenience, while for the Cornell students it was constituitive of the discourse itself. There are, however, many other patterns of paragraph organization besides the 'logical' one, and the complexities surrounding this matter will be explored in more detail in the next chapter.

Another reflection of the planned nature of Text is the expectation of parallelism of statement. Again, because we expect it, we find it, and it helps to order and integrate the material it displays. It is interesting that E. D. Hirsch treats both paragraphing and parallelism as meeting the natural tendencies and limitations of the mind (*Philosophy*, pp. 151–52). In the case of paragraphing, the limitation is that of being able to consider only one theme at a time. But surely this limitation applies as much when considering spoken discourse or casual letters, so, if that is all that is involved, paragraphing should not be a special problem for any student who is capable of communicating in any way. In the case of parallelism, the tendency is to expect the next event to be like the last one (which is met by parallel structure). But it may work just the other way: the appearance of things in parallel positions is a clue that they go together. In both cases, conventions of Text create obligations and opportunities for writer and reader.

Richard Lanham, in *Revising Prose*, remarks on the curious convention that when we read a passage, we assume it took about as long to write as to read (though we know the reduction ratio may be 10:1). The effect tends to make the writer seem extremely intelligent. This observation comes as close as anything I have read to explaining the fascination writing has for me: to read what I have written is to think faster, more sustainedly, coherently, and effortlessly than I do in composing. This effect explains why authors may be caught at odd moments reading bits of their own writing with a satisfied smile. It may also explain why some very good student writers find revision almost impossible.

4. *In Utterance, word senses are based on conversational exchanges and shared experience and are used without redefinition; in Text, word senses are based on formal written usage as recorded in dictionaries and are subjected to scrutiny and stipulative clarification.*

This fourth opposition reflects the familiar fact that words often bear senses in conversation that diverge from those listed for them in dictionaries. These differences can be sorted into three types: sheer lexical difference, difference in the realm of experience assumed as a backdrop, and treatment of word sense as implicit and fluid versus explicit and fixed.

The difference between word senses in Utterance and Text is more than a matter of contextual specialization of senses, which occurs in all discourses. It extends to actual differences in word meanings coded by speakers whose contact with the words is primarily by ear from meanings coded by speakers whose contact with them comes from reading relatively formal printed texts. The exact nature and extent of this divergence has not been systematically charted, and there are great obstacles to doing so, since it would involve the compiling of a dictionary of spoken English. Even dictionaries of slang and colloquial English wait for instances of terms used in print. Composition teachers, however (among others), gradually accumulate a goodly store of anecdotal data, which, unfortunately, is often viewed as evidence of vagueness, slovenliness, and imprecision in students' use of words. It would seem useful for instructors to call attention to differences between oral and written lexicons and to the need to master a second lexicon for the purpose of getting about in Text. *Unique,* my students tell me, means 'different' in their speech. *Extracurricular* means something done for pleasure. *Traumatic* means very tense or nerve-wracking.

A second, and possibly more pervasive, difference appears when students use words to evoke the realms of (presumably) shared experience in which they have learned and used the words, and again the composition instructor 'broadens' the horizons of the students by standing outside of this realm and reporting inability to grasp the associations the students may have in mind. When conflicts of this nature arise, the representative of Text (the instructor) appears to the student as the dull, inexperienced, and obtuse party. The realms of experience against which the words are used and interpreted are simply different, and, it appears, the gap between them is widening (at least as this instructor ages). Here are a few illustrative anecdotes.

The first is a description of a classmate written in the first meeting of a freshman composition course:

> She has long brown hair that is neat and well taken care of. She is attractive and seems to quite friendly. She smiles and laughs often. She is well dressed even though she's wearing blue jeans. She is probably around 19 years old but so is almost everyone else in the class.

I picked this out as one of the rare cases that would not succeed in identifying the classmate (at least three members seemed to me possible), yet the class was able to identify the person described. On discussing this, I found that *long hair* means straight hair falling free. *Long* in this use appears as a kind of code word shared by my students but not by me. Probably there are other codes and conventions involved in this description that I am not privy to. Here I am obliged to say that *long* in formal Texts cannot be depended on to carry so much particular weight.

The next example is from an essay on the topic "You Can't Always Tell a Nonconformist from the Way He Looks":

> You can't always tell the person that acts differently. If a nonconformist dresses different sometimes you can see this, but if he acts differently it is not so obvious. A boy that tells jokes in class may be right at home at the lunch table. Someone who would make a scene could be considered a nonconformist, but how can you tell how a person acts by the way they look?

The 'lunch table' contrast is clearly an example, but what is it an example of? If we take a clue from the succeeding sentence, we might suppose that nonconformity for this writer comes close to indecorous behavior (like telling jokes in class). One might suppose then that the lunch table contrast is one of misbehavior in one situation but appropriate behavior in another. Bearing in mind the evoked high-school context, however, one might think of the lunch room as a situation where anything goes, where being an 'animal' is the norm. And so I must tell this student that in written essays she should not assume that *lunch table* will evoke all the resonances of high-school culture that she expects it to.

The last example of dependence on cultural context comes from another paragraph by this same student—this one comes from the self-classification essay, which she chose to develop with an extended analogy to music:

> The very beat of my life is an exploding clash of the symbols at the height of the drum cadence.

Again, I objected that *beat* involves repetition and that this component conflicts with the single culminating clash, and I was told by several students that *beat* means 'essence' or 'intrinsic tendency,' and not just in this instance. To me, this seems vaguer than my sense of the lexical center of *beat* in formal writing, but it appears that I just am not privy to an altered sense of the word in the oral culture of my students. It remains my obligation as an instructor of Text to call attention to these divergences of word sense, but I would do well to rein in or abandon the notion that I think or express myself more precisely (in absolute terms) than my students do.

Word sense, by the way, is one of the points where learned discourse more resembles Utterance than Text: words function against a backdrop of shared, nongeneral experience which is partly face-to-face (in classroom, laboratories, corridors, and offices) and partly face-to-page (reading 'the literature'). Just think of the way the linguist's use of the terms *clause* and *noun phrase* baffles nonspecialists (or even dissenting specialists) or the curious complex of values surrounding the term *grammatical,* and so on. The writer of introductory texts exposes the learned discipline when she calls the students' attention to the specialized, nongeneral way key terms are being used; it is like opening the door on a backroom poker game, or functioning as an informant in a sociological study of street gangs: one jeopardizes one's solidarity with the special group.

The third difference in this general opposition perhaps springs from the solidarity theme in Utterance: the word senses the speaker knows are given and generally shared; the student writer reflects this attitude in a reluctance to define words commonly used without definition, much less to stipulate his/her own definition for the purposes of the essay. When told that they will find it helpful for an essay to define *nonconformist* or *socialism* or *liberated,* student writers will cite a dictionary or pamphlet and then return to using the word in common ways. This certainly does give the impression of muddled thinking and the inability to fix a single sense and hold it in mind, but such fluidity is typical of conversation, almost, one might say, necessary to it.

To put this matter in the terms of recent semantic theory, Utterance is quite comfortable treating words as having complexively organized senses—i.e., the view that a word like *socialism* stands for a bundle of related attributes and can be used appropriately when some of these attributes are present. The term can thus be used to refer to social systems that exhibit only a family resemblance. In this case, these attributes generally include state ownership of the means of production ('nationalization'), central planning ('regulation'), and state guarantees of a minimal level of subsistence to all citizens ('cradle-to-grave'). Text would prefer that senses be made up of sets of necessary and sufficient criteria for application of the terms; this is one reason Text encourages the stipulating of the senses of key terms as they will be used in the discourse.

5. *In Utterance, bridging premises are based in common assumptions and stereotypes and may be largely implicit; in Text, bridging premises and logical structure are to be made explicit.*

This opposition is closely tied to the preceding one in that the premises necessary to follow the argument and understand text connectives may often be part of what the speaker understands by particular words and phrases or be part of the common fund of stereotypes and values he believes will be activated by the words. Olson views the contrasting obligation of Text to be that all the premises of the argument should be made explicit, but here I think he is overstating the case. The noticeable lapses or gaps in student compositions do often require us to treat as given premises we do not in fact hold, but texts that are equally gappy are not noticed as such if the implicit premise is one we do hold, so the problem with the student gaps is not that they have failed to make a premise explicit but that they have mistakenly assumed that the instructor (as representative of the general readership) holds the views the writer does. The objection then should be phrased "you seem to be assuming p (the premise), but not everybody (I, for example) believes that p is so." If we write *obscure,* or *logic!* or *unclear* we are in effect blaming the student for not thinking as we do—and in most cases they are not even aware that they do not.

A few examples should make the point clear. The first involves the inferring of a bridging premise in classic syllogistic fashion:

> Since I come from a very large family, I treasure the moments I
> spend with them.

The main, assumed, premise is something like 'The more family you
have, the more you enjoy being with them.' This premise may in fact
be part of the ideology of Large Families, but it is certainly one I am
loath to grant. There would be nothing to catch my eye, however, if
the student had written:

> Since I come from a very large family, I find it easy to be part of a
> group.

The premise in this case evokes well-known notions about socialization and seems to be a genuine commonplace. It happens that I have
my personal reservations about the validity of this premise also, but I
suspect that I would be bucking the majority. Perhaps if I were feeling ornery and querulous, I might pencil in the margin "does this
always follow?" but I would be aware of obtruding my own views
rather than representing the puzzlement of 'the general reader.'
   The next example is a little murkier:

> Liberated means to be free not to be men. Many women want to be
> liberated. They want to open their own doors and pull out their own
> chairs, while other women only want to be equal with men.

(Previous context suggests a comma is warranted in the first
sentence). The connective word *while* signals an opposition between
being equal and opening one's own doors, which is an example of
being liberated. But how being free (liberated) is different from
being equal is hard to see. Possibly what has happened is a shift in
the definition of *liberated* from the 'true' sense given in the first
sentence to the specious one ('opening doors'), and the last reversal
to *equal* is a reversion to 'true' liberation. One could get this into
print so:

> *Liberated* means to be free, not to be men. Many women, however,
> want to be 'liberated': they want to open their own doors and pull out
> their own chairs, but other women only want to be equal to men.

If this is the right interpretation, then perhaps we do have an instance where the logical connections and shift of sense need to be
articulated more in print: the 'shudder' quotes help a lot and reflect
an intonational gambit that would make this much more intelligible
in speech. If this is not the right interpretation, however, the writer
is drawing on word senses and premises that I cannot even guess.

The last example is from another paper (one of the self-classifications) by the same student. Our interest is in the middle paragraph of the three cited—the other two paragraphs seem to provide some clues:

> My dream has always been to live in a log cabin in the Mountains
> . . . I know I sound like somewhat of an introvert, yet basically I am
> not. I love to help people, to feel needed. Currently—I am studying
> to be a nurse-midwife and I feel that I would fit in better in a moun-
> tain town. The healing of the mind body through diet and rest are
> very important to me.
> You could call me a "miss-goodie-two-shoes" (and they often do)
> because of my moral standards. But here I am—yet where am I. I
> love simple things. I don't care much for this *whole* Women's Lib
> thing.
> Emotional and extremely sensitive, yes, that is myself. I believe in
> big families, and loving and sharing and giving. . . .

The middle paragraph was discussed in class and two classmates (both female) were able to supply most of the unexpressed premises. Being mocked for one's moral standards (it means goodie-goodie; Oliver Goldsmith, lie still!) which presumably center on commitments to premarital chastity and marital fidelity, generates an expectation that one would be categorical and defensive about them, but the Cartesian 'here I am—yet where am I?' indicates self-questioning of the moral standpoint as an absolute, hence the *but*. 'I love simple things' attempts to find a reason for the preference for the 'moral standards.' Simple things contrast to the messy and complex lives that the writer associates with multiple and partial relationships and with a code of unrestrained pursuit of sexual gratification (the Sixties stereotype of the Liberated Woman). The love of simple things, then, provides the reason for the rejection of some parts of 'Women's Lib.' We can rephrase the passage on this interpretation as:

> Some make fun of me because of my commitment to chastity and
> fidelity. These are my values, yet I wonder why they appeal to me. I
> like simplicity in my relationships, and for that reason I don't think
> of being with only one man as bondage.

To put this together and then spell it out, one needs to plug into several complexes of attitudes and values, causes and effects (we will call them schemata in the next chapter) that the code words mark: *simple things, moral standards, Women's Lib thing* are the main ones. As noted at the beginning of this section, this is in a way a question of word meaning; here we see how it provides the connective premises (and conclusions!) to produce a coherent line of thought.

6. *In Utterance, speakers are expected to speak understandably; In Text, writers are to write correctly according to grammatical rules and follow the canons of usage given in the handbooks.*

Here we touch the much vexed matter of correctness, which, I would argue, has a place in the culture of Text equivalent to that of understandability in Utterance. In Utterance, one may speak in non-sentences, interrupt oneself, commit agreement errors, stumble over pronouns, say the wrong word, and so on without failing. In addition to the obligation to be understandable, the Text writer is expected to follow the grammatical rules and usage canons set forth in handbooks, and thus this convention of Text constitutes a restriction on the (syntactic) freedom of expression accorded a speaker in Utterance and requires the learning of the rules and canons of Text that differ from the rules and practices of his or her speech community. The differing commitments of Utterance and Text in this area are the source of conflict when the student defends some construction used in a paper as understandable, only to be told that it cannot be used in an expository essay. Many teachers obscure this difference by defending the rules and canons of Text as guaranteeing understandability or enhancing 'logic,' but there are a number of these rules that do no such thing, except in the obvious sense that one expects to find them being observed when reading texts, and their nonobservance is disruptive. Similarly, many teachers obscure from themselves the extent to which their own speech fails to conform to the rules of Text. English teachers try to speak the written language, and think they do, but the notion that there is an independent body of rules called Standard English that governs 'the careful speech of educated speakers' is, I think, quite illusory. Rather than constituting a basis for the rules of Text, such a Standard is based on the rules of Text: careful speech is speech that is trying to conform to the rules of Text, and speakers appear educated when they succeed. Academics carry this to extraordinary lengths, speaking forms usually encountered only in writing (*albeit, whereupon, the former/the latter, if and only if*) and even pronouncing the punctuation and outline of their spoken 'Text' ("The topic may be approached in three ways, colon, roman numeral one . . ."). This is often somewhat tongue-in-cheek, of course, and this manner of articulation may given us a clue to the proper pronunciation of Standard English. If teachers' consciousnesses could be raised on this point, they would not tell students to edit their own writing on the basis of the way it sounds to them. The sound in question is heard in the mind's ear, and the students who defend an incorrect construction by saying it sounds all right (or alright) to them are not being dunces—just taking the teacher literally. The solution is not to get the student to speak Standard and then base his ear on it, but to learn the rules and canons as a filter through which writing must pass as it is edited.

All of this is intended to counter E. D. Hirsch's claim that the standard language is also the standard 'grapholect' (*Philosophy*, p. 164) (which is manifested on television!—p. 48). It looks like a category error to equate a 'grapholect' with any dialect (blurring the distinction of speech and writing again), and it is monstrous to urge that the grapholect be taught as a new dialect to those who don't speak (!) it already (p. 164). To clarify the divergence of dialects and 'grapholect,' let us survey some points of likeness and difference.

The first and most obvious is vocabulary. There is a virtual second lexicon of words I recognize and occasionally write, the pronunciation of which is uncertain to me, partly because I never hear them pronounced, and partly because I cannot even imagine wanting to use them in speech. At least as large a body of words are those that I use in speech only with colleagues and intimates and only when I am being playfully bookish (*replete, redolent, recumbent,* just from the *re*'s). I do not recall having heard them on television.

Second are rules of grammar and usage. There is, of course, a common core of rules shared by Text syntax and by some or nearly all spoken dialects, and we can think of the problematic points raised in the composition handbooks as pointers to rules of Text syntax that do not correspond to rules of students' dialects. Students run afoul of the rules of Text in three ways:

First, they may use a form characteristic of nonprestige dialects only; these stigmatize the user as unschooled:

> *he don't, hisself / theirselves, have went, amount / number, there is sure a lot of people here, John and me got there late,* double negation, basic agreement, and the like.

Second, they may use a construction that is normal in the informal speech of prestige speakers rather than the construction characteristic of formal usage (spoken or written); using the first of each of these pairs makes the discourse distinctively colloquial:

> If I was / were to propose, would you accept?
> It is me / I.
> He drives like / as I do.
> Each of my cousins have / has their / his (his or her) favorite sport.
> This is one family (that) eats anything.

Elizabeth Traugott's observation on this last construction is appo-
site: "a sharp distinction must be drawn between the written and the
spoken language in the NE [New English=Modern English] period.
For most speakers the ENE [Early New English] system that permits
deletion of any relative still persists, though many educated speakers
who are more conscious of the way they write than the way they
speak may actually think that their use of this construction is considerably more limited than it is."[11] When speakers think that they use a
formal construction in speech, they do not regard it as distinctively
formal; to others it may be more obviously so.

Third, they may fail to observe one of the canons of editing that
principally govern the way a printed text looks. These canons are
observed if at all only in the careful speech of the most bookish
speakers; disobeying them does not make the discourse distinctively
colloquial:

> no dangling participles or other modifiers, no squinting modifiers,
> no ambiguous antecedents generally, no *which* or *that* with a whole-
> sentence antecedent, *whose* only with personal antecedents, *between/
> among,* no split infinitives, no *which* in restrictive relative clauses, no
> uncompleted comparatives (*more. . . than. . . ; so. . . that. . .*) or 'illogi-
> cal' comparatives (*He is smarter than anyone in his class*), no superlative
> in comparisons of two, no prepositions stranded at the ends of
> clauses, no contractions, no *I will* for predictions, no *who* for non-
> subject uses, etc.

These 'errors' do not spring from ignorance of standard usage or
avoidance of formality, but from the urgency of the composing process and the semi-planned nature of the sentences one sets down on
the page. These canons are not equally obligatory, fixed, and settled
by consensus: they continue to occasion much discussion, split votes
on usage panels, and friction between copy editors and authors.

It is important, however, in surveying all of this, not to give too
much of our attention (or efforts) to the rules and canons of Text.
These are rules governing most formal writing, and this may explain
why they receive so much attention in school: they are as it were a
lowest common denominator for written discourse of various types.
But if we view the task of a course in composition as teaching all the
ways in which writing an expository essay differs from uses of language more familiar to the student, not splitting infinitives is a very
minor matter indeed, though it seems to be established in the popular mind as the very essence of what English teachers do (or don't
do).

The language of Text is by convention Formal English. This tabulation of the special features of written Formal English is perhaps somewhat misleading in that it characterizes Formal English almost entirely in negative terms. Formal English can also be characterized positively, in terms of its special vocabulary and its preference for syntactic complexity, inversion, and parallelism. Indeed, Formal English has many of the characteristics of the High variant in a culture with *diglossa*. Charles Ferguson defines diglossa as

> a relatively stable language situation in which, in addition to the primary dialects of the language (which may include a standard or regional standards), there is a very divergent, highly codified (often grammatically more complex) superposed variety, the vehicle of a large and respected body of written literature, either of an earlier period or in another speech community, which is learned largely by formal education and is used for most written and formal spoken purposes but is not used by any sector of the community for ordinary conversation.[12]

Ferguson observes that the situation, though it is relatively stable, is likely to change under certain circumstances. The prestige of the High variant reflects its historical origins and the fact that mastery of it is accessible only to the elite who can receive an education in literacy (i.e., High literacy). As the franchise in literacy is broadened, the stable situation is subject to levelling pressures toward a 'standard,' with much polemicizing by conservative upholders of the glorious past and advocates of the people's speech. One could certainly view the current atmosphere of crisis about corruption and decline of literacy as reflecting a destabilizing diglossa.[13] From this angle, the notion of an established, uniform Standard English appears as a myth that obscures differences in the Formal (High) and conversational (Low) variants.

7. *Utterance aims at the sharing of experience; hearer interprets speech in relation to the speaker; Text aims at proving the correctness of its models of the world; reader interprets Texts in terms of what is on the page.*

When operating under the conventions of Utterance, we constantly and automatically evaluate and interpret what the speaker is saying in relation to what we know or surmise about his values and attitudes. On this point classical rhetoric shows its roots in face-to-face oratory in the notion of the ethical proof. To paraphrase the rhetoricians in the modern idiom is a bit jarring but faithful to their conception: we constantly relate what is said to our sense of where the speaker is coming from (the stance), how she is coming on (her style), and what she is getting at (her drift). One recognizes stances in terms of familiar types or stereotypes (schemata again, of a different sort), such as paternalistic liberal, feminist, friend/enemy of business, environmentalist, fundamentalist, Bircher, spokesman for the underdog, etc. These stances, of course, predict what the speaker is likely to be getting at. These stereotypes need not be applied absolutely. Even if the speaker does not make an issue of his stance, we keep a weather-ear tuned, because it will help us make sense of his discourse and decide how to take it, which amounts to deciding whether we like or can get along with a person like that—whether, that is, his viewpoint is one that we can provisionally adopt. Successful communication in Utterance is not based on speaker saying precisely and exactly what he means and hearer attending as closely as possible to what was actually said, but rather on a kind of tuning in between speaker and hearer, a concerting of interests and attitudes that the speaker must evoke and engage and that the hearer must attempt to activate and replicate in himself. One attends to the drift and contours of the conversation as much as to the words. Perhaps the appeal of highly charged and slanted writing for many composition students is that it bears with it the whole emotional aura and set of values against which the student's words can be interpreted: it engages the reader as a partisan. Succeeding in communicating is accordingly not convincing the hearer that one's conclusion is well-founded, but getting him to share one's stance. As Olson nicely puts it, the response sought from the hearer in Utterance is "how true!" And, we might add, the equivalent in Text is "I see."

Under the conventions of Text, the writer is responsible only for what he says, and the reader must concentrate on that and evaluate it on its own terms. Thus we allow ourselves the possibility of acknowledging that a writer whose views we generally reject 'has a point' that is valid in a particular essay. Further, the convention that one should focus on exactly what the text says and doesn't say seems essential to the presentation of novel arguments and viewpoints: if the reader is constantly interpreting, adapting, and enriching the text in terms of stereotypical stances, there is danger that the novelty and point of the discourse will be missed. In Text, then, we try to make a sharp distinction between understanding the point and adopting the stance of the writer. This, of course, involves an obligation on the writer's part to efface his personal self, or at least to mute it, and project the self of the dispassionate fair-minded inquirer. To signal a bias or personal preference is to limit one's freedom as a writer of Text (though it may add the pungency and spirit of Utterance). So Strunk and White, those venerable spokesmen for Text attitudes, advise the writer:

1. Place yourself in the background.
   Write in a way that draws the reader's attention to the sense and substance of the writing, rather than to the mood and temper of the author.[14]

From this it follows that the so-called subjective expository essay is not a pure type: whenever the writer begins to make an issue of his personal tastes, values, or attitudes, he is drawing the reader into a different kind of engagement, one that is in the direction of Utterance. Whenever we find ourselves evaluating an essay on the basis of our reconstruction of the writer's personality and other views, we are reading as if we were listening to him exhort us.

The notion of objectivity is tricky in two respects. First, the convention of Text here does not require 'voiceless' or committee writing (Walker Gibson's Stuffy style): any written discourse postulates an implied writer and reader, and Gibson argues very persuasively that our responses as readers are very much like our responses as listeners with respect to the assumptions writers make about us.[15] So there is a slight official fiction involved in 'just what is on the page.' Nonetheless, the convention of Text is that even if the implied writer seems brusque or obsequious or indifferent to us as readers, we will try to evaluate what he proposes on its own merits.

Second, students, especially those drilled to shun *I*, often confuse objective style of presentation with objective point of view—the latter is a virtual impossibility, though the term does turn up in some guidebooks. These students, if asked to develop an essay by means of classification use pre-established classes; if by definition, they go to the dictionary, if by comparison and contrast, they compare multiple sclerosis and muscular dystrophy. What is truly difficult for the student is to adopt the implied magisterial self as his own 'speaking' voice: the student does not feel judicious, informed, in command of material and audience. And so there may be an element of the fictional here, too, which is perhaps what is meant by statements that writers find or create selves by writing.

I do not mean to imply that this magisterial voice of authority is utterly unlike any of the voices the student enacts orally, or that speech provides no models for the 'voice in print.' There are indeed numerous ways that we speak, some of which approximate the ideal of Text more than others. Plainly, the manner of speaking in casual exchanges with friends is quite far from this ideal; not so obviously to some, the consultative manner, as Martin Joos calls it, such as one would employ in a business conversation, fails to meet the expectations of Text. It is a voice of some authority and, like Text, makes background information explicit rather than assuming it is shared, but it uses general nouns, filler phrases, and repetition to a greater extent than Text tolerates. Here is a sample cited by Joos from Charles Carpenter Fries's transcripts of telephone conversations (the italics indicate the remarks of the other speaker):

> I wanted to tell you one more thing I've been talking with Mr. Davis in the purchasing department about our typewriters *yes* that order went in March seventh however it seems that we are about eighth on the list *I see* we were up about three but it seems that type of typewriter we're about eighth that's for a fourteen-inch carriage with pica type *I see* now he told me that Royce's have in stock the fourteen-inch carriage typewriters with elite type *oh* and elite type varies sometimes it's quite small and sometimes it's almost as large as pica *yes I know* he suggested that we go down and get Mrs. Royce and tell her who we are and that he sent us and try the fourteen-inch typewriters and see if our stencils would work with such type *I see* and if we can use them to get them right away because they have those in stock and we won't have to wait *that's right* we're short one typewriter right now as far as having adequate facilities for the staff is concerned *yes* we're short and we want to get rid of those rentals *that's right* but they are expecting within two weeks or so to be receiving—ah—to start receiving their orders on eleven-inch machines with pica type *oh* and of course pica type has always been best for our stencils *yes* but I rather think there might be a chance that we can work with elite type. . . [16]

Except for the self-correction ("ah—to start receiving"), this passage closely resembles a certain type of bad student writing; the speaker presents himself as having considered the question from several angles, but not as having preplanned the actual telephone presentation, hence the notable lack of concision or subordination. Consultative style is a kind of amphibian between the casual, at times elliptical, informality of friendly conversation (Utterance in purest form) and the explicit, authoritative address to the educated reader (pure Text), and it is easy to see why it would be attractive to some apprentice writers as a model for writing. The manner of speaking closest to Text, however, is probably, as Roger Sale suggests, that which can emerge in a good classroom discussion. Sale's description is feelingly written and bears extensive citation:

> Any teacher and most students know that some of the finest speaking they have ever heard comes in a really good class discussion, a discussion that, for some mysterious reason, stops being filled with

ploys and attitudinizing and seems, for a little while, to express the
emphases and urgencies the students truly feel. On the one hand,
the style is better than that usually used by students among themselves, because the presence of the teacher and the organized circumstances of the classroom force students to avoid their usual
slackness and to complete their thoughts, to choose their words with
whatever care can be mustered. On the other hand, the language
does not have the stiffness and the awful mixture of hesitancy and
pompousness that are the usual result of the students' awareness that
they are students and speaking to a teacher. At such a moment,
speech is still speech, but it does not have the conversational voices
that encourage us to substitute vague personal good will for precision
of language. These moments are rare, yet everyone has known and
been excited by them. They cannot, of course, be self-consciously
achieved or repeated, but I have often felt that if we could acknowledge such moments as an ideal of style, everyone's writing would
improve.[17]

One reason discussions of speech and writing have proved relatively
inconsequential is that they have treated speech as a uniform phenomenon; here we see that some speech, namely that which occurs
in the specially contrived situation of the classroom, could come
quite close to sounding like uttered Text (and good Text, at that) and
provide a model for the voice in print.

Shifting the focus slightly from argumentative to more reflective
communication, we can see the bearing of some recent work by
Adrienne Lehrer on the semantics of terms describing wine.[18] When
people describe the taste and 'nose' of wine to each other, she observes, the terms used are heavily metaphorical and referentially
very shaky. That is, nonprofessionals do not agree about which
words are to be used to describe particular wines. But the purpose of
such descriptions is not to make a true or verifiable claim about some
part of the world but to share an experience, namely, that of tasting
the wine. Professional enologists, however, do have an obligation to
refer to properties of the wine in a way that other professionals dis-
tant in time and place can recognize and verify, and, by training,
they do come to agree among themselves in the terms they use to
describe particular wines more than nonprofessionals do, even those
who drink, describe, and discuss wines together over a considerable
stretch of time. Metaphor, it has often been noted, by its nature as
nonstandard use of language requires interpretation in terms of the
user's intention rather directly: how far and in which directions is it
to be taken? This is perhaps why Olson regards metaphorical and
figurative language as a characteristic of Utterance rather than Text.
Literature itself Olson regards as more in the camp of Utterance

than Text, aiming at the sharing of experience rather than the construction of verifiable models of the world, interpreted in terms of
the reader's interests and experience (unless the reader is a New
Critic) and in terms of an implied author, and achieving success in
the reader's "how true!" This is perhaps what James Britton means
by likening literature to gossip.[19] Text regards figurative language
with some reservation or even hostility (Strunk and White again:
"18. Use figures of speech sparingly"). Above all, figurative language
must not bear the weight of exposition or advance the argument,
though it may be used to summarize or concretize the line of
thought. So the little carbarn metaphor used earlier at the end of a
paragraph is acceptable there, but would be much less so at the beginning, or if it were not explicated by the rest of the paragraph.
Utterance achieves much richness by letting words and images resonate, but in Text we must spell it all out. When we assign students
the task of writing an explication of a poem, we are essentially asking
them to render a piece of Utterance into Text.

Gibson's claim about encountering voices poses an interesting
theoretical question: "The experience of reading, then, is a confron-
tation with a voice, or personality, clear or confused. . . ."[20] The
question is whether voice is a category or dimension of all reading,
or whether certain types of writing (e.g., official documents, scientific
articles, 'encyclopedia prose,' instruction manuals) are properly
exempt from it—i.e., to criticize them for being voiceless would be
inappropriate. Perhaps we need to distinguish between an implied
author as a category or construct posited in the comprehension process and a personalized implied self—between, that is, 'voice' and
particular voices. Then we can say that a writer may choose a relatively depersonalized, public, 'objective' ('flat') voice and so approximate or attain the 'voiceless' and hence 'toneless' effect. In such a
case, we might conclude that attending to the voice will not give us
much guidance to the perspective, evaluation, meaning, or human
implications of the information presented; in short, 'voice' fails to
function as a useful category in our construction of the text. The
widespread contempt and vituperation heaped upon the official, or
stuffy, or bureaucratic style, however, suggests that our tendency to
expect and seek a human, responsible voice is very strong and may
override any conventions exempting certain types of discourse from
having a voice. In any case, such types are rather rare and marginal
in the universe of discourse (many encyclopedia articles are quite
personally 'voiced,' as, for examples, the *Encyclopaedia Britannica* article on Gustav Mahler) and should not be taken as any sort of reg-
ulative norm for expository prose.

A closely related issue is how concretely the notion of voice should be taken. Gibson's alternative—"personality"—is abstract enough to suggest a construct that may have little sense of physical presence attached to it, and, similarly, the 'voices' may be 'heard' with the mind's ear rather than heard. For the latter to be in the case, one would actually have to vocalize (i.e., read aloud) or perhaps sub-vocalize the text. Interestingly, there is considerable evidence that people reading relatively difficult texts do subvocalize, and this sub-vocalizing does assist comprehension.[21] The 'great revolution in reading' (silent reading) described by many scholars (e.g., E. D. Hirsch and Richard Lanham) may be incomplete or even illusory.[22] Further, skilled readers might be able to realize the auditory aspects of a text by a kind of secondary capacity like that developed by musicians who can 'read' a score without humming it. Other writers speak of the mediating of reading by 'auditory imagery' rather than detectable subvocalization.[23] Perhaps, also, we can switch the audi-tory decoding on and off, or engage in it to various degrees (for instance with or without lip movements) as we choose. Introspection tells me that I alternate modes when reading freshman essays. Perhaps, too, the sense that some professors experience of being defiled by freshman compositions comes from (re)producing the student's language in the process of reading the essay. 'Readability' thought of in these terms is clearly an aesthetic notion, not a utilita-rian one. This discussion must remain speculative, given our present state of ignorance, but it does seem that 'hearing voices' is not neces-sarily as metaphorical as many have assumed.

We have come quite a distance with Olson's single polar opposi-tion. On two points, however, it will clarify matters to split things a bit more by introducing some categories of James Kinneavy and James Britton.

The first point is Olson's sober-sided account of the explicit, un-ambiguous language required in Text. Olson lumps the essay tradi-tion of Montaigne, Bacon, Locke, and Hume with the 'scientific lan-guage' movement also foreshadowed in Bacon's *Advancement of Learning* and developed by the Royal Society and Bishop Sprat. Kin-neavy observes, however, that as the exploratory motive comes to the fore in exposition, so, characteristically, do aphorisms, paradoxes, figurative language, and even puns. We might think of this as a shift of focus from setting out the product of inquiry toward engaging the reader in the process of inquiring. (Kinneavy views the Platonic dialogues as a natural written form of exploratory discourse.) It is really only exposition in its most public, decorous, and demonstra-tive aspect that Olson is describing.

The second point is the relation of essay to literature, which, James Britton suggests, is not a proper instance of the opposition of

Text to Utterance, since literature is as much governed by conventions that distinguish it from, say, conversation, as is the expository essay. He suggests a quasi-developmental model with an early, undifferentiated 'expressive' use of language out of which literature and essay develop, or, as he calls the matured opposition, language in the role of spectator (poetic, presentational, display-text) versus language in the role of participant (transactional, discursive, instrumental).[24] Though his view of 'the poetic' is perhaps excessively formalist, he is certainly right that 'the poet' does not address his audience, seeking to accommodate himself to their needs, interests, and knowledge in the way that the essayist does: the poem is overheard, not heard, and does not exemplify face-to-face Utterance any more than it does Text. This characteristic helps explain the resistance, often virtual hostility, on the part of some composition teachers toward including 'creative writing' in composition courses.[25]

On the other hand, the essay is often regarded as a type of literature and is certainly susceptible of 'literary' treatment. Literary theorists like Wolfgang Iser and Umberto Eco distinguish between open and closed texts in terms of the involvement of the reader that is presupposed or sought and the degree of precision or definiteness in the meaning.[26] Similarly, Martin Joos distinguishes between formal style, which is committed to explicitness of meaning, and frozen style, which is many layered and requires rereading.[27] Encyclopedic or scientific writing is usually cited as the extreme of closedness (along with apologues and much popular fiction): it is clear what it is about, and no analogizing to one's own experience is necessary. An 'open' essay, then, would be one that signified something beyond itself and sought constructive engagements in that direction from readers. Perhaps *Walden* would furnish an extended example. The handbook obsession with getting it down on the page and controlling the reader's response seems to point directly toward a closed text and away from the richer and more interesting relations to texts that English departments are supposed to value. Similarly, the advice to 'consider your reader,' if taken as an instruction to project an image of an actual body of people, exactly misses the point that open texts create their readers: Thoreau did not do a market survey, but brought his reader into existence, and the reader implied by *Walden* is a triumph of the imagination. As conveyed by assignments, the closed/open difference is that between "Describe the production of PVC" and "Describe something you know how to do in a way that will suggest what is satisfying or meaningful about doing it." Certainly we do tend to warm to and value writing that shows richness, resonance, and a sense of larger implications; if we do want our students to attempt to write literature, in this sense, we ought to tell them so, for much in the handbooks and school lore of composition tells them not to.

In general, approaches to composition that emphasize writing from personal experience, such as Ken Macrorie's or Lou Kelly's, tend to focus on the sharing of that experience rather than the analysis or interpretation of it, and thus to treat the college writing course as a sort of halfway station between Utterance and Text. Macrorie's critics find him either irresponsible or subversive, for they suspect, probably rightly, that he would like to 'loosen up' the conventions of Text for all academic discourse.

In the course of sketching in these seven oppositions, we have touched on many of the real problems of student writing: faulty assumptions about the audience, lack of originality, stridency, uncritical use of stereotypes, clichés, punctuation errors, obscure, vague, and faulty diction, leaps in logic, weak paragraph structure, wavering word sense, usage violations, inconsistencies of tone, and boring, 'objective' writing. Though incomplete, the list is daunting, and the ineptitude it catalogues threatens to appall. But at least we can see these problems not as crudities or diseases but as manifestations of an incomplete substitution of the conventions of Text for those of Utterance. These problems are like the accent of one who is trying to speak Received Pronunciation with the phonological rules of Yorkshire. The analogy is useful, because the dialect speaker can usually begin to hear the difference before he is able to produce it easily and habitually.

The analogy is good, too, in that it leads to the one significant qualification I feel is necessary to the general explanation of writing problems in terms of missed or misunderstood conventions. Human limitation does play a role, I think, as well as convention, but the significant limitation is that involved in the composing process, not in reading. It has often been remarked that thought comes more quickly than the words can be written down—at least at the good times—and to keep getting it down fast enough we need ways of abbreviating it, quick marks that will later require expansion. Jargon and clichés seem to function this way for many writers, underdeveloped general terms for others. Many omitted premises and unstated consequences doubtless occurred to the writer but were crowded off the page in the rush of ideas. This is the case, I know, in my own writing. Just so, the dialect speaker's accent becomes worse under the stress of communicative urgency, and having something to say often involves the writer in more faults. But the writer has one advantage the non-native speaker does not: he can revise, and his initial telegraphic stutterings need never come before the public's eye.

CHAPTER THREE

Ideas of Order

By a curious division of labor, linguists have been content for most of the last twenty years to study the structure of sentences and to leave the study of larger units of discourse to rhetoricians and composition teachers. Virtually every handbook in print contains extensive description of paragraph structure (unity, coherence, and emphasis), connective words, patterns of development, and essay structure. These treatments are prescriptive to varying degrees according to the taste of the writer, and the pedagogical assumption seems to be the old-fashioned one that description of the patterns plus exercise in their use will give form and bounds to student writing just as instruction in traditional grammar will guarantee the correctness of the sentences. It is the rare handbook writer indeed who assumes that students can acquire a competence for the larger structural patterns in the same way that they acquire sentence competence, and that textbook descriptions are simply attempts to formulate what the student already knows. The only handbook to openly advocate such a "Chomskyan" interpretation of paragraph development, for example, is W. Ross Winterowd's *The Contemporary Writer*. Recently, however, William Irmscher has also suggested that students have intuitions of order that instructors should aim at fostering.[1] But there is also a trend, particularly in the area of 'basic writing,' toward what we might call neo-hard-nosed drill in formulaic composition, the assumption apparently being that for 'basic' students at least, the faculty for language does not extend so far and the intuitive sense of order is feeble at best.

It might appear that this matter turns on the degree to which the ordering patterns are natural to discourse and the degree to which they are special conventions of particular, unfamiliar discourse types with little or no relation to the way we usually think or discourse (like the MLA bibliographic citation form or the standard forms of a business letter). There is a sort of Neo-Ramist school, most vigorously championed by Frank D'Angelo, which treats the standard patterns of development, for example, as processes of thought and ways of inventing ideas. Hence 'the traditional paragraph' (by which

D'Angelo means the paragraph as traditionally described) is a unit of 'logic' and represents, as well as assists, clear thinking.[2] Other writers who give advice on thinking and invention, however, assume that these processes are not isomorphic with those implicit in the standard patterns of development.[3] Equally important, and obscure, is the degree to which readers employ and rely on these formal patterns: some handbooks justify the teaching of the patterns in terms of the reader's needs and expectations. But little is known about these expectations—what they are, how they are activated, and how they function in comprehension. A strict intuitionist, I suppose, would maintain that readers also have intuitions of order that can be fitted over texts. Perhaps the primary fact is a sense of a piece's working or not working, and all explanations are after that fact.

The intuitionist position has its appeals, not the least of which is that it does not claim to describe (and, in an institutional setting, prescribe) how we think. But without some characterization of possible intuitions of order, the position seems to precipitate us headlong into obscurantism.

Recent work in language processing and cognitive science suggests certain perspectives on these possible orderings. I stress the *possible:* what the cognitive scientists offer us is a model of (part of) what comprehension is on the higher levels. The empirical evidence for it as reflecting real processing is fragmentary, and much of it is subject to the reservations expressed in the first chapter. And it is content-oriented. Its usefulness lies in its ability to explain certain experiences of texts—the sense of something having been explained, of course, may be another intuition.

The key notion we will borrow from the cognitive scientists is that of a *schema* (plural is *schemata*). Basically, a schema can be understood as a model or pattern by which the mind analyzes and interprets experience. Schemata come in varying levels of generality and operate in different ways.[4] For our purposes, it is most useful to divide them into those that give form or structure to experience and those that interpret its content. Since part of experience is experience of discourse, we have schemata that apply to the form or structure of discourse and to its content. We know, for example, that stretches of a discourse may have the pattern of a generalization plus illustrative examples; this is a formal schema that may be fitted over a particular stretch we are reading or hearing. Similarly, we know that there is an activity called golf made up of certain parts, and, by virtue of this content schema, we may interpret a particular sequence of facts and details as an instance of 'playing golf.' Part of this interpretation involves filling in many particulars and shaping understanding of individual words, as in this case, for example, *the ball*. These are patterns we may bring to texts—or may not, if we do not know them—and that we may or may not apply in interpreting the text. They form a basis of communication insofar as writers (and speakers) assume that they can and will be applied by readers (and hearers).

We can think of schemata as performing three functions in the process of text construction—organizing, integrating, and predicting material. An example of an organizing schema is the one that Charlotte Linde and William Labov found being used by the vast majority of the people they asked to describe their apartments.[5] Almost all of them chose to order the material in terms of a walking tour through the apartment, beginning with entering the door. Another organizing schema appeared in descriptions of 'a hassle with a bureaucracy' that Wallace Chafe collected (he calls it the 'runaround schema').[6] Unlike 'golf,' these two schemata are formal rather than content-oriented; we will see below, however, that content schemata can also perform an organizing function, as indeed the golf schema does at the beginning of *The Sound and the Fury*. An example of an integrating schema is the 'graphthink' in Frank Bormuth's article on reading research discussed in chapter one: it draws together and fills in the assumptions of such phrases as *linear* and *varying degrees of curvature*. Patterns of Generalization-plus-Examples or Problem-plus-Solution illustrate the integrating function of formal schemata: we know what 'to make of' the material that follows a Generalization. As an example of this pattern and its imperfect handling, consider the following brief paragraph of self-classification written by a student in class at the start of a freshman composition course:

> I am an introvert. I have no problems with making or keeping friends. I am very rational, easy going and most of the time I like to be alone. Although sometimes I find it strange not communicating with my peers. There may be a reason for my being this way. I am constantly thinking, often about a number of things that may occur on any day of the week, things of the pass; but, most of all question and mysteries of our world and universe that may never be answered. I enjoy it and the time I spend with myself. I am slowly uncovering the inate ability of my minds-capacity to understand and reason; which is a big plus for me.

Some classmates commented that the paragraph seemed to be built on the Generalization-plus-specifics schema, but that it did not go together as an illustration of the 'introvert' generalization as well as it would with another term like *meditative* or *contemplative* (the last term supplied by the instructor). Notice, by the way, the interaction of content and form here: one interprets, or reinterprets, the content in terms of the apparent form, shaping the understanding of the specifications and the generalization so that they 'fit' each other. This example leads directly into the third function of schemata, which is to allow predictions of what is coming next to be made. From the reader's side, these predictions reduce uncertainty and allow the assimilation of extra detail. From the writer's side, these predictions function as leads to what is to be said next and how the pattern he is embarked on must be completed.

We can think of schemata, then, as ideas or models of order, patterns of coherence that we expect to find, and seek to find, in discourse. As noted in the previous chapter, the type of discourse one is engaged in bears with it conventions of the kind of schemata that should prove relevant in constructing the particular text. It is only by reading and practice that one learns how to wield the schemata special to certain types of discourses. To indent, for example, is to make a commitment to writing 'a paragraph,' and students who do not indent on placement tests and on in-class writing (see the example just discussed) are signalling their uncertainty about making this commitment. One might say that the student's sentences of self-classification cited above in their original, unindented form are hesitating on the verge of becoming a paragraph.

Labored reading, miscomprehension, and sheer incomprehension occur when the reader cannot find the schema or must wrestle with interfering incorrect schemata that he does find. These difficulties are not always the writer's fault, however, since ignorance, inattention, and wayward associations on the part of the reader will also produce them. Further, since many schemata are essentially stereotypes and conventionally held beliefs, the passage of time may produce readers who no longer come to texts with the assumptions the original readers did. Thus many teachers of Renaissance literature feel that some description of the Elizabethan world picture is now necessary so that students can put Renaissance texts together as they could be put together when the relevant schemata were more on the order of common knowledge. Similarly with biblical allusions: readers ignorant of scripture will lack the schemata that make sense of portions of works of earlier literature.

The notion of failed comprehension must not lead us into thinking that schematizing always comes to a clear-cut Succeed/Fail termination. We may think of schematizing as aiming for a 'best fit' of schema to details of the text, but in practice we may settle for relatively good or less good fits. David Rumelhart puts it nicely: "As we discover increasingly more specific schemata to account for the passage, we have an increasing amount of structure in the schema and we find that the more specific schemata yield better fits to more of the detail of the passage. Depending on our knowledge and our purpose in reading we may settle for a more or less specific schema corresponding to a more or less deep understanding of the passage."[7] He goes on to add another qualification, which is that one schema need not crowd out the others. Typically, in fact, several may be applicable: "Finally, it must be emphasized that more than one schema must be used to account for the various parts of a situation at any one time. In fact, a configuration of mutually consistent and interrelating schemata are normally found to account for a situation in its entirety." Complete incomprehension, then, is one extreme of a continuum, and, I think, a very rare occurrence.

The distinction between formal and content-oriented schemata probably cannot be drawn in an absolutely categorical fashion, and for our purposes it need not be. For one thing, content schemata may have internal structures that can be described in formal terms, as for example the general/particular, permanent/fleeting, universal/idiosyncratic opposition employed by Johnson in the sample from the *Preface to Shakespeare*. A schema with dichotomous or antithetical structure is often worked out in the form of Contrast. Similarly, the 'rape' schema has an action/narrative structure. We may think of formal schemata as types of relations between concepts in content schemata. What attention to formal structure does is to give a recipe for constructing super-schemata for essays. Many word definitions have the form of a generalization plus specifics, and by carrying this process out over several sentences, we in effect fabricate a similarly structured configuration on a higher (i.e., more comprehensive) level.

Second, there may be interaction between levels, so that perception of the formal relations intended between elements may be a clue to their proper interpretation as parts of the larger content schema. For example, the first sentence of the second paragraph of the first Macaulay sample reads: "The character of Milton was peculiarly distinguished by loftiness of spirit; that of Dante by intensity of feeling." As the passage unfolds, this difference turns out to be an absolute opposition; the parallelism suggests a major division—particularly to those familiar with Macaulay's use of it. That is to say, his way of using parallelism to signal antithesis is partly a convention established with the reader. Those who are not in on the convention, however, can take the sentence as expressing two very similar qualities (reading *loftiness* as 'height') and miss an important clue to the relevant interpretive content schemata.

The main point to bear in mind is that form is not something we pour a plastic content into; getting material schematized is the fundamental structuring operation.

Traditional handbooks and rhetorics have concerned themselves chiefly with describing and prescribing formal schemata. This is a reasonable procedure insofar as these are the ones that are not conditioned by the particular matter the writer wants to set forth. We too will spend the bulk of this chapter discussing them. But this procedure tends to exaggerate the actual importance of formal patterns and indicators of pattern. Good content schemata will often carry the day: one can paragraph 'rhetorically,' omit transitions, leave topic sentences implicit, and so on through the whole list of ways that real texts deviate from the prescription of what one should do. In fact, as we all know, transitions, connectives, and topic sentences are not always necessary, though sometimes one loses one's bearings and craves signposts. The mistake often made, however, is to think that the formal structure is weak at the points where these needs arise: in fact, it may be the content schema that has run out (or broken down) or is understood in a different way by the reader. Before turning to formal schemata, I want to discuss three passages that some readers have found difficult for reasons of content rather than form. These experiences of difficulty reflect the organizing, integrating, and predicting functions of schemata (respectively), though here by partial absence and failure.

1. *Content schemata*

The first passage is "Exhibit J" from Richard Hofstadter's *Anti-Intellectualism in American Life*.[8] The book was published in 1962, and the chapter from which this exhibit is taken details manifestations of anti-intellectualism in the immediately preceding decade. The preceding exhibits are right-wing attacks by Senator McCarthy, Billy Graham, red-baiting congressmen, and the like. Here is Exhibit J:

> In the post-Sputnik furor over American education, one of the most criticized school systems was that of California, which had been notable for its experimentation with curricula. When the San Francisco School District commissioned a number of professional scholars to examine their schools, the committee constituted for this purpose urged a return to firmer academic standards. Six educational organizations produced a sharp counterattack in which they criticized the authors of the San Francisco report for "academic pettiness and snobbery" and for going beyond their competence in limiting the purposes of education to "informing the mind and developing the intelligence," and reasserted the value of "other goals of education,

such as preparation for citizenship, occupational competence, successful family life, self-realization in ethical, moral, aesthetic and spiritual dimensions, and the enjoyment of physical health." The educationists argued that an especially praiseworthy feature of American education had been

> the attempt to avoid a highly rigid system of education. To do so does not mean that academic competence is not regarded as highly important to any society, but it does recognize that historically, *education systems which stress absorption of accumulated knowledge for its own sake have tended to produce decadence.* Those who would "fix" the curriculum and freeze educational purpose misunderstand the unique function of education in American democracy.

This exhibit does not 'speak for itself' for many readers today. It is hard for some people to get the good guys sorted out from the bad guys, the intellectual position from the anti-intellectual one. This is largely a result of a shift in alignments that has occurred since 1962 with 'back to basics,' 'firmness' and 'rigidity' now associated with the right wing (which remains associated, as ever, with anti-intellectualism). Applying this schema to Hofstadter's passage, we end up identifying the 'professional scholars' as right-wing anti-intellectuals and the 'educationists' as intellectuals. This of course jars with the rather loaded terms *professional scholars* and *educationists*. So the passage is hard to get one's bearings in, because we bring the wrong political schema to it, one that Hofstadter cannot be blamed for not taking account of. Indeed, Hofstadter may be said to have put an expiration date on the whole passage with the phrase 'the post-Sputnik furor over American education'—this is no longer part of 'common knowledge' any more than 'post-Lindbergh developments in aviation.'

The next example, which illustrates an integrative failure, occurs in Robert Stockwell's *The Foundations of Syntactic Theory* in his chapter on "Types of Syntactic Rules." Stockwell enumerates four properties of rewrite rules, the second of which is

> 2. Each rule applies regardless of the structure around the item to which it applies.[9]

He then gives an example (with diagram), enumerates the other two properties, and then expands on each one of them as conditions that guarantee the result will be a sensible grammar. When he gets to the second condition, he says,

> The second condition defines a particular type of phrase-structure rule, what is known as a *context-free* rule. At some point in a deriva-

tion, it is necessary to examine the context and make decisions which are SENSITIVE to that context. For our purposes that point can be postponed until the bottom of the derivation, where words are looked up and attached to the category symbols; we will then be employing *context-sensitive* rules.

One of my best and most conscientious linguistics students proclaimed herself unable to fathom what a *context-free* rule was. This was perplexing to me, since it seems clear that Stockwell indicates by very explicit formal signalling that the 'second condition' was to be read in terms of (or integrated with) the 'second property.' That is, *context-free* = 'applying regardless of the structure around the item.' Despite the clear signals, she did not make this identification. Finally we discovered that by *context* she understood 'preceding sentences and situations.' This is certainly the most common use of *context* in a grammar class and in earlier chapters of Stockwell's book, and his discussion of context-sensitive rules was not clear enough to her to push this first sense of *context* away (she was still quite unsure about what a derivation is). And as long as that first sense stays in mind, it blocks seeing the symbols flanking the 'item' in a tree as constituting its context in the required sense. In short, the schema of 'examining the context' that she applied prevented a necessary integration. Stockwell, of course, might have indicated that *context* in this chapter is being used in a different and more technical sense than in previous chapters.

My illustration of a breakdown in the predictive function of schemata is based on a sentence from a widely anthologized piece of Tom Wolfe's, "O Rotten Gotham: Going Down the Behavioral Sink." In citing this passage, I do not suppose that it will be experienced as extremely difficult by most of the readers of this book. It was, however, absolutely baffling for large numbers of students in a midwestern state university in 1979:

In everyday life in New York—just the usual, getting to work, working in massively congested areas like 42nd Street between Fifth Avenue and Lexington, especially now that the Pan-Am Building is set in there, working in cubicles such as those in the editorial offices at Time-Life, Inc., which Dr. Hall cites as typical of New York's poor handling of space, working in cubicles with low ceilings and, often, no access to a window, while construction crews all over Manhattan drive everybody up the Masonite wall with air-pressure generators with noises up to the boil-a-brain decibel level, then rushing to get home, piling into subways and trains, fighting for time and for space, the usual day in New York—the whole now-normal thing keeps shooting jolts of adrenalin into the body, breaking down the body's

defenses and winding up with the work-a-daddy human animal
stroked out at the breakfast table with his head apoplexed like a cau-
liflower out of his $6.95 semi-spread Pima-cotton shirt, and nosed
over into a plate of No-Kloresto egg substitute, signing off with the
black thrombosis, cancer, kidney, liver, or stomach failure, and the
adrenals ooze to a halt, the size of eggplants in July.[10]

When it became apparent that the passage as written was unreadable
for my students, I assigned the task of rewriting it to make it clearer,
omitting details or modifiers if they seemed to clutter things up and
obscure the main point. Here are two typical revisions:

> Everyday life in New York is no easy or pleasant experience. Just
> getting to work in massively congested areas can be very difficult.
> The cubicles with their Masonite walls and high pressure generators
> producing continuous noise are typical of New York City's offices
> during the working hours. Getting home from work is also a very
> trying experience. The rushing to save time and the scramble for a
> seat on the subway or train are typical situations in New York City.
> The continuous cycle of New York City life, with its everyday
> traumas draining adrenalin into the body, along with poor daily di-
> ets, brings about an early death from cancer, or kidney, liver or
> stomach failure. Life goes on for the rest of the lawn with one less
> blade of grass.

> Everyday life in New York is the same, day-in and day out. The
> days start with a person getting up and going to work in a congested
> downtown. The people work in small rooms with low ceilings and,
> often, no access to a window. Construction crews all over Manhattan
> drive everyone up the wall with the noise from their jack-hammers.
> At the end of the day everyone rushes home. They all pile into sub-
> ways and trains, fighting for time and space. This kind of fast pace
> living finally takes its toll, by bringing death to those who live it.

What is germane to our purposes about these passages is the chunk-
ing up into sentence units and the use of summarizing, evaluating
words. The revisions present the materal as new to the reader—they
are presenting it, not presupposing it as Wolfe does. (The sense of
presuppose that is relevant here, by the way, is that conveyed by the
phrase *of course*: we will use this concept extensively in chapter five
when discussing Given information.) Wolfe assumes that the 'life is
hell for the Manhattan commuter' schema is entirely familiar, as are
'Grand Central Station at rush hour,' 'jackhammers,' and so on.
These are instances of the conventionalized 'knowledge' and attitudes that one shares as a member of the New York community. The
prose is not burdened with conveying any of this as new. Once we

plug in the relevant schemata, the direction is wholly predictable, and we can appreciate the ingenuity of the expression of what are, in fact, well-worn schemata. This is the general principle sanctioning baroque, involuted, suspensive syntax touched on in chapter one: the syntax is suspended, but the reader is in little doubt about where it's all going. But my students simply lacked the relevant schemata. This passage was new information to them—perhaps their first exposure to applied urban sociology—and, lacking the knowledge to predict where it is going, they found the suspensions and elaborations along the way simply overwhelming.

The conclusion to be drawn from these three experiences of difficulty is not that the passages are poorly written. All writing is interpreted against a background of beliefs, knowledge, and concerns that the writer believes are accessible to the reader; to imagine an audience involves deciding what you can take for granted. It is certainly not Hofstadter's fault, or Wolfe's, for example, that pieces of their work intended for special audiences should occasion difficulties when presented to an undergraduate audience in a textbook on reading and writing a decade later. Indeed, one might make a reasonable pedagogical point by calling attention to the dependence of these pieces on their cultural milieus. What the concept of schemata adds to our understanding here is a means of identifying the sources of difficulties at a level well beyond the sentence, or even the paragraph. Notice also that the problematic schemata—the 'right-wing–anti-intellectual–non-academic' configuration and the 'Manhattan commuter–rat race' are not premises or missing links in the chain of argumentation; these cases do not involve inexplicitness in that sense.

The problem with the altered meaning of *context* in the Stockwell excerpt is a little different, because the passage is from a textbook addressed to the undergraduate (or graduate) nonlinguist. The art of writing a good introductory textbook lies in communicating not just the main definitions and procedures of a subject, but the whole conceptual framework and way of thinking that constitute the discipline—what, in fact, all linguists (in this instance) take for granted. But the textbook writer must do so by tying these specially defined schemata into the more common or general-purpose schemata the student already has while not obscuring the difference. This is an extraordinarily difficult task, principally because one is less aware of the overarching assumptions that organize and make sense of one's thinking than one is of the thinking itself. In this respect, schemata correspond to the 'scripts' or 'images' of depth psychology.

2. Formal schemata as organizers

Like schemata of content, schemata of form come in varying levels
of generality and comprehensiveness. They range from the relatively
large or higher-order ones, such as the patterns of paragraph, paragraph block, and essay development marked by things like transitional paragraphs and 'traffic signals' (*Turning now to the second point
. . .*), to relatively more restricted ones that operate over stretches of
two or three sentences, or even within sentences. These include the
connective relations (additive, adversative, temporal, and causal),
patterns of parallelism and antithesis, correlative pairs (*not only/but
also, not this/but rather that, as/as, neither/nor,* etc.), and even punctuation. With the global patterns, the organizing function of schemata is
most salient; at more local levels, the integrative and predictive
functions come to the fore.

A writer's style may be regarded as the pattern of choices or preferences for certain formal schemata over others. In this light, it
seems curious that treatments of style are usually confined to preferences on the fairly local (even the one-sentence) level, as if the way a
writer chooses to organize the text is not a stylistic choice. In this
section, I will examine options among organizing schemata, drawing
on a number of studies that suggest that certain patterns may present material in an easier, more assimilable manner than others. The
following section will shift the focus down to patterns of development on the one-and-two-sentence level and engage in a more familiar sort of 'stylistic' analysis.

Perhaps the largest choice facing the writer is the type of schema
to use to organize his material. One might think that as long as the
material lies in an unschematized state, the choice of overarching
schema should be relatively free, though in practice, of course, there
is a kind of interplay between the way pieces of things take shape
and the initial intention; certain patterns seem to suit the material
better than others as it struggles toward articulation. Normally, the
form serves the meaning, and it is quite artificial to instruct students
to write an essay of a certain form, since they must find matter to
suit the form, instead of the other way around. The purpose, of
course, is to sensitize and exercise the students in the conventions of
form. While schemata of form are conventional, they are also, as
noted above, natural inasmuch as they are immanent in content
schemata. What is conventional about them is the manner and the
degree to which they are highlighted in an essay. They codify expectations that readers bring to essays. Or should bring—there is an
implicit assumption in the freshman composition handbooks that the

formal patterns of classification, definition, comparison and contrast, cause and effect analysis, etc. need to be taught, that they are not as easy for students as narration and description. Numerous considerations suggest that this is true, and that this difference reflects an even deeper tendency of adult readers, what is sometimes called a 'bias toward narrative' or toward thinking of things according to the pattern of human actions. Ultimately, it may underlie the well-nigh universally expressed preference for the active voice and for a vividly verbal style.

The first of these considerations is the developmental commonplace that we master narrative both as readers and writers before we master the more abstract, analytic patterns. James Moffett makes this notion one of the keys of his ordered K–13 writing program.[11] Freshman composition teachers, and especially remedial teachers, know how fluent struggling students can become if they can work a piece of narrative into an essay. As readers, too, freshmen seem to approach model essays as if they were stories; they try to wrestle them into narrative schemata—their calling the essays 'stories' is, I think, revealing, though it may partly reflect the use of the term for articles in a newspaper, many of which are only rudimentarily stories.

Some interesting light on this preference for narrative is shed by an ingenious study conducted by Arthur Graesser et al. with psychology students at California State University at Fullerton.[12] The subjects, who were under the impression they were waiting for the experiment to begin, were placed alone in a room with a sheet from the *National Enquirer,* which the previous 'subject' (a confederate) had been avidly reading as the new subject came in. Remarkably, eighteen of the twenty subjects picked up the sheet and read around in it. When they had finished reading, the experimenter came in and gave them a second sheet to read, telling them that they would be tested on its contents. They were given as much time to read the second sheet as they had taken on the first. Graesser and his group found that the subjects remembered more narrative material than static facts under both conditions and significantly more narrative material than facts when reading for their own purpose (to kill time) than when reading to be tested. Graesser et al. conclude that when reading what they choose to read, "individuals tend to select and construct active, narrative conceptualizations more than static descriptions during the course of comprehending a selected passage" (p. 368).

This conclusion will not surprise very many people: it is the way that this study isolates and confirms the intuitions of teachers and writers that is interesting. One can perform informal experiments on oneself and friends that suggest that a good narrative structure facilitates storage (or retrieval) of facts. Consider, for example, how the Big Bang theory of the origin of the universe organizes facts and is known by people who don't know a nebula from a galaxy or a comet from an asteroid. Evolutionary theory provides a way for the biology student to keep the various phyla in order. One could argue, in fact, that a science must develop a good story if it wants to win the layman's mind.

Writers aspiring to explain technical notions to an audience of nonspecialists are aware of this bias toward narrative and use narrative patterns whenever possible. Two of the sample passages are from works of this nature. Rachel Carson continually organizes descriptions of oceanographic facts in terms of tours, origins, cycles, and processes (the sample was deliberately chosen for its lack of narrative structuring, but even there it is an undercurrent). George Miller, when reporting a psychological experiment, always shifts into a strongly marked narrative mode. Look at the second paragraph of the sample, which describes Pavlov's experiment(s) with inducing neurosis in dogs: four successive sentences beginning with time adverbials! How dramatically different this is from the conventional abstract of a scientific article. Compare, for example, Graesser et al.'s own abstract:

> This study explores what information is selected and acquired when readers genuinely want to read textual material. College students read sheets from the *National Enquirer* news magazine in both Self-induced and Task-induced reading conditions. In Self-induced conditions they read the new [sic] sheets voluntarily and did not expect to be tested on the contents. In Task-induced conditions the students knew they were in an experiment that would assess memory for the material they read. In the Self-induced reading condition the subjects tended to select articles on familiar topics and they extracted more active, narrative code than static descriptions. In contrast, article selection was not guided by familiarity and there was no "narrative bias" in Task-induced reading conditions. The differences in information extraction between Self-induced and Task-induced reading conditions suggest that it is important to examine knowledge acquisition and text comprehension in ecologically valid reading conditions (p. 355).

This synopsis does try to present things in a sequence, but it jumbles up the story line a bit, and by concentrating on the difference of Task-induced and Self-induced 'conditions' gives the misleading impression that the subjects were divided into two groups and participated in one 'condition' or the other but not both and not in immediate sequence. But at least we have some idea of who did what and what happened; notice the sequence of sentences with *the students* as Subject of active verbs telling what they did. This is quite unusual for a psychological abstract—compare the following abstract of another article in the same issue:

> Inferential comprehension and recall of stories by children, 5 and 8 years of age, were studied where the story protagonist's motivation and other referential information crucial to understanding the story were varied. The inclusion of negative or positive protagonist's goals versus a "neutral" goal led to qualitatively different and better inferential comprehension as measured by probe questions. However, these manipulations did not affect how well the children recalled the stories. In addition, when the children in the two age groups were matched for retrieval of propositions crucial to the inferences, the older children made more inferences. These data suggest that inferential comprehension may be independent of surface recall of text and that inference probes are better measures of comprehension than free recall measures.[13]

A great reconstructive effort is necessary to get a story out of this. In addition, an extremely misleading action sequence is suggested involving some sort of contest between the older and younger children that spurred the older children to make more inferences (this didn't happen—the recalls were matched). Of course it is true that the Abstract is a highly conventionalized signalling device designed for the use of other specialists; it makes no attempt to engage the layman; but perhaps we are justified in complaining that we are all laymen at heart. Roger Schank and Robert Abelson maintain that much of our knowledge is organized and stored in the form of episodes rather than being abstractly categorized.[14] If so, we may find it easier to assimilate material organized as an episode to our knowledge. Viewed in this way, the passages from the USDA report and the insurance policy cited in chapter one are difficult not because their syntax obscures their content but because they shun a natural and easy way of schematizing the material in favor of an abstractive, classificatory one.

Another kind of writing that mixes narrative and other ordering patterns is how-to-do-it instruction. Cookbooks, for example, use a basic narrative line, but sometimes put things out of actual temporal sequence to emphasize the component subprocesses. Very few cookbooks actually tell you what to do in the exact order you should do it. Every novice cook learns to distrust the 'preheat the oven' instruction that so often precedes half an hour of chopping, peeling, trimming, sautéing, etc. One learns to read a cookbook much as one learns to read any author—by tuning in on the characteristic ways things are said and developing the needed set of interpretive conventions to map from the cookbook 'narrative' onto a plan of execution. One of the reasons people like one cookbook or another is the relative ease they experience in constructing this mapping.

Some recent work by Bonnie Meyer and associates suggests that preferences differ even among the nonnarrative structural patterns. Meyer and her group worked chiefly with ninth graders but with junior college and graduate students and retired people as well.[15] Their basic strategy was to analyze the free-recall accounts of paragraphs the subjects had read, looking for the structure of the original passage in the recall. They found that much more material from the original passage appeared in the recalls that reproduced the formal structure of the original passge, suggesting that the pattern is useful in retrieving the material from memory (both immediately after reading and after a week's delay) and hence that it must have been used in coding material. There was a marked difference, however, in the usefulness of different patterns. Each passage had one of four possible structures: 'attribution' ("relates a collection of attributes to an event or idea"), 'response' ("relates a problem or question to a solution"), 'adversative' ("relates what did happen to what did not, or a favored view to an opposing view"—close to contrast), and 'covariance' ("relates an antecedent condition to its consequent"—cause and effect). For most of their subjects, the second two patterns brought back more information than the first two and were more often reflected in the recalls. This was true even when essentially the same material was presented in the different forms. Meyer suggests that this effect may reflect the greater amount of structure the contrast and cause/effect schemata give to the material. Other interpretations are possible, however: Meyer reports that two groups of subjects did not show this preference for contrast and cause/effect over attribution and response, namely, the retired subjects and relatively poor-reading ninth graders. This suggests that the purposes for reading may make some difference. The generally more useful patterns are those of analytic and critical thinking, and retired persons are often content to seek confirmation for their views in their reading rather than to seek to enlarge or sharpen them. They have accordingly less use for the analytic patterns. A similar explanation might be offered for the parallel preference of the less able ninth graders. It is possible, too, that the bias toward narrative discussed earlier enters in here by favoring cause/effect or 'what happened versus what did not,' but without examining the passages used it is hard to tell.

Two other findings from these studies bear mention. One is that the efficiency of formal schemata in recall is reduced when the material read is familiar and interesting. One of the tests was run on a passage discussing killer whales just after the class had completed a unit on the ocean and just before a trip to Sea World, and on the delayed recall, use of the structural pattern of the original did not produce the usual dramatic increase in the amount of material recalled. Meyer concludes:

> It seems plausible that use of the top-level structure would be a less crucial strategy for this highly familiar and motivating content. With extensive prior knowledge of a topic, the propositions from the passage are integrated into propositions stored in memory. The rich network on the topic provides many cues and links (Anderson, 1976) which facilitate recall independently of the use of the author's top-level structure (p. 14).

It is also perhaps reasonable to suppose that this sort of assimilation is always likely to occur to various degrees and to occur more if the reader is interested in the material and has some reason to integrate it into his working knowledge. Form is more important as a way of assembling things that are kept 'out there.' Content becomes meaning-for-the-reader when it bears on his existence. A similar effect was observed by P. Clements with regard to a passage on psychosurgery read by some subjects who happened to have recently viewed *One Flew Over the Cuckoo's Nest:* sentences dealing with psychosurgery were far more salient than their formal prominence would predict.[16]

The last point concerns the teaching of these formal patterns. One of Meyer's graduate students (D. M. Brandt) demonstrated that pre-teaching the structure of individual passages did *not* increase the use of the author's structure in the recalls. Another, more fortunate, graduate student (B. J. Bartlett) did discover a way to stimulate the use of structural patterns by teaching them an hour a day for a week and building the student's ability to abstract them. Apparently, for the structuring to be effective, the student must learn to do it for himself—it must be a pattern he finds and uses. And presumably the same can be said about writing. At the same time, the evidence for a preference for or bias toward narrative seems strong enough to warrant the general piece of advice: Organize your material into a narrative or at least a quasi-temporal sequence whenever you can. Indeed, as noted earlier, the advice given in so many books and articles to use finite clauses with specified Subjects instead of abstract nominals seems to address the syntactic symptoms of the underlying non-narrative illness.

3. *Formal schemata as integrators*

As mentioned in the introduction and in chapter one, we cannot predict the actual constructive acts a particular sentence form or pattern will trigger in a reader's mind, principally because the processing of syntactic units interacts with the body of text already read, and the predictions or expectations can render the intake of material easier (or harder) than would be the case if syntactic processing were something that had to be done first (bottom-to-top). Nonetheless, we can identify certain patterns in the ways writers present material on the one- and two-sentence level and can link up aspects of our experience of these texts with the appearance of these recurrent patterns. Again it should be stressed that these effects are not directly caused by intrinsic properties of the syntactic patterns: rather, it is their recurrent use that enables readers to base their expectations and integrative maneuvers on them. Reading a writer becomes easier as we become familiar with (i.e., learn) his or her characteristic modes of carrying forward the line of thought.

The sort of stylization I am referring to here is well within the reach of the freshman writer. Indeed, composition classes that focus on patterns such as the cumulative sentence or sentence embedding are often temporarily too successful in getting students to pattern their prose. Most writers pass through stages of excessive fondness for certain constructions and suffer occasional attacks in later life. The excess, by the way, lies in using the same formal pattern to signal what are diverse relationships and in repeating the same pattern to call attention to it rather than allowing it to accomplish its work inobtrusively. Students are usually surprised to discover the formal patterns described in handbooks in the works of the most polished writers; what also must be remembered is that they did not notice them before.

Traditional stylistic analysis has attempted to describe differences in the kinds of integrative experiences writers set up by distinguishing between periodic and loose (or cumulative) styles. Some analysts (such as Francis Christensen) have given this distinction a fairly narrow definition in terms of syntactic units, but customarily the opposition is treated in the fuzzier terms of material necessary to the completion of 'the thought' being delayed or not delayed. There is wisdom in this woolier view, though one of its consequences is rarely spelled out: we cannot be sure how effectively suspensive a particular syntactic suspension will prove to be. Also, the same sort of integrative pattern may have several different syntactic manifestations. We need to approach this matter from the point of view of the integrative act rather than the syntax, and to discuss the interaction between them. As long as we are focusing on this 'micro' level, we can work fairly sensibly with snippets, though all the examples instanced below are drawn from the samples, and the reader can refer to the larger context as he or she wishes.

One noticeable trait of Edith Hamilton's style is a two-clause sequence in which the second clause restates the first, perhaps specifying it further or explaining the strong claims of the first sentence. Consider, for example, these sequences:

> There is no danger now that the world will not give Greek genius full recognition. Greek achievement is a fact universally acknowledged.

> Rather it is the fashion nowadays to speak of the Greek miracle, to consider the radiant bloom of Greek genius as having no root in any soil that we can give an account of. The anthropologists are busy, indeed, and ready to transport us back into the savage forest where all human things, the Greek things, too, had their beginnings; but the seed never explains the flower. Between those strange rites they point us to through the dim vistas of far-away ages, and a Greek tragedy, there lies a gap they cannot help us over.

> This is what we know as the Oriental state today. It has persisted down from the ancient world through thousands of years, never changing in any essential. Only in the last hundred years—less than that—it has shown a semblance of change, made a gesture of outward conformity with the demands of the modern world. But the spirit that informs it is the spirit of the East that never changes. It has remained the same through all the ages down from the antique world, forever aloof from all that is modern.

> They were the first Westerners; the spirit of the West, the modern spirit, is a Greek discovery and the place of the Greeks is in the modern world.

> Many things there pointed back to the old world and away to the East, and with the emperors who were gods and fed a brutalized people full of horrors as their dearest form of amusement, the ancient and the Oriental state had a true revival.

The pattern here is dominantly that of a sharp, slightly cryptic statement, just arresting enough to get one's attention, and then an explanatory unpacking. The first example cited, however, is almost a filler or rehearsing use of this strategy, which is the basis of the entire second paragraph. Note that this pattern has several syntactic manifestations: the simplest is the sentence pair in the first example; in the second, we have the appositive infinitives

> to speak of the Greek miracle,
> to consider the radiant bloom . . .

and the expansion in the last full sentence of the slightly gnomic conclusion of the preceding: *but the seed never explains the flower.* A little later this pattern is repeated with only a semicolon separating the expansion:

> but in truth the way across is not impassable;
> some reasons appear for the mental and spiritual activity which made those few years in Athens productive as no other age in history has been.

The semicolon juncture is repeated in the other examples, varied in one by simple coordination (. . . *to the East, and with the emperors* . . .). The syntax, in other words, does not directly match the formal pattern, but the pattern is so sustained that it is its own clue: one quickly adjusts, begins to expect further expansions of the cryptic statements (instead, for example, of looking back to see if one has missed something) and to interpret incoming material as a rephrasing of the point just made.

If we have only two terms to describe this sort of patterning—cumulative and periodic—we would have to call this cumulative, but it is not cumulative in the same way that standard examples with appositives and participles following the main assertion are. There are examples of this type also in the passages cited (e.g., *It has persisted down from the ancient world through thousands of years, //never changing in any essential; It has remained the same through all the ages down from the antique world, //forever aloof from all that is modern*). The added material in these does not justify or explain the main assertion as the second clause in Hamilton's basic pattern does; rather, it fills in details of the statement outlined in the first clause. This distinction is reflected in the dispensability of the second unit of material: if the first stands and functions in the argument without the second, then it is the standard cumulative type.

This detail-filling is the dominant function of the added material in the classic cumulative pattern described and catalogued by Francis Christensen.[17] This pattern is one of Rachel Carson's favorites. Here are a few examples from the sample:

> It [the continental shelf] is scored by deep troughs between which banks and islands rise—further evidence of the work of the ice. The deepest shelves surround the Antarctic continent, where soundings in many areas show depths of several hundred fathoms near the coast and continuing out across the shelf.
>
> Biologically the world of the continental slope, like that of the abyss, is a world of animals—a world of carnivores where each creature preys upon another.

Like river-cut canyons, sea canyons are deep and winding valleys, V-shaped in cross section, their walls sloping down at a steep angle to a narrow floor.

According to one theory, there were heavy submarine mud flows during the times when the glaciers were advancing and sea level fell the lowest; mud stirred up by waves poured down the continental slopes and scoured out the canyons.

Only in the last example does the second unit of material significantly explain something left incomplete in the first unit. The integrative strategy signalled by the Carson-type cumulative sequence is therefore different: the second unit of material really is an afterthought that can be attached, sometimes loosely, to some part of the first unit (or skipped, if one wishes). Accordingly, the second unit never provides the point of departure for the next clause or sentence as it frequently does in Hamilton.

Here is a double example of the cumulative, detail-filling type from the first Macaulay sample that raises a difficult theoretical point:

It was a loathsome herd, which could be compared to nothing so fitly as to the rabble of Comus, grotesque monsters, half bestial half human, dropping with wine, bloated with gluttony, and reeling in obscene dances. Amidst these that fair Muse was placed, like the chaste lady of the Masque, lofty, spotless, and serene, to be chattered at, and pointed at, and grinned at, by the whole rout of Satyrs and Goblins.

The strings of modifiers in each sentence follow the pair of entities they describe and spell out the points of the comparison that has already been declared. The pattern of the two sentences is extremely parallel: adjectival modifiers precede verbal ones (i.e., participials and infinitives), about three of each in each sentence. Macaulay's writing is in general marked throughout by this sort of meticulous, almost fanatical, attention to syntactic detail. Note, however, that there is a double likeness in the last sentence: Muse, like chaste lady, is lofty, spotless, and serene; she is placed there, like the chaste lady in Comus, to be chattered at, and pointed at, etc. Possibly, however, this distinction between 'Muse' and 'her being placed there' does not correspond to a real difference in the way the two sets of phrases are integrated into the composite 'image' of the Muse amidst the satyrs. This is essentially a question of whether the integration here is done in terms of syntactic units and relations or in some other way. This sentence doesn't seem to me any more taxing or complex than the preceding one, though that may be because the preceding one rehearses the integrative maneuver. At the very least, we should leave this matter open and should not assume, as I have previously done, that the integration of material that involves a syntactic relation of modifier-to-head must necessarily be carried out by matching each phrase to its syntactic head.

It is interesting to note that parallelism, like apposition, is usually a backwards-looking integrative signal. That is, when we see a second phrase or sentence unfolding in a pattern like the preceding one, we may take it 'in the light of' the previous phrase or sentence—we can be relatively sure that it will not carry us into a new stage of thinking. Other examples of parallelism functioning this way are rife in the nineteenth-century samples and can be checked by inspection.

The classic periodic sentence is but one type of suspensive pattern. The pattern is essentially one of interruption or delay before some unit that has been started is completed. When the unit is a syntactic one, and the completion occurs at the end of the clause, we have a periodic sentence. The following examples are grouped according to type of unit delayed. The first group have complex subjects:

> To bring a lover, a lady, and a rival into the fable; to entangle them in contradictory obligations, perplex them with oppositions of interest, and harass them with violence of desires inconsistent with each other; to make them meet in rapture and part in agony, to fill their mouths with hyperbolical joy and outrageous sorrow, to distress them as nothing human ever was distressed, to deliver them as nothing human ever was delivered, is the business of a modern dramatist. (Johnson, 5)

> That critical discernment is not sufficient to make men poets, is generally allowed. (Macaulay, II, 3)

> That which distinguishes the modern world from the ancient, and that which divides the West from the East, is the supremacy of mind in the affairs of men. . . . (Hamilton, 4)

As every student of transformational grammar knows, there is an alternative pattern in which *it* is used as a dummy filler in Subject position and the complex infinitive or *that*-clause is shifted to the end of the clause, following the main predicate. This second alternative lowers the suspensive tension of the first form. Another delaying strategy is beginning a sentence with a good bit of adverbial or other qualifying matter:

> In all the branches of physical and moral science which admit of perfect analysis, he who can resolve will be able to combine. (Macaulay, II, 2)

In the moment in which the skill of the artist is perceived, the spell of the art is broken. (Macaulay, II, 3)

Between those strange rites they point us to through the dim vistas of far-away ages, and a Greek tragedy, there lies a gap they cannot help us over. (Hamilton, 2)

Wherever the line is drawn by this or that historian between the old and the new the Greeks' unquestioned position is in the old. (Hamilton, 3)

In a world where the irrational had played the chief role, they came forward as the protagonists of the mind. (Hamilton, 4)

Another suspensive arrangement has a block of material lodged between Subject and Verb:

while another, employing the same materials, the same verdure, the same water, and the same flowers, committing no inaccuracy, introducing nothing which can be positively pronounced necessary, shall produce no more effect than an advertisement of a capital residence and a desirable pleasure-ground. (Macaulay, II, 2)

This is one thing to be kept in mind. Another is, that the exercise of the creative power in the production of great works of literature or art, however high this exercise of it may rank, is not at all epochs and under all conditions possible; (Arnold, 2)

Shakespeare is, above all writers, at least above all modern writers, the poet of nature. . . . (Johnson, 2)

Venal and licentious scribblers, with just sufficient talent to clothe the thoughts of a pandar in the style of a bellman, were now the favourite writers of the Sovereign and of the public. (Macaulay, I, 3)

Another, highly suspensive, place to insert material is between a subordinating conjunction and the rest of the clause it subordinates:

Hence it was that, though he wrote the Paradise Lost at a time of life when images of beauty and tenderness are in general beginning to fade, even from those minds in which they have not been effaced by anxiety and disappointment, he adorned it with all that is most lovely and delightful in the physical and in the moral world. (Macaulay, I, 4)

Finally, material can be inserted between the copula and a Subject Complement or between auxiliary and main verb:

It was not, as far as at this distance of time can be judged, the effect of external circumstances. (Macaulay, I, 2)

His mind was, in the noble language of the Hebrew poet, "a land of darkness, as darkness itself, and where the light was as darkness." (Macaulay, I, 2)

It is almost too much to expect of poor human nature, that a man capable of producing some effect in one line of literature, should, for the greater good of society, voluntarily doom himself to impotence and obscurity in another. (Arnold, 1)

the creative has, for its happy exercise, appointed elements. . . . (Arnold, 2)

The distribution of these examples suggests that certain patterns are preferred by certain authors; on the whole, Arnold is the freest with his suspensive inserts (I didn't cite many of them because they are so long). Although all these examples involve delays in the business of assembling the syntax, the strain of reading them is reduced by several factors: one is that the domain of suspension is confined to the clause; another is that the relative status and function of the delaying material is indicated (as parenthetic, adverbial, concessive, and so on); a third is that the main clause material is usually not terribly novel: these sentences tend to repeat or recapitulate material introduced in previous sentences. The one noticeable exception to these generalizations is the *Hence it is* . . . sentence from Macaulay that begins a paragraph where it is not clear at the outset what conclusion is being "henced." That sentence is a challenge to the reader, and only one who has paid full and acute attention to all that has gone before will be able to get it integrated into the argument the first time through.

The suspensions surveyed so far depend on basic syntactic patterns. Other special patterns such as cleft sentences ("It is by giving faith to the creations of the imagination that a man becomes a poet") also set up one term that looks to the second for completion. Our 'periodic' authors are equally fond of creating their own suspended patterns by using correlative markers like *as/as, as/so, so/that, such/such, the more/the more, if/then,* and *not/but.* Many of these correlative pairs, which signal a dependence on the second member to complete the pattern, are fairly small-scale structures, but at times the muscle developed on them is extended to its limits. Consider this gorgeously intricate summary sentence in the first Macaulay sample. (I hope that the reader has become sensitized enough to suspensions and formal patterns to enjoy the patterning without any explication of it):

Such as it was when, on the eve of great events, he returned from his travels, in the prime of health and manly beauty, loaded with literary distinctions, and glowing with patriotic hopes, such it continued to be when, after having experienced every calamity which is incident to our nature, old, poor, sightless and disgraced, he retired to his hovel to die. (Macaulay, I, 3)

One is reminded of the Tom Wolfe passage discussed earlier. The information here is very low: Macaulay has already reviewed the salient reverses in Milton's fortunes (and indeed presumes even in that review that the basic facts are known), so the formal ordering is free to become, for the moment, the center of attention.

Generalizing about the effect of periodic sentences on readers, then, is tricky business. To say they require more concentration from the reader, or that they are emphatic, ignores the degree of predictability of the completing member. The most pleasing (and emphatic) ones in my view are those in which the concluding material can almost be guessed, as with *to die* in the last example from Macaulay. Too much predictability and they seem just a variation (as in some of the first examples cited with complex Subjects); too little, and they pester the reader whose need to know distresses him. And, of course, the predictability is not entirely in the writer's control; the purposes, attention, interests, and knowledge of the reader will have a lot to do with the way the pattern is experienced.

The *not/but* pattern repays special attention for, unlike the others, it is not limited to the sentence level and is one of the patterns most heavily used in the samples, especially those from Macaulay and Johnson. It is plainly suspensive in its nature, since you say what something is not before you say what it is. This difference, however, may be more apparent than real, because saying what something is not usually helps to mark out what it is. Some theorists view word meanings as essentially negative in that saying what something is amounts to excluding the things it is not: if someone walked, then he didn't hop, skip, or run, and to say he walked is to mark out a zone of locomotion in which falls whatever he did.[18] In this view, all definition is exclusion anyway, so spelling the exclusion out with *not* is giving an implicit definition. This principle applies on levels higher than the word as well.

The *not/but* construction brings the predictive function of formal schemata into prominence. Since it is pointless to negate possibilities that nobody would think of (What I am writing with is not a lampshade or a cougar or a dishtowel . . .), we can project from a statement of what something is not a fairly narrowly restricted set of things that it is likely to turn out to be. We might say of the *not/but* pattern that it formally delays positive statement but may fairly directly lead one to it. Rather than examine local instances of this pat-

tern that run through the nineteenth-century samples, let us look at
three examples of the pattern operating over several sentences. Here
is one from George Miller, where the *but* part has itself a *not/but*
pattern nested in it:

> Pavlov did not make any direct observations of the processes going
> on in the brain. He based his opinion of them entirely upon infer-
> ences from what the animals did in his experiments. What he looked
> at directly was not the animal's brain, but the animal's behavior. (Mil-
> ler, 1)

The overarching pattern of Miller's last three paragraphs, by the
way, is a *not/but* one: false assessments of Pavlov's importance versus
a final, just one, and within that, the false view of Pavlov (and Freud)
as anti-intellectual leading to a corrected view of them as anti-
optimistic.

The second example is really the entire second paragraph of the
Hamilton sample, where the foolish view of the Greek achievement
as a miracle is sketched, the inability of Cambridge school anthropology to account for it noted, and then the possibility of explaining it asserted.

As one would expect, at this level of generality, the particular
markers of the *not/but* structure are more various, and 'tuning in' on
this pattern is less mechanical than noting an *as* . . . or a *so* . . . . Once
we are tuned in, however, the pattern can get us over some rough
spots. Consider, for example, the first paragraph of the first
Macaulay sample:

> To return for a moment to the parallel which we have been attempt-
> ing to draw between Milton and Dante, we would add that the poetry
> of these great men has in a considerable degree taken its character
> from their moral qualities. They are not egotists. They rarely ob-
> trude their idiosyncrasies on their readers. They have nothing in
> common with those modern beggars for fame, who extort a pittance
> from the compassion of the inexperienced by exposing the naked-
> ness and sores of their minds. Yet it would be difficult to name two
> writers whose works have been more completely, though unde-
> signedly, coloured by their personal feelings.

The sentence *They are not egotists* can pose a problem; if the reader
tries to link it back to moral qualities evident in their poetry, he may
get something like 'modesty' or 'humility' and begin to think
Macaulay's mind is softening. As one reads on, however, finally reading the *yet,* one realizes that the first sentence essentially means 'their
personalities [not virtues] are manifested in their work' and the pas-

sage continues 'not obtruded but revealed undesignedly.' The rule of thumb that helps us here is, "seeing a *not,* expect a *but,*" i.e., "look forward for clarification, not back." An author's style can thus become a guide to construction of the text once we learn the rules of thumb that apply.

When isolated and collected for study, these formal patterns stand out clearly, yet one scarcely sees them at all until he begins to look for them, partly, I think, because we normally attend to constructing what is being said and adjust with as little thought as possible to the way it is being said. Possibly the myth of a plain, simple, direct style arises from this usual experience of formal transparency. In any case, many of the constructions and patternings used by the authors in our samples do not appear to be syntactically simple and direct. These styles are widely admired, however, which suggests that the doctrine of the plain style (described, for example, by Richard Lanham[19]) is narrow-minded and probably falsely grounded. In part, it seems to spring from a naïve confidence in positive statement; E. D. Hirsch for one cities some experiments supposedly demonstrating that sentences with negatives are 'harder to process' (*Philosophy,* p. 150). It is probably this attitude that makes it so hard for many students to develop an idea or shape, modify, or criticize a definition: they do not see that one specifies a concept by excluding plausible but not intended alternative understandings. This attitude in turn reflects an assumption that the reader is an essentially passive receiver of concepts cloaked in words, not an equally active constructor of the intended meaning. A similar view of readers' limitation seems to underlie the belief in simple, uninverted, uninterrupted sentences. Along with this pessimism about the reader's resources and degree of involvement goes a deeply ingrained distrust of artifice and ornament as something that would put off readers and isolate the writer. Commonly freshman writers will disclaim awareness of having written a parallel construction—especially if it is discussed in class. And indeed, one may write them without awareness, for the matter often falls out so, and then all the writer need do is let it happen, or, perhaps, sharpen it just a little. The curious fact is that writing that exhibits care and artfulness in the details of its expression flatters the reader and evokes a willing appreciation for the writer's craft; writing that suggests a low estimation of the reader's attention and involvement projects a dull writer. All of this seems to reflect a primary social reality that other people are generally more interesting, and interested, if you assume that they are.

4. *Making and marking connections: punctuation and connective words*

One of the points where handbooks refer to the intuitions and
judgment of writers is on the matter of marking relations of clauses:
a semicolon, for example, should be used if the 'thoughts' of the two
independent clauses are 'closely related'; a dash marks an abrupt
change in 'thought,' and so on. Similarly, in advising the use of connective words, many handbooks recommend their use 'where helpful
to the reader.' Unfortunately, the notion of mechanics seems to
undercut the call for the use of judgment, and the impression is
often given that the connective words create the connection, so that
all one has to do to write connected, coherent, consecutive, lucid,
explicit prose is to put a connective in each sentence. If we think of
these words and marks only as signals to the reader to guide him or
her toward the type of assembling the writer intends, we will not fall
into these errors.

A number of writers have attempted to classify the types of formal
relations that may exist between two main clauses. There is general
agreement on a basic four-term division into Additive, Adversative,
Causal, and Temporal; disagreement begins at the point of how
many and which subdivisions to make of each class. If we wish to
subdivide very delicately, we may do so down to each connective
word (i.e., each connective word spells out its own special link). John
Locke went even further centuries ago in claiming that there are
even more connective relations than words to express them.[20] If,
however, we allow the number of relations to swell to infinity (i.e.,
each relation between two clauses is unique) we lose the intuition of
type-relatedness and the practical point that it seems useful to have
general indications of how incoming material is to be fitted onto that
which is already assimilated. Each connection is in a sense unique,
insofar as the thoughts are, but we can generalize upwards or specify
downwards to suit our purposes. Connective words and marks are
not the actual links, but indicators of the direction to go in constructing them. We will return to this matter after a brief survey of the
general conventions governing the marking of connections.

The first of these general conventions is that connective words can
indicate links and shifts between groups of sentences as well as between pairs of main clauses; they may be used, in other words, to
articulate larger units. Arnold, for example, makes unusually heavy
use of such 'traffic signals.' (*This is one thing to be kept in mind. Another
is. . . . Now in literature. . . . ; in short; Or, to narrow our range, and quit
these considerations of the general march of genius and society. . . .*) He may
in part use these instead of paragraphing. This firm steering of the

reader contributes to the flavor of public lecture in many of Arnold's writings, probably because heavy use of them is more characteristic of lectures (which do not, effectively, have paragraph indentation).

The second convention is that not every connection needs to be marked: we can make the necessary integrative step without being guided. W. Ross Winterowd nicely illustrates this point (p. 116) by adding to each sentence of a passage the connective words that spell out the integrative connections he automatically made while reading it. There is no small art, in fact, in deciding which links to spell out and which to leave out. The handbooks seem to think that student writing needs more connectives in it. But still—which ones? One partial answer here, which I have never seen in a handbook, is that adversative ('but') connections conventionally require spelling out. The additive ('and as one might expect') relation is the unmarked one: when there is no connective, the reader will take the next clause or sentence as a relatively expectable continuation of the first—or try to. The 'but' relation, however, is counter to expectation in just the sense we have been using the term: if the material following is not going to fall within the set of expectations the reader is projecting, this fact should be signalled. Omission of an adversative connective is a common fault of student writing, and it is a fault because the reader tries to integrate the material additively. Consider the passage of self-description cited early in this chapter:

> I am an introvert. I have no problems with making or keeping friends.

Here the 'introvert' schema (or stereotype) projects an expectation sufficiently contrary to what the next sentence says to attract a *but* rather strongly. Similarly in this passage:

> The life of a cosmetologist is like riding the biggest merry-go-round in the world. Many girls and some boys dream of making other people look nice or even beautiful. It takes a determined person to search for the best merry-go-round with bright lights, music, movement, and a story behind its colorful background.

It seems that a contrast is intended between the dream of many children and the dedicated few who struggle to achieve it, and again a 'but' seems called for.

Another sort of connection that needs marking is the looser connection or aside. It is, of course, not true that everything one wants to say in a paragraph (or paper) is equally relevant to the main point, and it is often helpful simply to mark a portion as incidental or by the way, either with these words or with parentheses. For reasons unknown to me, some teachers tell their students not to use parentheses and treat a student's *by the way* as a confession of inexcusable irrelevance. The result of suppressing these conventional devices, however, is often that the work of sorting out the relevance or centrality is left to the reader. Of course, the reverse is also possible: one may explicitly state that something is 'related' when it is not. This use of 'fake' connectives was nicely satirized by Wayne Booth in his CCCC address in 1979. Saying something is 'related' is fake because it says nothing: any statement is presumably related to what has gone before unless marked otherwise.

The fake connective depends for its deceptive power on a naïve faith in the word to make the connection. This mistaken view is widespread, though few voice it as baldly as Patricia Carpenter and Marcel Just:

> Intersentential connectives relate the sentences of a paragraph to each other much as verbs relate the constituents of a sentence. In cases where the connective does not appear in the text, the reader must infer the relationship between the sentences by drawing on his knowledge of the referential situation. The integrative process should be shorter in duration when connectives do appear and thus make the inference process unnecessary.[21]

The inference process is not complete when the general type of relation has been marked or inferred: the particular connection intended must still be constructed by the reader. More formally stated: texts are interpreted in a particular domain of interpretation (or 'possible world') in which various individuals, laws, and forces are assumed to exist. Plugging into or activating this body of knowledge and assumption is necessary to interpret causal chains, probable inferences, individuals referred to, and intended senses of words, as will be dealt with in succeeding chapters. The depth and range of this inferring of causes and relations will vary with the type and purpose of the discourse. Thus in a fairy tale, typically, the psychological motivation stepmothers have for being cruel is generally not relevant, and the text will be adequately constructed even though it does not motivate such things (say in terms of the feelings or behavior of the father or children). This is an extremely complex and obscure theoretical problem.[22] Its bearing here is simply that the connective words and marks only point the direction for the reader, narrowing the range of possibilities; it is still up to the reader to construct as much of the connecting detail as he deems necessary in the particular instance. To give just one illustration of this point, consider the following sequence:

John belched; Mary blushed.

This suggests a causal ('and so') link, which could be variously written

Mary blushed because John belched.
John belched, and so Mary blushed. (*consequently, inevitably,* etc.)

but what is still necessary is to construct the linking inferences about why John's belching made Mary blush (one may try the stereotypic social convention that, assuming John is Mary's consort, Mary is or feels tarred by the same brush). As noted in chapter two, we can never be totally explicit; we just have to arrange things so that the needed extra-content schemata come readily to mind. This specific interpreting is required for the other connective links as well. Consider, for example, the following sentences:

Voter apathy is the norm and only diminishes when the stands of the candidates are dramatically different on bread and butter issues. For example, the turnout in the 1976 election was very light.

We infer that this example is an example of prevailing apathy and that the writer expects us to supply the information that the stands of the candidates (Ford and Carter?) were not noticeably different. Seeing that something is an example is not enough: we must see in what respects it is. If the writer is inexplicit on this point, he has not spelled it out enough for the reader. This is a besetting vice of my own writing. Sometimes, I suspect, teachers prescribe extra doses of connective words as a cure for a more deeply rooted inexplicitness. In my own case, at least, I know this tendency to leave connections unmarked reflects a fear of insulting the reader's intelligence, or explaining and spelling it out too much and thereby putting the reader off. Further, I hate to manhandle readers, preferring to let them choose to drink the water I have led them to, or even some related and slightly unexpected stream of their own finding. Also, I want to treat the reader as an intimate, and few things destroy intimacy as much as repeating yourself or pointing out the obvious. This would seem to be one of the dangers attending Brooks and Warren's notion of projecting yourself as your reader; no one, after all, is as intimately familiar with the characteristic turnings of your thoughts as you are. The antidote, for me, has been to recruit intimate friends whose intelligence is beyond question, who assure me that more explicitness would be most welcome. This is one of the functions teachers can perform for students, as long, of course, as the students respect their teacher's intelligence and as long as the teachers, by precept and example, show that they have no hidden respect for obscurantism.

A final small point about connective words: *and* and *but* can function as connective words as well as conjunctions, both following a semicolon and sentence-initially. Some college composition handbooks (e.g., Harbrace) even advise students to try beginning sentences with *and* or *but* because they know the students are told (still told!) not to do this in high school. What they do not tell the students is the special effect of such usage. Since the alternative is to coordinate the sentence to the preceding one, the decision not to do so means that the sentence is connected not just to the preceding one but to the preceding two or more sentences. With *And,* the sentence following is often on another plane of generality (usually upward) or somewhat loosely attached as a further comment on the preceding material (see Miller's last paragraph in the sample; the second paragraph in the Arnold sample).[23] Similarly with *But,* the shift in direction is often against the direction of two or more previous sentences—a shift, in other words, in the line of thought (there are many examples in the samples).[24]

Turning now briefly to end punctuation, we may note that the period is the unmarked connector; the semicolon, colon, and dash can convey special clues to integration. As the handbooks say, the semicolon indicates that the 'thought' of the second clause is closely related to that of the first. That is, it signals integration in a fashion rather like parallel structure, and, not surprisingly, many of the parallel clauses in the samples are joined by semicolons. The colon is even more specific in that it indicates two specific types of close relatedness: specification ('namely') and consequence ('it follows that'). The use of the colon as a mark of end punctuation is not common. The dash one might call a disintegrative signal, in that it signals an afterthought, break, or shift in the line of thought before it is completed. As often noted, the cause of comma splices in student writing is an intuition of relatedness that makes the student shun the full stop. A partial cure is effected by introducing the semicolon, and this treatment is potentiated by introducing the dash. The dash is rarely taught in the schools, perhaps out of a fear that it would give too easy a solution to many syntactic problems, but this not only denies the student a useful indicating mark—it limits the ways in which end punctuation can be practiced as part of the art, and not mechanics, of writing.

It may seem preposterously rarefied to insist on the incompleteness of the marking of connection by punctuation and connective words. Many, if not most, freshmen, after all, seem to read with no awareness of the varying shades of punctuation and connectives, and surely calling their attention to that would at least be a step in the right direction. With that I vehemently agree. My quarrel is with the theoretical assumption that too often appears in discussions of these matters, namely, that once one has got the right word or mark one has nailed the connection down and put the text together. And the view I have tried to sketch in this chapter has its own general pedagogic usefulness: when students realize how open, complex, and various the processes of constructing individual texts can be, they should be more inclined to give their readers as much guidance as they can marshall.

It is useful in concluding this chapter to pose the question: what do formal schemata do? On the one hand, one might say 'nothing essential,' in that they can at most point to the structure of the content; they don't create that structure. So some authorities (Richard Lanham, for example) treat paragraphing and paragraph structure as distinctly secondary to a well-conceived argument. The more traditional approach, however, treats paragraphing and planning ('outlining') as the very structure of the argument itself, probably reflecting the building-blocks view of discourse structure ("there's no point in having them writing three pages when they can't write a decent paragraph"). Supporting the first position is the consideration that structure is not usually the most memorable feature of a text (unless it is exceptionally bizarre[25]). Also, content is remembered equally well from different versions of 'the same' passage, as long as the content is fairly familiar or ordinary and follows a conventional format: Robert de Beaugrande reports this result for descriptions of a V–2 rocket launching, Perry Thorndyke for several news stories; the findings of Bonnie Meyer and P. Clement suggest this also.[26] The *as long as* qualification is important, however, for novel ideas and arguments are just what an expository essay should present—not highly esoteric material, to be sure, but arguments of some subtlety and perhaps intricacy—and here formal indicators may be relatively more helpful by supplying the lack of familiar content schemata.

In his article on news stories, Thorndyke speculates on another function of formal schemata. Some 'stories' are interesting because their material is rather shaggy and amorphous and lends itself to different shapes: a narrative, or a topical ordering, or the conventional journalistic pattern of 'timely, important information, then supporting background and details, in descending order of importance.'[27] Thorndyke found that all three forms got their material across quite efficiently, but he remarks that the type of structure one would prefer would depend on the interest one took in the 'facts,' whether as a political scientist or economist and so on. That is, each version gives saliency to different points and relations of points and so suggests a different perspective or point of view with regard to the material. Here we encounter one of the limits of the 'memory of content' approach to language processing. 'Content' is usually defined as a relatively unstructured list of propositions, and so such experiments provide no direct evidence at all about higher-order understanding of the texts read. We will come up against further limitations of this memory approach in chapter five. It would be a mistake, then, to think of the function of schemata purely in terms of facilitating intake and assimilation of content: they establish not only a pattern of content but a pattern of significance as well.

CHAPTER FOUR

Specificity and Reference

The composition handbooks clearly identify specificity and reference as problems afflicting student writing, but they provide no suggestions why these should be problems except for the implication of laziness and insufficient attention to the details of expression, nor do they, in pointing out passages that don't work, explain to the student wherein artful handling of these matters lies. It is perhaps too much to expect handbooks to provide such an account, but advice like Be Specific, Watch Your Pronouns, and Repeat Key Terms appears to be attacking symptoms, not causes. It is not entirely obvious, in fact, why specificity or coreference should pose difficulties in student (and other) writing, since they are not noticeably troublesome in speech. Native speakers generally have a fairly acute sense of how much specificity is normal for a given conversational exchange,[1] and hence of when someone is evading the issue or wringing some secondary meaning out of unexpectedly detailed or general language.[2] Likewise, we commonly enrich our understanding of texts according to our knowledge or surmises, or by what Richard Anderson calls instantiation of general terms. Anderson and his associates gave subjects sentences like the following:

The animal chased the cat up a tree.

When they later tested various words as 'prompts' for recall of the sentence, they found that *dog* was a better prompt word than *animal!*[3] It seems likely, therefore, that difficulties in these areas have to do with conventions of particular discourse types rather than with effective expression in general. This is plainly so with fine points of the punctuation of modifiers, but I think it is equally true of specificity, repetition/variation, and the management of coreference. Writers typically do things in prose that have at most an analogue in speech, and when the student is ignorant of the special possibilities and expectations of prose, or mistaken about them, 'faults' are likely. This chapter will be divided into three sections, the first dealing with large-scale questions of specificity, the second with description and modification in noun phrases, and the last with reference to things already introduced into the discourse ('later mention'). As before, we will try to understand these matters not as aspects of text structure but as elements of the constructive processes of writers and readers.

1. *The appeal of the general*

As Mina Shaughnessy convincingly argues in *Errors and Expectations,* the principal convention of 'academic discourse' bearing on specificity is that the writer should move flexibly through levels of generality and specificity: sustaining for too long the same level of generality, whether high or low, is a fault. She mentions that 'Basic Writers' are often said to be unable to ascend the ladder of generality but notes that even they seem to have more trouble getting down the ladder than up. Excessive, sustained generality does seem the main problem for writers in 'regular' college composition sections. Here, for example, is the first paragraph of a paper on the topic (chosen by the student) "How to Handle Emotional Trauma":

> One thing in my life that I've always wanted to maintain is optimism, and even with minor setbacks I have usually found this positive attitude easy to adhere to. There have been rare occasions, however, when both my usual pattern of life and my optimistic ways have been challenged by more than just a minor setback. This larger, more damaging setback is emotional trauma, which can show itself in many forms and which can leave its mark on any person. Emotional trauma can do great damage to a person that is vulnerable to its effects. So through the "eyes of experience" I've combined and put into order some steps that I think will prove helpful in understanding and handling traumatic situations. Hopefully these steps will help not only the vulnerable, but also anyone else who may experience some sort of tragedy in the future.

A traditional response to this sort of prose is to suppose that the writer has either not thought very much about what he wants to say or is deliberately leaving the door open to allow discussion of whatever may come to mind in later paragraphs (i.e., a 'first-draft introduction'—common under timed, impromptu conditions like placement tests but considered to reflect inadequate planning in a paper prepared out of class). In short, this might be said to be a paragraph of throat clearing; the student is simply not getting down to business. Unfortunately, in my experience, papers that begin like this rarely do get down to business, or only do so in sporadic flashes. This paper continues:

The first thing that must be realized in a traumatic situation is that your state of mind is not at its best functioning level. Therefore, you will probably tend to be upset, confused and irrational, and will not be able to make important decisions of any sort. You will also find it harder to take anyone's advice, no matter how good the advice may be. Worse yet, the thought of anything optimistic will more than likely turn your stomach. To state the point more concisely, you are not functioning as you normally would, and your confused and upset state of mind is the reason. So if you find everything in life disagreeing with you, just remember that it's a result of the detour life is taking you on at this time. It's a phase, not a new streak of bad luck, and will probably disappear when the situation at hand has straightened out.

The paragraph attempts to step down the language a bit (and into clichés) and to make the advice-giving sound real, but the pitch of generality is unrelenting. One begins to suspect that the problem is not careless or thoughtless first-draft writing—indeed, there is an almost painful stylistic self-consciousness and laboring of transitional words. The generality here seems *willed,* and students who write this way are usually earnest and obedient, the papers long and well typed. The suspicion arises that the student is striving to make a Significant Point and believes that such points must be general— "philosophical" in sweep, as it were. The serious and authoritative voice sounds to these students like a Neo-Classicist. Such writers seem to doubt that particular experiences can or should be communicated, or they distrust them as a distraction and, similarly, seem to doubt that the reader can be trusted to infer the generalization and evaluation—he must be handed it outright. The tendency to repeat words and whole phrases (optimism/istic, [minor] setbacks, vulnerable, functioning, [traumatic] situation, confused and upset) may reflect a parallel distrust of the reader's ability to integrate the text by matching synonyms, finding antecedents, and supplying ellipsed material, or it may reflect instruction to repeat Key Words. These students have taken their training about thesis and topic sentences to heart.

So there are at least two sources of excessive generality—the notion that the more important a point is, the more generally it should be stated, and the view that the best way to ensure that the reader gets the point is to state it directly. And these amount to misconceptions about the ways essays work: we do not know, and cannot appreciate, how comprehensive a generalization is until we know what is under it—how largely and with what central focus, that is, the general term is being used; general terms are less determinate than specifics, not more, Anderson et al. notwithstanding. Likewise, it is

easier for readers to assimilate material into their knowledge and
beliefs ('relate to it') if the text gives entries at several levels of generality and if the reader is invited to recapitulate the process of
thinking that led to the generalized product.

It is worth considering a third possible line of explanation, however, which is simpler than the foregoing, namely that the source of
this kind of writing is a particular bent of mind (or mindlessness)
and not a misunderstood convention about how to unfold a
significant point. Perhaps such writers simply do think top down and
have trouble getting very far down, treating ideas as unexamined
counters in an intellectual game. This may characterize the imagined
author of these passages; the question is thus essentially whether this
author is an accurate reflection of the writer or is the unfortunate
product of a mistaken editing effort. It is probably impossible to decide this question, but the tendency to generalization appears even in
descriptions of personal experience, suggesting that the experience
is being edited upward to meet the expectation of generality. Here,
for example, is the concluding paragraph of a paper comparing and
contrasting two friends:

> Our weekend in Palm Springs turned out to be an enjoyable expe-
> rience. Mark and Mike got along fantastically and found so many
> interests that both of them shared. Before our vacation and before
> both of them had met, I had had a feeling that they would enjoy
> talking with each other and spending the weekend together. Being
> from different countries, they were each curious about what it is like
> to live in another country. Both Mike and Mark found that people
> from seperate countries can have surprising similarities and differ-
> ences. Both are great friends to have because both are so encourag-
> ing to me. By this I mean that if I were to hold a certain viewpoint
> about something, even if either of them disagreed with it, they
> wouldn't criticize me for that viewpoint. Instead, they would prob-
> ably want to know why I feel that way and compare positions. It's
> nice to have one friend that you can really trust and talk with but
> when you have two friends like this it is extremely fortunate. I have
> shared many different experiences with both of them, especially
> since we are all from different parts of the world, and since we don't
> see each other except on special occasions we've always got new ex-
> periences and stories to share with each other.

Well, yes, perhaps the generality here is a defense or curtain of
modesty drawn over matters felt to be too personal to reveal, but it
seems to me that it springs from the desire to give a dignified public
treatment to the Value of Friendship. Another reason to think that it
is not just the particular matter that calls forth this treatment is that
such students tend to employ it on *any* topic. Following is a para-

graph from an earlier paper by the same student describing his previous training in composition:

> As they say "save the best for last." My most favorite teacher and the teacher that has helped me out the most was Jean Bush, my Psychology teacher in my senior year of high school With the information I acquired through her class, I came to have an increased understanding towards other people and especially myself. I learned so many things about peoples behavior and why they act in different ways. I was exposed to many new ideas and thoughts from Mrs. Bush and from other psychologists and guest lecturers. Some things such as meditation and self-hypnosis were taught. I also learned such things as assertiveness training and ideas such as "looking out for number one" as Mrs. Bush explained it. She had such a positive outlook on life, and this tends to rub off onto others. The course was fantastic for me because it had such a practicle application; things I learned in the classroom I could apply to my overall general behavior especially in my views about others.

There is an attempt to specify what was learned in the psychology class, but the parts do not really explain the generalization that the class has had great impact on his relationships. Here again appears the desire to tell the reader the meaning and significance of the experience, rather than presenting it and letting the reader draw the intended evaluation. Somehow these writers must be convinced that readers can draw general conclusions and overall assessments and that they prefer to do it; to get the conclusion without the specifics that led up to it is to be asked to endorse the writer's point of view without being allowed to share it. If this diagnosis of the problem is correct, then the taste for the general does not reflect a mental inadequacy on the one hand, or a local, stylistic problem on the other, but is a confusion about the medium of exchange in essay writing.

2. *Modification*

Just as the student with a passion for generality often stubbornly resists exhortations to be specific, so some student writers prove notably obtuse about the punctuation of modifiers, especially the restrictive/nonrestrictive distinction and the rule about adjectives in a series. Some students seem to have figured the conventions out for themselves, but those who have not seem to find instructors' and handbooks' explanations obscure and unhelpful. There is a reason for this, I think, which is that the standard explanations are based on an inadequate model of how modification works in essays. This model begins with the logico-semantic notion that the function of

noun phrases is to make contact with the world by identifying individuals (or sets of individuals) in the world (or subpart of some
world that constitutes the relevant domain of interpretation for the
discourse) by using a category name (common noun) plus modifiers
to further pick out the individual from the other instances of the
category that might be lying about. So the phrase the *all-night market
on Fifth Street* identifies one market by mentioning two extra properties that eliminate all the alternative markets that one might be referring to.[4] This is the model of how all modification works that
underlies handbook advice about restrictive/nonrestrictive modification. One is supposed to distinguish restrictive from nonrestrictive relative clauses, for instance, in terms of whether the information in the clause is needed to identify (i.e., specify the references of
the phrase) or not. Teachers of grammar and composition know that
this point is difficult to convey to freshmen: either the terms of the
explanation are hard to apply, or the freshmen are reluctant to
apply them. I think there is a tendency to waffle on this distinction
even in the work of polished, professional writers, and that this reflects a sound intuition that a good bit of officially restrictive modification is not really restrictive anyway. And I would suggest also
that with relative clauses, the basis of the distinction is not
identifying/nonidentifying but relevant/less relevant (or background) to the topic under discussion. The comma offsets of the
nonrestrictive relative clause, that is, are parenthetic in nature; the
distinction teaches well in terms of whether *incidentally* or *by the way*
could be inserted in the clause.

The restriction or subset-of-larger-set notion is even carried to the
adjective-noun sequence and is the basis for the extremely confusing
advice given about inserting commas between two adjectives preceding a noun. Properties may be mentioned simply because they are
salient or relevant to the topic at hand. The writing in Aesop's fables
is sprinkled with adjectives that emphasize a quality that would
readily be inferred by an adult reader ('A thirsty ant went to a
stream for a drink'—surely not in opposition to all the unthirsty
ones). Children's stories often use phrases like *the wide ocean* to emphasize a property particularly relevant at the moment. But before
we class all of this as an oddity of writing for children, we should
note uses in scholarly writing of phrases like *This surprising conclusion,
these interesting observations, Such an appalling attitude,* which often
smuggle in an interpretive categorization via the adjective. And
surely it should not be

This surprising conclusion, which we have just come to, is. . .

If one adjective is supposed to narrow the set of objects denoted by the base noun, an additional adjective is supposed to narrow it again. Thus

  a large brown bug

takes the set of bugs, narrows it to the set of brown bugs, and then narrows it again to the bigger brown bugs. If not, the adjectives should be separated by commas so: *a large, brown bug.* In essence, so the account goes, the adjectives could be joined by *and* or reversed in order, since priority of order does not reflect the subset/set distinction here.[5]

This 'rule' is even more widely and freely disregarded than that governing relative clauses. We need to reopen the question of the actual function of a comma separating two adjectives before a noun. The samples do not help us very much on this point because adjective-adjective-noun sequences are not common and most that do occur have the adjectives joined with *and* (or *or*) or have no comma (e.g., *free creative activity, creative literary genius*). What we need is a writer who punctuates both with and without commas so that we can infer the difference in his usage (at least). Henry James is one such writer. Here are some contrasts from the early pages of *The Wings of the Dove:*

a knitted white centre-piece wanting in freshness	a small, salutary sense of neither shirking nor lying
the vulgar little street	mere mean, stale feeling
the narrow black house fronts	the faint, flat emanation of things

What stands out here immediately is that the nouns on the right denote abstractions, those on the left, physical objects. The adjectives on the right, we might say, are there to construct the 'feeling' ('sense,' etc.), not to help pick it out from the domain of possible feelings, and each adjective is a way of catching some quality of the feeling, which has no existence apart from these impressions. This gives us a clue to James's use of commas and, I think, the usage of many other writers as well; namely, adjectives joined by commas look appositional, and in essence they are: each identifies the same set and suggests a close relation, even identity, of the qualities attributed. Thus *mean* clearly means "low, shabby," not "cruel," because we align it with *stale,* and *flat* means "insipid" because it aligns with *faint.* So Rachel Carson joins *deep* and *internal* with commas (*deep, internal waves*) because the qualities denoted are not to be taken as different, but rather two ways of stating the same referring function. Descriptions of physical objects, however, are less likely to attract the appositional adjective treatment than descriptions of impressions and other abstractions. We tend to assume that physical objects exist in the real (or postulated) world quite apart from their descriptions, and so expect that they may be 'reached' by different and unrelated referring functions ('the author of *Aspects of the Theory of Syntax*,' 'the Ferrari P. Ward Professor of Linguistics at MIT,' 'Mrs. Chomsky's little boy'). There is more doubt about the existence of abstractions apart from their descriptions: if two descriptions (e.g., mean feeling/stale feeling) reach the same set (the feeling in question), it must be because the descriptions are themselves equivalent. Consider the following phrases from the samples:

> the haggard and woful stare of the eye
> the sullen and contemptuous curve of the lip
> a baneful and injurious employment

If we replaced the *ands* with commas here, we would suggest a greater identity between *haggard/woful, sullen/contemptuous, baneful/injurious* than the phrases as printed do—we would simply adjust our understandings of the senses of the words in ways to be discussed in the final chapter (e.g., the kind of wofulness that makes you look haggard, the kind of haggardness that looks woful—as opposed to overworked and underfed). As printed, however, the texts instruct us to regard these as distinct, though of course related, properties.

With physical objects, however, this identity of sense is not suggested; one can scarcely take adjectives describing perceptual qualities of physical objects as equivalent. So with

> a large, brown bug

we cannot take 'large bug' and 'brown bug' as in some way identical referring functions. Here using a comma may have more the force of the handbook account (i.e., it makes it clear that the existence of a larger set of brown bugs is not implicated). Thus the comma does not look appositional here, but it often does with abstractions (clearly this has to do with the abstract nature of the qualities as well as the object described, but I am assuming these go together). In the case of adjectives modifying abstract nouns, the comma rule should be: "Don't replace the *and* with a comma unless you mean to suggest an equivalence of the qualities." With respect to adjectives before concrete nouns, we should note that using the comma blocks off the suggestion that the first adjective narrows a potentially larger set, but that this nicety is widely disregarded as not communicatively relevant.

If we turn our attention for a moment to 'hedging' or qualifying modification, we can see another point at which conventions of abstract discourse override the official doctrine. Part of the decorum of essay writing and especially academic writing is not to claim, or appear to claim, more than you know or can prove. This might be phrased as the maxim "Be Modest" or "Don't Force the Reader." This convention, by the way, is already in some conflict with hand-book advice to be forceful and direct in your assertions. Good aca-demic writing, however, is dotted with *probably, perhaps, seems, suggests, indicates, at least, hardly/scarcely, in this case, some, somewhat, rather,* and so on. Like many conventions, however, this one does not work at face value, for, according to the official doctrine, all these hedges should imply (or implicate) that much is uncertain, unclear, and unproven, but in fact they simply certify the writer as a modest, careful scholar whose tentative conclusions are probably of wider application and greater likelihood than he feels he can claim. Thus the qualifiers fade out: a theory that is "hardly proven" or "scarcely sustained" by the evidence is wrong; an explanation that is "proba-ble" or "likely" is the one he believes is right; "fairly clear" is clear beyond a reasonable doubt; and so on. Students who are apprentice academic writers are ill-served by categorical advice to be positive and forceful by omitting 'weakening' qualifiers. The student writing I have read more often stands in need of a delicate qualifier here or there rather than the removal of them, though there is the occa-sional student who is so intimidated by the august solemnity of learned discourse that he is afraid to say boo on the page.

This section has been more negative than positive. The official view of modification (and specification generally) as narrowing the set of possible referents to identify the one(s) meant is so firmly ensconced in handbooks and even grammatical studies, however, that it is something of an accomplishment just to see around it or budge it. The official account is designed, as we have seen, to de-scribe modification in regard to physical objects, but even in that domain it seems fairly clear that speakers and writers often overspec-ify (i.e., give more specifics than those needed to identify and in fact give specifics that are not meant to identify at all). In the domain of abstractions, the whole account seems to miss the point that one is often constructing a 'thing' that is not to be understood as an in-stance of some familiar entity or set of entities.

3. *Later mention*

The previous section focused on introducing things into the discourse, with 'things' broadly construed to include properties and relations as well as individuals. In this section the focus will be on how those things, once introduced, are mentioned later in the discourse, and here discussion will center more narrowly on the reference of nouns and pronouns. Just as language processing models have been concerned with establishing reference to objects with sufficient specificity, so in regard to later mention they have been concerned with establishing coreference between the introducing phrases and phrases occurring later that have the earlier ones as antecedents (i.e., that refer to one of the entities already introduced by one of those phrases). There have been many studies of portions of the system of coreference (e.g., pronominal reference, definite articles, variation/ repetition of phrases), and, despite the prevading anxiety about coreference and integration, the work is more helpful than that on specificity. In this section, I will review and codify some of it, making crucial use of the notion 'foreground of consciousness,' which will figure prominently in the next chapter as well.

It is generally agreed that personal pronouns share the property of definiteness with the article *the* and in fact are more strictly definite than *the,* since *the* sometimes introduces an entity not previously mentioned or present in the situational context ("I found out what was the matter with the car. The carburetor was gummed up."). Pronouns, along with ellipsed material, are governed by the strictest constraints on 'recoverability' because they contain so little inherent information about what they refer to (number and, in the singular, gender). They can refer, as it were, only by coreferring, though it does not follow from this that their processing necessarily involves finding the syntactic antecedent—we may identify the referent simply in terms of an entity already in mind. Clearly, however, pronouns do signal that the entity they refer to has been recently mentioned; they are the usual things to use when you have introduced something and want to go on talking about it. Grammarians have spent copious amounts of time and ink trying to specify exactly where antecedents have to be in order to avoid obscurity or awkwardness or oddity.[6] Out of this work an interestingly fuzzy conclusion seems to emerge, which is that the antecedent of a personal pronoun should be currently fairly well in the foreground of consciousness. Wallace Chafe made this point some years ago and Dwight Bolinger has found evidence for it independently of Chafe, as far as I know.[7] Bolinger calls attention to sequences that have a perfectly placed antecedent but seem a little forced, like:

If there were sun, I'd put them out in it.

In this example *sun* is a syntactic antecedent but may not get established as an entity in the foreground of consciousness, since the *if*-clause is equivalent to "if it were sunny." If you want to refer to something already introduced (and therefore within the awareness or consciousness of the reader/hearer) that is not currently in the foreground of consciousness, then more strenuous marking may be required. In speech one can often stress the pronoun,[8] and sometimes writers try to capture this stressing by italicizing the pronoun, as in the following sentence I came across in Thoreau's "On the Duty of Civil Disobedience": "I could not but smile to see how industriously they locked the door on my meditations, which followed them out again without let or hindrance, and *they* were really all that was dangerous."[9] Thoreau shifts the antecedent of *they* from the townspeople who imprisoned him to his meditations, indicating the shift by the emphatic italics. Some stylists frown on italics used to transcribe a voice inflection as an easy way out of a writing problem, and English does furnish other means of indicating that the antecedent may not be in the foreground, most notably the demonstrative pronoun set. So Arnold uses *these* in the following passage (as well as the inversion of shifting *these* to the front of the clause—of which more in the next chapter): "But it must have the atmosphere, it must find itself amidst the order of ideas, in order to work freely; and these it is not so easy to command" (Arnold, 2). Stephen Isard observes that answers to the instruction

Take the number 19, square it, and then cube it.

will often be either "361 and 6859" or "6859" rather than "47045881." If the last answer is the one sought, the instruction should be phrased:

Take the number 19, square it, and then cube that.[10]

Usually *this/these* is used to signal that the antecedent has just been introduced (it is 'here,' freshly arrived), but of course Isard's example 'the square of 19' is something the reader is supposed to 'find.' Demonstrative forms can work this way to signal a special focusing among antecedents even when they occur as articles, as in this example from M. A. K. Halliday and Ruqaiya Hasan's *Cohesion in English:*

The first row of cottages looked empty and decrepit. But behind them stood another row, well kept and with small bright gardens. Whoever lived in these cottages lived well enough.[11]

Robert Kantor points out that demonstrative forms are used also
when an entity is redescribed with other words than those used to
introduce it—a matter we will take up shortly.[12] Usually an item that
is redescribed is not in the foreground, but the extra attention called
up by the demonstrative form in these uses seems related to the
change of 'name.' We touch here on the notorious matter of 'non-
reference *this*,' that is, *this* used sentence- or clause-initially to refer to
all of the contents of the preceding clause. The old hard line was
that this usage is a fault that should be repaired by adding a noun to
the pronoun, changing

> At the end of the first week, 14 rats were dead. This was unexpected. . .

to

> . . . this result . . .

Many of the nouns that one can add, however, like *idea* or *concept* or
occurrence, do not really give much additional help identifying the
antecedent of *this*, and their obligatory insertion seems a point of
purest pedantry. The line is softening nowadays out of recognition
that many writers use a bare *this* now and then without occasioning
any difficulty at all. We leave this point now and turn to a less subtle
matter of later mention that lies between first introduction and pronominalization.

Various writers, notably Halliday and Hasan, Charles Osgood, and
Dwight Bolinger, have pointed out a pattern of later mention that
involves the gradual shedding of modifiers before going to a pronoun. Here is an example from Halliday and Hasan:

> She found herself in a long, low hall which was lit up by a row of
> lamps hanging from the roof. There were doors all round the hall,
> but they were all locked. (*Cohesion*, p. 72)

Here *the hall* in the second sentence is a shortened form of the introducing phrase (*a long, low hall which was lit . . .*). (Notice, by the way,
the use of the pronoun *they* referring to the things just introduced as
doors.) Charles Osgood found that the writers he studied were less
inclined to shorten a description if they felt the modifiers were
necessary to maintain a contrast with other things, as, for example, if
one is talking about a large blue ball but there is also a small orange
one and a small blue one around. Also, Osgood found that the tendency to shorten the phrase diminished as its distance from the pre-

vious mention increased—it is as if the thing fades from immediate consciousness and must almost be reintroduced.[13] Dwight Bolinger suggests that it is not just the distance but the amount of complexity intervening that creates the need to reintroduce.[14] Here again, then, we come upon the notion of the foreground of consciousness as an irreducible explanatory concept. It is worth noting that the problem for the writer, whose consciousness (under optimal conditions) is crowded with material, is how to estimate and defer to a reader who is not full of the thought but only filling with it. Student infelicities in the handling of later mention are almost always in the direction of assuming too much about what the reader is holding in his consciousness and how he is attending to it—i.e., infelicities run to excessive pronominalization and brevity rather than the reverse, except in the very rare case when a student has been traumatized about pronouns (and see the comments on legal language below).

One variation on the use of a pronoun is the substitution of a general noun (*the thing, the man, the building,* etc.). Dwight Bolinger points out that the noun must be so general as to be virtually empty of content (making it somewhat pronounlike). Compare, for example, his contrasts:

How did you know that shark was after you?
—I could see $\left\{ \begin{array}{l} \text{i. the creature's} \\ \text{ii.? the fish's} \end{array} \right\}$
outline in the water.

He threw the wrench away because $\left\{ \begin{array}{l} \text{i. the thing} \\ \text{ii.? the tool} \end{array} \right\}$ wouldn't work.

The more specific noun is distinctly odd on the intended coreference reading and tends to suggest that another fish or tool is involved.

The definite article is essential to signal that the noun is indeed coreferential and does not introduce a new entity. P. DeVilliers constructed a rather bizarre pair of 'texts' (sets of sentences presented one at a time), which differed only in the presence of the definite or indefinite article:[15]

(a) A man bought a dog.
    A child wanted an animal.
    A father drove to his house.
    A cottage stood near a park.
    A boy was delighted with a gift.
    A twosome went exploring along a path into a woods.

(b) A man bought a dog.
    The child wanted the animal.

The father drove to his house.
The cottage stood near the park.
The boy was delighted with the gift.
The twosome went exploring along the path into the woods.

Subjects presented with the (b) set reported that the sentences seemed to form a story, and they recalled more of the sentences than subjects presented with the (a) set. They also misreported sentences from (b) with the words from one sentence substituted in another (e.g., *the dog* for *the animal*). It seems that the definite article is a potent stimulus to integration of material, the more so because the 'definite' 'text' mixes up the pattern of specific-to-general (dog–animal) with general-to-specific (man–father, child–boy, house–cottage), and this second pattern has been shown by Simon Garrod and Anthony Sanford to be much more difficult for subjects to follow than the specific-to-general pattern.[16] Just on the face of it, it is not obvious why one pattern is better than another. Garrod and Sanford propose an ingenious explanation in terms of matching of semantic features, but any explanation will, I think, have to take more account of the status of the specific-to-general sequence as a convention of later mention.

The last major type of later mention is the redescription of an already-introduced item by means of a new phrase. This differs from the use of a general noun because it predicates new (or more) properties of the thing rather than picking out one general property. Here we enter the much-vexed area of repetition and variation, which is for some students (just the small number that take the advice they are given about writing seriously) a no-man's-land where they are caught in a crossfire of Never Use the Same Word Twice on a Page and Repeat Key Terms, Use Your Thesaurus to Find Synonyms and Avoid Needless ('Elegant') Variation. This is one area where a single-minded concern with integrating a text via coreference blinkers the understanding. The standard view is exemplified by E. D. Hirsch, who vehemently advocates the use of thematic tags, including the repetition of key words, though he will allow substitution of a 'synonym' (*Philosophy*, pp. 123–26, 156). Indeed, if one's concern is for integration, why should even synonyms be allowed? Just to avoid monotony? And when do you sprinkle in the comic relief?

There seem to be two major functions of redescription that are not recognized by an account the sole concern of which is establishing coreference: call them word/thing and stereoscoping. By word/thing, I mean to invoke the main thesis of the General Semantics

movement—the word is not the thing. One way to see what is involved on this point is to examine texts where redescription is
scrupulously avoided. Roger Shuy and Don Larkin observe that this
shunning of redescription is characteristic of insurance policy prose.
The following passage, for example, thumps the word *furnish* as if
no other word would do as well:

> Written notice and proof of claim must be furnished to the Home
> Office while the Insured is living and remains totally disabled. In
> event of default of payment of premiums, such notice and proof of
> claim must also be furnished within 12 months from the due date of
> the premium in default. Failure to furnish notice and proof as re-
> quired above shall not of itself invalidate or diminish any claim
> hereunder if it is shown not to have been reasonably possible to have
> furnished such notice and proof and that such notice and proof were
> furnished as soon as was reasonably possible.[17]

(Note also the mind-numbing effect of the writer's refusal to pro-
nominalize later occurrences of *notice and proof*.) Shuy and Larkin
note that this practice begins to stretch and distort the meaning of
the term selected as it is pressed into service in contexts where a
subtly shaded synonym would be more natural. I would add that
avoiding synonyms suggests that there is something special about the
concept involved, since it is commonly the case that ordinary concepts can be reached by more than one expression and the use of
more than one expression reassures the reader that the terms are
being used in their normal, quasi-substitutable fashion. The passage
makes me think there must be something special about the furnishing to be done—registered mail, at least (contact your insurance
agent for instructions). Using only one term, that is, contributes to
the impression that the word is the thing, since the thing can only be
expressed by the word. The simple truth is that for many things, any
one of several words will do. Composition teachers, with their (our)
concern for the best word, will not be the first to grant this point;
nonetheless, it holds, I believe, for many types of discourse and some
parts of most discourse.

There is, however, a convention of learned writing that tends in
the opposite direction, namely that when concepts are being defined
and discussed, the term selected for the concept should not be varied. The reason for this seems clear: in such areas, one's commonsense grasp of what is being talked about doesn't help much, though
another factor that may be involved is that abstract nouns do not
take articles, so the usual signal of identity is not present. Here is an
example from the hand of a notable writer:

I quote F. H. Bradley neither to praise nor blame his stand on analytical judgment, but to applaud his accuracy in describing our normal
use of language. His denial of synonymity in "Man is man" is surely
accurate for most conceivable uses of that phrase, even though it is a
point that has no necessary application to logical systems. But fortunately synonymy does not stand or fall on examples like "East is East
and West is West," for which Bradley's observations hold. . . . But
Bradley's reasoning would not necessarily deny synonymity to the
following two sentences:
    A rose is the flower of a dicot.
    A rose is the flower of a dicotylednous plant.
Nor, on Bradley's principles, would there be any grounds for denying synonymy in "A rose is *eine Rose.*"[18]

The author alternates very freely between *synonymy* and *synonymity,*
and it is difficult to find the basis for any distinction between the two
things. I recall experiencing dismay, uncertainty, annoyance, and
disappointment with the author, whom I had come to trust as a most
competent craftsman and obeyer of this convention. In fact, the
example is a trick, constructed by the author (E. D. Hirsch), as he
later discloses, to show that two words can be used as absolutely syn-
onymous in some contexts for some purposes. So Hirsch is flouting
the convention here; such vacillations in terminology are most un-
common, though lapses do occur in books written by more than one
person or over an extended period and are often severely censured
by reviewers. The convention appears to hold preeminently in types
of discourse where definitions are abstract or stipulated, as, for
example, in the law. Because of it, a different word much more
strongly signals a change in concept than it does in other types of
discourse. It would seem, however, that the convention principally
governs key terminology; in matters of commonsense meanings, redescription is the rule.

    The second major function that redescription can perform is what
can be called stereoscoping, to suggest the illusion of a third dimension by means of a double perspective. This effect is quite related to
the first (word/thing), though in this aspect we are concerned with
the enhancement of our understanding of the thing via the changed
or doubled perspective. This enhancement may be of a fairly low
level, simply using different terms to tie into different conceptual
networks (as when Johnson uses *persons, personages,* and *characters* in-
terchangeably in one paragraph), or it may bear more communicative load. Some writers will change the description as different properties of the thing become relevant. A small example is Halliday and
Hasan's

There's a boy climbing along the rafters.
a) Those beams aren't very strong.
b) That wood isn't very strong. (*Cohesion,* p. 280)

Either shift picks out a property relevant to the question of safeness to walk on (i.e., beams support loads; wood is less strong than steel—'they're only wood, after all'). A few more interesting occurrences in the samples will be discussed in the next chapter.

A third use of redescription is to add more information about the thing, semicovertly, as it were. Newscasters and some sports writers are fond of this usage; these days many articles about Henry Kissinger introduce him by name and then switch to *the former Secretary of State,* a property that is often relevant to the news item and that people can be reminded of in this fashion. This usage, carried to the extreme of motiveless variation, deserves the contempt Henry Fowler heaped on it, but used with motive, it can be a useful way of sketching in background information. That may even have been the motive for one of Fowler's main examples: "There are a not inconsiderable number of employers who appear to hold the same opinion, but certain owners—notably those of South Wales—hold a contrary view to this"—of course, without the context, it is hard to know if the fact that employers are owners is becoming more relevant for what is to follow.[19] In any case, this usage seems distinctly tied to the world of journalism, and it is curious how the school directive "Don't use the same word twice" prepares the student to write for the school paper, not English class. Sometimes, of course, this instruction has the ulterior motive of getting the students to learn more words and think of their shadings of meaning. If it is done for that reason, however, its propaedeutic nature should be made explicit.

Probably the most useful and interesting kind of redescription is one that summarizes or refocuses what has gone before. In many cases, these redescriptions do not have a noun phrase antecedent at all, as is the case with the following example of Robert Kantor's:

> When so many age-old institutions had been violently overthrown, men began to place a new value on the continuity of historical tradition and turned to the study of the past as a means of diagnosing, and possibly finding cures for, their present ills. Out of this intensified interest in history there grew a deeper understanding of historical causes.

Note the demonstrative *this,* which indicates that the integrative effort of finding an antecedent is going to be more strenuous here. It would certainly make for easier integration of texts if writers didn't do things like this. That is, good writing is not always concerned with giving the reader the easiest way. It just does not seem to be the case that the prose of good writers takes the facilitation of integrative matching as the summum bonum; indeed, it may require more of the reader in that regard than more workaday prose.

Quite clearly then, redescription has functions other than keeping monotony at bay. Written or printed text, moveover, allows more liberties of redescription than speech, since readers can scan back for antecedents and, if Patricia Carpenter and Marcel Just's research on eye movements is any indication of natural reading, they do.[20] Still, the basic constraint for pronouns, shortened descriptions, general nouns, and redescription seems to be that the item referred to be in the foreground of consciousness, and that would not seem to vary much whether the discourse is heard or read. In this chapter, we have simply assumed that things may or may not be within that foreground at any particular moment; there is much that can be said about how writers can manage that foreground, and that is the topic of the next chapter.

If there is a general moral to be drawn from the inadequacies of traditional and psycholinguistic accounts of specificity and later mention, it is that there appears to be no one true doctrine in these areas. An account of modification in the physical domain does not provide an adequate way of describing the modification of abstracts, and all accounts must acknowledge the importance of relevance of detail to the purposes of the discourse. The difference between abstractions and concrete objects parallels the tendency in later mention, to some degree conventionalized in the learned essay, to vary descriptions more with concrete, or at least ordinary, things than with key abstractions. Running across these differences, furthermore, are conventions of special types of discourse that considerably modify such general-purpose maxims as "Be Forceful and Direct" and "Use Synonyms to Avoid Repetition." So again we see the need to tie our rules of good writing to the type of writing we are trying to teach.

CHAPTER FIVE

Focus, Emphasis, and Flow of Information

Once again, the terms in the chapter title refer to stylistic precepts and intuitions seeking a theory. Impressions that sentences flow together well or jump around, that emphasis falls where it should or it doesn't, are readily voiced by composition students. Describing these characteristics as properties of the text, or of sentences, probably reflects the common illusion that takes aspects of the reader's experience to be aspects of the text. Numerous linguists have used terms like Topic/Comment, theme/rheme, Given/New, and Functional Sentence Perspective to describe aspects of the structure of texts that give rise to these impressions. Terminological problems abound, and systematic application of these concepts to the analysis of particular texts has been very scanty. The question most in need of clarification, however, is how these structural properties of texts enter into discourse processing and text construction. Some suggestions have been made in terms of facilitation of coding into memory—i.e., the 'flow' is the intake of new information as it increments known material already in memory—but this model, I think, is inadequate, illustrating the reductionist tendencies of channel limitation thinking in a particularly clear way. There is an alternative approach to these matters, however, that is implicit in the discussions of linguists: here the use of the terms perspective, background, and foreground suggests a visual metaphor for the display of information in texts, and this will be the basis for the model to be put forth in this chapter. First we will examine versions of the memory model that have been advanced and sketch the rudiments of the alternative, 'consciousness' model. Then analysis of texts in terms of topical progressions will be illustrated, and finally the function of cleft sentences in controlling perspective will be rather extensively discussed.

1. Topics and their function

Herbert Clark and Susan Haviland have introduced the basics of the memory model.[1] Beginning with the observations of linguists such as M. A. K. Halliday that sentences usually contain some information already familiar to the reader (or hearer, but our concern is with readers) from the preceding context or context of situations and some information that is new, they suggest that the 'Given' (or known, or old) information in a sentence provides the address in memory where the new material should be attached or integrated. The assumption seems to be that texts are made up of statements about individuals and are integrated and stored in memory in that way; hence any phrase in a sentence that refers to an individual previously introduced is counted as old, given information. This view seems inadequate, for reasons that will emerge. The model so far is too broad, for it suggests that any piece of knowledge might be the address of a sentence and that a succession of sentences might each address a different piece of knowledge. But texts are more tightly organized than this would imply. Sentences tend to bear on the Topic under discussion, or to shift to a new or a related one, not just to any piece of known material. Patricia Carpenter and Marcel Just accordingly introduce the notion of a Discourse Marker, which indicates the currently activated piece of information in memory.[2] As we come to the end of any sentence, some piece of material will be marked in memory as the currently activated site, and if the Given portion of the next sentence repeats or refers to this piece, then the New material will flow easily in. On the other hand, if the Given portion refers to some other piece of material in memory not currently activated, the reader will have to search for it and activate it to integrate the New material. This search should take longer and should give the sense of a hiatus or break in the flow of information in the text, perhaps even impeding integration altogether. The Topic of a sentence, then, is just this Given portion, and if it matches the item currently activated, the sequence is well-formed and easily processed (it flows). Obviously there has to be some way to shift the Discourse Marker to another element, or every sentence in a sequence would have to have the same Topic. Carpenter and Just talk briefly about certain constructions that may 'reset' the Discourse Marker.

As a rather simple example of how this model works, consider the following two versions of a passage on 'four first ladies' studied by Charles Perfetti and Alan Lesgold:

Normal Version

Each of the first ladies made a special imprint upon the White House. Eleanor Roosevelt's life was filled with visitors from early morning until late at night. Mrs. Roosevelt believed in physical exercise, and encouraged her staff to do calisthenics. At meetings Mrs. Roosevelt spoke out whenever an idea caught her imagination. Mrs. Roosevelt served beer in the foyer at parties for the press. The favorite flowers of Bess Truman were talisman roses. A keenly intelligent and well-educated person, Mrs. Truman knew her politics. Unsuspected by many in government, Mrs. Truman entered into almost every decision the President made. Mrs. Truman was very conscious of economy in housekeeping. In Mamie Eisenhower, the public saw a friendly and outgoing lady. Mrs. Eisenhower slept late and generally breakfasted in bed. Mrs. Eisenhower never treated the White House as government property—it was hers. Mrs. Eisenhower took an interest in everything that happened in her staff's lives. Lady Bird Johnson remained a very private person in the swirl of public activity. An avid T.V. fan, Mrs. Johnson never missed her favorite show, "Gunsmoke." Mrs. Johnson was extremely well-organized and mapped out every day in advance. When she was worried, Mrs. Johnson often hummed a tune.

Scrambled Version

Each of the first ladies made a special imprint upon the White House. Lady Bird Johnson was extremely well-organized and mapped out every day in advance. At meetings Eleanor Roosevelt spoke out whenever an idea caught her imagination. Mamie Eisenhower slept late and generally breakfasted in bed. When she was worried, Mrs. Johnson often hummed a tune. A keenly intelligent and well-educated person, Bess Truman knew her politics. Mrs. Eisenhower never treated the White House as government property—it was hers. Mrs. Roosevelt believed in physical exercise, and encouraged her staff to do calisthenics. An avid T.V. fan, Mrs. Johnson never missed her favorite show, "Gunsmoke." Unsuspected by many in government, Mrs. Truman entered into almost every decision the President made. Mrs. Roosevelt's life was filled with visitors from early morning until late at night. The favorite flowers of Mrs. Truman were talisman roses. Mrs. Eisenhower took an interest in everything that happened in her staff's lives. Mrs. Roosevelt served beer in the foyer at parties for the press. In Mrs. Eisenhower, the public saw a friendly and outgoing lady. Mrs. Johnson remained a very private person in the swirl of public activity. Mrs. Truman was very conscious of economy in housekeeping.[3]

The scrambled version is plainly harder to integrate than the normal version because one has to keep hopping from address to address. Subjects recalled significantly less of the scrambled version (p. <.003) after reading the passage once at their own pace. The subjects were grouped into high and low reading ability groups, and, while the groups took about the same time to read each version, the high ability group recalled significantly more than the low ability group (p. <.001). Interestingly, the low ability readers remembered almost as much of the scrambled version as of the normal one (i.e., the version-effect was produced by the high-ability readers), suggesting, as so many studies do,[4] that readers of identified low ability do not structure the text as much as better readers do; hence they are less responsive to differences in the text that would facilitate or impede structuring. Although these contrasting versions illustrate the general notion of activated address fairly dramatically, it is well to note how contrived and simplified even the 'normal' text is. Since it is designed to allow scrambling, each sentence includes the relevant first lady's name, with the result that there is less pronominalization than would occur in a natural text. Also, the Topical structure is very loose and vague: *special imprint* is obviously a cover term, the facts about each first lady are almost all unrelated, and so the names of the four first ladies provide the only basis of integration. Thus the experimenters force the readers to take that route and then make it difficult for them in the scrambled version. The danger of taking this passage as a paradigm case is that it has no 'point' that ranks information in terms of interest and importance; the kind of perspective that can be established in a sentence that is employed to make a point is here flattened out, so that even the 'normal' version is a relatively unordered set of sentences conveying bland and trivial gossip.

The basic idea of the 'intake' model is thus quite a simple one based squarely on the channel limitations of the needy reader. It is a little surprising, therefore, that Clark and Haviland discuss it as a matter of convention (or "contract," as they say), since in one sense all the convention does is say 'Meet the needs of your needy reader.' It appears that they treat Given and New distribution as a matter of convention because they want to give it what one might call a Gricean twist—there are numerous instances where texts do not conform to pattern (e.g., where there is no obviously Given material in a sentence), and they want to maintain that such violations function the way violating a maxim of conversation (as described by H. Paul Grice) does, which is to indirectly convey a meaning. Invoking Grice's notions here seems excessively elaborate; the idea is simply that the reader will assume the writer is trying to link things into consecutive discourse and will try to infer the necessary missing links—i.e., that patterns of Topical progression constitute expectations (essentially formal schemata) that will guide the reader in the process of text construction. The model now has some flexibility and plausibility, and I confess that at one time I thought it pretty well captured all there was to be said about the function of Topical progressions in text construction.

But it does not. The problem with it is that it implies a very tight and linear linkage of each sentence with the immediately preceding one, and there are many Topics that mark shifts or subdivisions of a larger Topic. They function as markers of a hierarchical rather than a linear structure. The model is impoverished in having only two statuses of material, Known (in long-term memory) and 'Activated' (in working memory). The Topic portion of a sentence frequently keys in to some item that may be 'in consciousness' (Given, in the sense of Wallace Chafe[5]) but not in the immediate foreground of consciousness (what the Discourse Marker marks). The Topic progression of a passage may impose some hierarchical structure on the items in consciousness and indicate where in that hierarchy the incoming material fits (but not necessarily what item in memory it says more about). Chafe uses the rich metaphor of 'background' in talking about Given information—i.e., the material in consciousness constitutes the immediately relevant background for the understanding of the sentence—and the notion of Topic should be related to that. We may think of the Topic as the standpoint that defines the background and the foreground—not the target of attention, but where attention is directed from. We can then think of the linguistic devices for marking and shifting the Topic as devices that orient the reader and thereby direct his attention. The root metaphor here is that of visual perspective rather than linear incrementation, with the field of view corresponding to what is in consciousness (or awareness) and with Topic being where we stand as we look toward the rest of the sentence. Further, we move in relation to the field of view, for a while holding the same standpoint and then shifting it. My claim is that this metaphor captures aspects of the experience of reading texts that are not reducible to the simpler memory model. It is with this basic understanding of the importance and interest of Topical structure that we should approach a more detailed analysis of the types of progressions and the ways that writers establish them.

2. *Topical progression*

The Topic structure of texts has been most intensively studied by linguists of the Prague Circle. The essence of Topic structure is patterns of liaison and shift of Topic from sentence to sentence. Once we describe these, we can explain the placement of elements of the sentence, including inversions or normal order, as satisfying one of these patterns or in some cases signaling that one pattern rather than another is operating. František Daneš has described four such patterns of Topical structure, each of which is readily exemplified in the passages of our samples.[6] The first is to have two or more sentences with the same Topic; that is, the succeeding sentence(s) sustain the Topic of the first sentence and make further Comments on it.[7] This pattern may be diagrammed (following Daneš) as:

It can be found many places in our samples:

> The melancholy of Dante was no fantastic caprice. It was not, as far as at this distance of time can be judged, the effect of external circumstances. It was from within. (Macaulay, I, 2)

> Yet both men, Pavlov and Freud, were true children of the Enlightenment; both believed that the search for knowledge must never stop, that only knowledge allows reason to function, that only reason can make men free. Both were loyal to the highest values of their positivistic education. (Miller, 6)

(See also Macaulay II, last paragraph; Hamilton, 3). As appears in these examples, the normal form for later mention of the sustained Topic is a definite pronoun (*it, both*). In this pattern, the initial Topic remains in the foreground and is not displaced from it by material appearing in the Comment.

Such displacement, which is quite common (as in this sentence), gives us the second, chaining, pattern representable as:

$$T_1 \longrightarrow C_1$$
$$T_2(=C_1) \longrightarrow C_2$$
$$T_3 \; (=C_2) \longrightarrow C_3$$

(etc.)

This pattern too can be found many places in the samples:

> But it must have the atmosphere, it must find itself amidst the order of ideas, in order to work freely; and these it is not so easy to command. (Arnold, 2)

The slopes are the site of one of the most mysterious features of the sea. These are the submarine canyons with their steep cliffs and winding valleys cutting back into the walls of the continents. (Carson, 8)

That which distinguishes the modern world from the ancient, and that which divides the West from the East, is the supremacy of mind in the affairs of men, and this came to birth in Greece and lived in Greece alone of all the ancient world. The Greeks were the first intellectualists. (Hamilton, last par.)

If ever despondency and asperity could be excused in any man, they might have been excused in Milton. But the strength of his mind overcame every calamity. Neither blindness, nor gout, nor age, nor penury, etc. (Macaulay, I, 3)

(The first two examples do not carry the chain to a third step.) Note in the last two examples that this sort of chaining does not require strict coreference of noun phrases (*Greece / Greeks; Milton / strength of his mind, every calamity / blindness, gout, etc.*). The occurrence of the demonstrative pronoun (*these, this*) in the first three examples is typical and illustrates Robert Kantor's claim that a demonstrative is generally a signal that extra effort is needed to locate the antecedent; one source of extra effort is a shift to a new Topic (i.e., the antecedent is not the Topic of the preceding sentence).

Richard Eastman calls this second pattern "dovetailing," giving as an example:

What we must never neglect is the will to win. The determination to survive can extend a man's resources up to 50 percent, perhaps even more.[8]

On the interpretation where *will to win = the determination to survive,* the second sentence takes the Focus (the high point of the Comment) of the first as its Topic. (We might take a hint from Kantor and improve this example by changing *the determination* to *this determination.*) Carpenter and Just, modifying Eastman slightly, note that the order in Eastman's example is better than one in which the second sentence is made passive:

What we must never neglect is the will to win. A man's resources can be extended by the determination to survive.[9]

The reason for this is that sentences are often passivized just to get the Topic material to the left and the New material to the position of end-Focus; here, however, use of passive results in just the opposite effect and seems motiveless and disruptive. (Note that Eastman's first sentence is a *Wh*-cleft—the significance of this will emerge in the next section.) This example is also complicated by the redescription in *the determination to survive*. It is as if this redescription creates an extra obligation on the writer: if he wants to trigger the equating of this phrase with *the will to win*, he should place it where Given material is usually found (i.e., initial position) to suggest that it does not introduce a new entity but continues one already given. Other optional placements (or inversions) can be used to get material conveying the Topic to the left.

These first two patterns embody the simple linear flow of material that the memory model accounts for, and, if we looked only at them, we would probably find little wrong with the model. Daneš's third and fourth patterns, however, carry us beyond the linear into the hierarchical. The third pattern involves a subdivided larger Topic; Daneš diagrams this as:

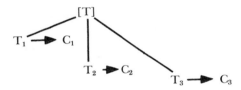

Here the subdivisions are all recognizably that: there is a shift of Topic, but in a specifiable direction, namely, downward in generality, or whole-to-part. Here is an example from the beginning of the Hamilton sample:

> But this little remnant preserved by the haphazard of chance shows the high-water mark reached in every region of thought and beauty the Greeks entered. No sculpture comparable to theirs; no buildings ever more beautiful; no writings superior. Prose, always late of development, they had time only to touch upon, but they left masterpieces. History has yet to find a greater exponent than Thucydides; outside of the Bible there is no poetical prose that can touch Plato. In poetry they are all but supreme; no epic is to be mentioned with Homer; no odes to be set beside Pindar; of the four masters of the tragic stage three are Greek. (Hamilton, 1)

Often, of course, the [T] does not initiate the discourse as a Topic but is introduced in a Comment, as in the following example with *source of material things:*

> Of all parts of the sea, the continental shelves are perhaps most directly important to man as a source of material things. The great

fisheries of the world, with only a few exceptions, are confined to the relatively shallow waters over the continental shelves. Seaweeds are gathered from their submerged plains to make scores of substances used in foods, drugs, and articles of commerce. As the petroleum reserves left on continental areas by ancient seas become depleted, petroleum geologists look more and more to the oil that may lie, as yet unmapped and unexploited, under these bordering lands of the sea. (Carson, 1)

This passage is particularly intricate because the initial Topic (*continental shelves*) reappears in subsequent sentences, suitably varied (*their submerged plains, these bordering lands of the sea*) so that the characterization of the shelves is being developed to correspond to what is predicated of them (e.g., they are *plains* from which the seaweed 'crop' is gathered). Thus there is inflow of New information here on two planes at once, on the sentence level and via the redescription of the continental shelf. This double flow is even more notable in the redescription of 'the will to win' as 'the determination to survive'—surely this is an unpredictable equation and therefore the second phrase is to some degree New information. In the next section, we will examine other instances of informative redescription, which in some cases bring the whole distinction of Given and New into question.

The final pattern is somewhat like the third in that the initial Comment introduces a kind of split or divided pair, each member of which is developed separately as the Topic of subsequent sentences. Daneš diagrams this as:

$$T_1 \longrightarrow C_1 \ (= C'_1 + C''_1)$$
$$T'_2 \qquad C'_2$$
$$T''_2 \longrightarrow C''_2$$

Paragraphs five through seven in the Carson sample are organized this way; the last part of paragraph five—

the starkness of a seascape in which all plant life has been left behind and there are only the unrelieved contours of rock and clay, of mud and sand.

—introduces 'life' and 'geography,' each of which is made the Topic of succeeding paragraphs and marked as such by the introductory adverbials *Biologically* and *Geographically*. As Daneš notes, Topic shifts in this pattern (as, for example, to T''_2) often require special marking; the new sub-Topic is scarcely in the foregound of consciousness. Carson uses paragraphing as well as the initial adverbs to point out the shifts. The Johnson sample probably contains an illustration of this pattern in the second paragraph, where the sentence ending "a faithful mirror of manners [personality types] and of life" is expanded in the next two sentences, the first dealing with manners and the second with life. Possibly the shift from *His characters* to *His persons* in the second sentence is a signal of change of Topic to 'life.'

Obviously this sort of pattern can extend over considerable stretches of text; we can view the organization of the early paragraph in the Miller sample as introducing a doubled Topic (Pavlov's impact on physiology and on psychology), explaining the reasons for his lack of impact on the first, and then explaining the reasons for his impact on the second.

These Topic progressions constitute patterns of expectation, and we have already touched on the ways adverbs and passive sentences can be used to signal and meet them. We have also noted that these signals do not always serve to link the incoming sentence to what is in the immediate foreground of consciousness; rather, they indicate where you stand in the landscape of ideas and conduct you through it. In the following example, the successive initial time adverbials set up a subdivided Topic network, but it is straining a bit to say that they indicate the address in memory where the contents of the sentences are to be integrated. Essentially, they indicate the subsections of the 'systematic observations':

> The first systematic observations of this emotional reaction were made in 1914. A dog was trained to salivate when it saw a circle. Then an ellipse was presented without any reinforcement by food; the discrimination was easily established. On subsequent days the difference between the ellipse and the circle was reduced progressively. Finally the two were so much alike that discrimination failed. After three weeks of unsuccessful training the whole behavior of the dog changed abruptly; (Miller, 2)

We turn now to examining how placements, especially the unusual ones known as inversions, are used by the particular writers to link Topics and signal shifts. The samples contain examples of adverbial fronting to sustain a Topic (Pattern 1) (the Topic link in the second sentence is italicized):

> It was a loathsome herd, which could be compared to nothing so fitly as to the rabble of Comus, grotesque monsters, half bestial half human, dropping with wine, bloated with gluttony, and reeling in obscene dances. *Amidst these* that fair Muse was placed . . . (Macaulay, I, 2)

More commonly in the samples, however, the fronting of adverbial and other prepositional phrases, along with demonstrative forms, signals a shift of Topic. In the following examples from Johnson, the introductory adverbials signal the shifts back and forth between the split Topics 'Shakespeare' and 'other dramatists':

> His persons act and speak by the influence of those general passions and principles by which all minds are agitated and the whole system of life is continued in motion. *In the writings of other poets* a character is too often an individual; *in those of Shakespeare* it is commonly a species. (Johnson, 2)

> *Upon every other stage* the universal agent is love, by whose power all good and evil is distributed and every action is quickened or retarded. To bring a lover, a lady, and a rival into the fable; to entangle them in contradictory obligations, perplex them with oppositions of interest, and harass them with violence of desires inconsistent with each other; to make them meet in rapture and part in agony, to fill their mouths with hyperbolical joy and outrageous sorrow, to distress them as nothing human ever was distressed, to deliver them as nothing human ever was delivered, is the business of a modern dramatist. *For this,* probability is violated, life is misrepresented, and language is depraved. (Johnson, 5)

The Topic of the second sentence in the last example is 'love,' which is detailed in the long infinitive Subject. *For this* is an inversion that continues, rather than shifts, the Topic of the preceding sentence. In the next example, this time from Macaulay, the fronting of the long prepositional phrase signals a dovetailing shift and facilitates recognition that *the great men . . .* are the leaders of *his party*:

> Milton was, like Dante, a statesman and a lover; and, like Dante, he had been unfortunate in ambition and in love. He had survived his health and his sight, the comforts of his home, and the prosperity of his party. *Of the great men by whom he had been distinguished at his entrance into life,* some had been taken away from the evil to come. . . . (Macaulay, I, 3)

Macaulay, like Johnson, is fond of using an introductory adverbial to indicate a shift of Topic. Here is a dovetailing example followed immediately by a fairly major shift of Topic:

> Almost everything that we have said of him applies equally to Falconbridge. Yet *in the mouth of Falconbridge* most of his speeches would seem out of place. *In real life* this perpetually occurs. (Macaulay, II, 2)

It is interesting to note in passing that one of E. D. Hirsch's examples of syntactic inversion to facilitate integration, a passage from

Edward Sapir's writings, is in fact a Topic-shifting inversion of the type we have been looking at:

> Probably the most important single source of changes in vocabulary is the creation of new words or analogies which have spread from a few specific words.
> Of the linguistic changes due to the more obvious types of contact, the one which seems to have played the most important part in the history of languages is the "borrowing" of words across linguistic frontiers. This borrowing goes hand in hand with cultural diffusion. (Cited in *Philosophy,* p. 156)

That is, Sapir has been discussing types of causes of change in language, has completed 'internal change,' and now shifts to 'changes caused by contact with another language.' Again, the paragraph inset underlines the Topic shift.

The next examples are cited in a block to illustrate the interaction of inversions with *but,* which often signals a shift of topic:[10]

> It is true that the man who is best able to take a machine to pieces, and who most clearly comprehends the manner in which all its wheels and springs conduce to its general effect, will be the man most competent to form another machine of similar power. *In all the branches of physical and moral science which admit of perfect analysis,* he who can resolve will be able to combine. But *the analysis which criticism can effect of poetry* is necessarily imperfect. One element must for ever elude its researches; and *that* is the very element by which poetry is poetry. *In the description of nature,* for example, a judicious reader will easily detect an incongruous image. But *he* will find it impossible to explain. . . . (Macaulay, II, 2)

In all the branches signals a shift of Topic in the direction of generalizing the previous mechanical analogy. The next sentence signals a shift with *but* to the analysis of poetry. *One element* in the next sentence is a reversal of the usual pattern, since it is New information, but it becomes the Topic for the next 'sentence' (appearing in it as *that*). *In the description of nature* then signals a new Topic, which is identified as an example of one of the sciences. If we do not see this phrase as recalling 'branches of physical and moral science,' we may try to dovetail *the descriptions of nature* to *poetry,* making it an example of one type of poetry (nature poetry). But Macaulay has just used the introductory adverbial *In* . . . to signal a shift of Topic, and when he uses it again, we can expect it to have the same signaling force.

There are in the samples a few instances of the inversion often called Topicalization, which fronts a noun phrase that would normally occur later in the sentence. This is actually quite appropriate as a name for its effect, which is very often to shift to a new Topic.

Macaulay is fond of it and uses it in the next example to introduce the Topic of succeeding paragraphs:

> It seems that the creative faculty, and the critical faculty, cannot exist together in their highest perfection. *The causes of this phenomenon* it is not difficult to assign. (Macaulay, II, 1)

We may ask how it is that *the causes* can be treated as if it were Given information here; it seems to spring from the body of actually Given information somewhat as if the description of a puzzling situation automatically calls forth the question of its cause. Topicalization can also be used for dovetailing, as it is in this example by Hedrick Smith:

> Ironically, this new Citizen of the World is a man who seemed to want his Mother Russia to pull back from the world and abandon the globalism of a messianic ideology adopted from the West.
> *Marxism* he has thrown off without choosing a new political doctrine. Neither capitalist nor Communist economics does he regard as a source of good.[11]

As before, placing *Marxism* in initial position may help skilled readers make the intended identification of it with "a messianic ideology adopted from the West."

As a final, recapitulating example, I will cite a rather long connected passage from the Arnold sample that illustrates many of the liaisons and shifts discussed so far:

> . . . for the creation of a master-work of literature two powers must concur, the power of the man and the power of the moment, and *the man* is not enough without the moment; *the creative power* has, for its happy exercise, appointed elements, and *those elements* are not in its own control.
> Nay, *they* are more within the control of the critical power. It is *the business of the critical power*, as I said in the words already quoted, 'in all branches of knowledge, theory, philosophy, history, art, science, to see the object as in itself it really is.' Thus *it* tends, at last, to make an intellectual situation of which the creative power can profitably avail itself. *It* tends to establish an order of ideas, if not absolutely true, yet true by comparison with that which it displaces, to make the best ideas prevail. Presently *these new ideas* reach society, *the touch of truth* is the touch of life, and there is a stir and growth everywhere; *out of this stir and growth* come the creative epochs of literature. (Arnold, 2–3)

There is a clear and simple dovetailing sequence in the first part of this example from *appointed elements* to *these elements* and then from *critical* power to *the business of the critical power*. The critical power re-

mains the Topic for two sentences before giving way to *the best ideas,*
which becomes the Topic as *these new ideas; the touch of truth* is a kind
of redescription of Topic ('the arrival of these relatively more true
new ideas'). "There is a stir and growth everywhere" essentially expands on *touch of life* and becomes the Topic for the last sentence via
the adverbial fronting. One could hardly construct a tighter and
neater example of liaison and dovetailing over an extended stretch
of text than this passage, and the way they steer this reader is so
evident as to require no further comment.

Clearly it would be hard to assign a single function to any particular syntactic placement or inversion. Initial position is the Topic slot,
but that Topic may be the same as the one of the preceding sentence
or not. Certain inversions, notably Topicalization, seem to be more
'strenuous' than others and perhaps by calling attention to themselves often signal a shift of Topic. But much remains up to the
writer to work out his own ways of directing the reader's perspective.
Some writers, for example, do not use Topicalization at all; others
use it fairly heavily and for their own chosen purposes.[12] A great
deal of careful descriptive work should be done in this area and
should yield interesting comparisons and insights into authors' styles.

Along with the call for further research, it is well to acknowledge
three of the complexities and uncertainties of Topic-Comment
analysis. First of all, not all texts maintain Topic-Comment progressions entirely in the referential or presentational domain; that is,
in most of the cases Daneš examined and in our samples also, the
author is relatively effaced (to borrow a term from literary criticism),
and the text carries out its business of talking about the world. In the
Arnold sample, however, and to a lesser degree in Miller, the author
calls attention to the act of discoursing itself, either by pointers to the
line of argument (*certainly, consequently, we may conclude that* . . .) or by
references to the author's 'saying.' More broadly, whenever *I* or *we*
appear, or the reader is addressed (with or without *you*), there is a
second plane, one that represents a writer writing and a reader reading the presentation, that may overlay or intersect the Topic
progression, or we might speak of the discourse itself as a sort of
alternative theme that can interweave with the referential Topic
progression, representation with presentation.

Second, not all Topics are in initial position in sentences. They are
initial in all of the standard examples and in most of the instances
from our samples, and the initial phrase is the first place to look for
a Topical signal, but some writers do occasionally set up inversions,
for example, for rhythm, variety, or ornateness. Also, initial subordinated elements such as participials do not appear to participate in

Topic progressions. The flow of information, then, in most cases is not radically disordered if some initial phrases are not obvious Topics.

Third, the Topic progression of a text is not always a direct reflection of and guide to the line of argument or significant point. Topic progressions can be faked, as it were, or used to produce a superficial impression of orderliness. And, too, Topics are sometimes allusive in nature, establishing a relationship between the comment and some previously discussed idea, without implying a tight integration on the order of coreference. That is, the Comment is not necessarily to be referred back to the previous material in memory to be integrated with it as the memory model implies. All these complexities suggest that while the progressions described by Daneš can explain some choices on the sentence level and capture something of what it may mean to say that the sentences follow easily and naturally, they should not be turned into recipes for a flowing style.

3. *Clefts*

Otto Jespersen it was who first described the *it*-cleft (or 'true' cleft) sentence form and characterized its function. A cleft sentence is generally regarded as a transform of a basic sentence in which some sentence element (normally a noun phrase, but adverbial words and phrases are also possible) is shifted to a position following *It is / was*, with the rest of the sentence then following *that* and resembling a relative clause. So, for example,

> Burglars stole our *OED* last night.

can be alternatively phrased:

> It was burglars that stole our *OED* last night.
> It was our *OED* that burglars stole last night.
> It was last night that burglars stole our *OED*.

Writing before positivism took hold in linguistics, Jespersen used the word *attention* unblushingly in describing the function of clefts: "A cleaving of a sentence by means of *it is* (often followed by a relative pronoun or connective) serves to single out one particular element of the sentence and very often, by directing attention to it and bringing it, as it were, into focus, to mark a contrast."[13] Contemporary treatments of clefts generally follow this line of thought, though they differ in subtle and important ways and sometimes lack Jespersen's touch for the well-placed qualification (*often, very often*). So Quirk,

Greenbaum, Leech, and Svartvik: "The usefulness of the cleft sentence partly resides in its unambiguous marking of the focus of information in written English, where the clue of intonation is absent. The highlighted element has full implication of contrastive focus: the rest of the clause is taken as given, and a contrast is inferred with other items which might have filled the focal or 'hinge' position of the sentence."[14] Because they define *focus of information* as the most prominent portion of New information, they are claiming that the cleft sentence always directs attention to a piece of New information. This is not accurate for the texts we will examine and seems to spring in part from an unfortunate ambiguity in the term *focus*. In another statement, Jespersen explicitly argues that the attention-focusing of the cleft cannot be equated with emphasis, which from his example appears to be what Quirk et al. mean by focus (and here, even contrastive focus):

> It is often said that the insertion of *it is* serves to give emphasis to the word thus singled out. But this is not quite correct. Emphasis is better given by stress and (or) intonation, and these phonetic means generally accompany the construction we are dealing with, but they might have been—and often are—used with effect even without employment of the *it is*–construction. Emphasis (and stress) is even frequently laid on another word than the one singled out by being made the predicative of *it is,* thus the adverb in "It is always the wife that decides" or "It is never the wife that decides." I should, therefore, rather say that the construction with *it is* serves as a demonstrative gesture to point to one particular part of the sentence to which the attention of the hearer is to be drawn especially.[15]

It is perhaps worth noting in passing that Jespersen's descriptions of English grammar were based on written texts, whereas more recent descriptions show the modern bias toward the spoken language. Nevertheless, his example sounds quite conversational, and his claim holds, I think, for spoken as well as written English.

Robert Stockwell adds to the characterization of clefts (among other 'focusing constructions') by noting that they not only foreground some material but background other: "Focusing rules introduce special marking into the Surface Structure to set off some element or elements as new or important; they assign PROMINENCE to that part of the message which the speaker wants to place in the foregound, and they destress (place in the background) that part of the message which merely provides continuity with what preceded or which confirms the presuppositions that are shared."[16] Although he avoids equating foregrounded with New information (by means of the qualifying *or important*), Stockwell introduces an equally dubious equation of backgrounded with Given information.[17]

I am sorry if the reader finds this tracing of grammatical vagaries tedious, but it is important for our purposes not to conflate the foreground / background distinction with that of Given / New information. What we want to say is that information being Given or New is one reason it might be backgrounded or foregrounded by means of clefting, but the function of clefting is not to mark information as Given or New; indeed, it is not always a reliable indicator of Given and New. Lest our terminology swamp us with too many *foregrounds*, let us use the term *focus* (of attention) for the foregrounding effected by clefts. It is, of course, quite possible that as one reads forward, focused elements move from the foreground of attention into the foreground of consciousness.

Contemporary grammarians have given a very similar account of *wh*-clefts (or pseudo-clefts: *What burglars stole last night was the OED*), where the final noun phrase (*the OED*) seems to be made extra prominent, in a fashion similar to the material following *it is* in an *it*-cleft, and the material in the *wh*-clause backgrounded. *Wh*-clefts seem to be a recent innovation in formal written English: Jespersen does not discuss them, and only our more recent samples have them.

Patricia Carpenter and Marcel Just have produced some rudimentary experimental evidence for the attention-shifting effect of *wh*-clefts by determining that the identification of ambiguous antecedents could be strongly biased by a *wh*-cleft (their example required the variation for animate referents, *the one who* . . . , instead of *what* . . .):

> The guard mocked one of the prisoners in the machine shop.
> He had been in the prison for only one week.[18]

The antecedent of *he* was remembered as *the guard* almost twice as often as it was remembered as *the prisoner,* but if a *wh*-cleft was interpolated:

> The guard mocked one of the prisoners in the machine shop.
> The one who the guard mocked was the arsonist.
> He had been in the prison for only one week.

the *arsonist / prisoner* was remembered as the antecedent of *he* twice as often as was *the guard,* thus reversing the preferences. Since, as argued in the previous chapter, foregrounded entities (i.e., entities at or near the center of attention) are the likeliest antecedents of personal pronouns, the results point to the *wh*-cleft as focusing on *the arsonist* and placing it in the foreground. It comes to mind, then, to ask whether this foregrounding amounts to establishing the element as a new Topic to be developed in the next sentence (as Carpenter and Just assume). This does not quite seem to be the case. That is, the focusing or direction of attention accomplished by clefting does not always result in a shifted Topic ('resetting the Discourse Marker'). One rather simple group of counterexamples are clefts that occur at the ends of paragraphs or chapters (etc.): the centering of attention in these cases would seem to involve having reached one's goal in the particular stretch of text. Another counterexample occurs in the article of Wallace Chafe that I have been drawing on in this chapter:

> They speak of the listener building a "bridging structure," and in Clark and Haviland (in press) they say that "when the listener cannot find a direct antecedent, most commonly he will be able to form an *indirect* antecedent by building an inferential bridge from something he already knows." Certainly what they are talking about is the establishment of the definiteness of one particular by inferences from another particular. The finding that this process takes time is of considerable interest, but it is not the process of accepting new information into consciousness.[19]

Here *the establishment* . . . doesn't become the Topic of the next sentence, though it is prominently enough introduced into the foreground to yield an easy antecedent for *this process*. The same sorts of observations apply with *it*-clefts—these too are sometimes used to hammer home a conclusion and do not always introduce the Topic for the next sentence. Of course, they sometimes do: having focused on an element and brought it into the foreground, one might be expected to want to comment further about it, but we cannot say that the function of clefts is to shift the Topic to the focused element.

Thus far we have concentrated on the attention-shifting or focusing force of clefts. What is to be said about the other part of clefts, namely the backgrounded, so-called Given portion? The standard statement that when a writer puts material in the *that* or *what* clause of a cleft he is signaling that it rephrases something in the zone of consciousness is, I think, basically correct. These constructions do have the power to stimulate a 'bridging' effort on the reader's part to see this material as at least implicitly present in consciousness. As Wallace Chafe puts it, they can "treat material as Given" and induce the reader to do likewise, though, as Ellen Prince notes, the *wh*-cleft is somewhat more powerful in this regard than the *it*-cleft. Prince cites a statement by a bookbinder from Studs Terkel's *Working*:

> So I learned to sew books. They're really good books, it's just the covers that are rotten. You take them apart and you make them sound and you smash them in and you sew them up.[20]

(I find I tend to take *covers* as the antecedent of *them* in the last sentence; however, the antecedent remains *books*, despite the focusing on *covers*.) She notes that 'something being rotten' can't really be said to be 'in consciousness' here; at best it is inferable from the knowledge that repairing books is required when 'something is rotten' about them. The tighter commitment of the *wh*-cleft to material in consciousness makes it awkward in this context:

> So I learned to sew books. They're really good books, what's rotten is just the covers.[21]

An important fact about clefts, especially *wh*-clefts, is that while they signal the Givenness of the material in the *what* or *that* clause, that material is only very rarely a verbatim repetition of earlier material. If the function of clefts is to facilitate matching to material already in memory, it is hard to explain why this should be the case. At this point it is useful to turn to the samples to see just what is going on there.

As noted earlier, *wh*-clefts are a relatively recent innovation; they are a marked feature only in the sample from George Miller's *Psychology*. The question we may ask about the first instance is in what sense the *wh*-clause material (italicized) is Given:

> Pavlov did not make any direct observations of the processes going on in the brain. He based his opinion of them entirely upon inferences from what the animals did in his experiments. *What he looked at directly* was not the animal's brain, but the animal's behavior. Consequently, all his statements about waves of excitation and inhibition that irradiate over the surface of the brain are little more than plausible fictions;

(Again I have cited the sentence following the *wh*-cleft to check whether *the animal's behavior* becomes the Topic. It does not.) The Givenness of the *wh*-clause seems to arise from a rather extended *not x but y* patterning (without the *but*, but with a kind of keying emphasis on *directly*): talking about what he didn't do brings into the background of consciousness the question of exactly what it was that he did. The next example, from a little later in the sample, is more extended and elaborate:

> Pavlov has often been classed with Freud as a major source of anti-intellectualism in the twentieth century. In their hands Sovereign Reason, benevolent ruler of the eighteenth-century mind, crumbled into unconscious reflexes and instincts, automatic processes that are the very antithesis of ratiocinative thought. Reason seemed

to refute itself. Yet both men, Pavlov and Freud, were true children of the Enlightenment; both believed that the search for knowledge must never stop, that only knowledge allows reason to function, that only reason can make men free. Both were loyal to the highest values of their positivistic education. *What they both attacked* was not sovereign reason, but foolish optimism about the inevitability of human progress. To dismiss them as anti-intellectuals is a dangerous oversimplification.

Viewed purely as a matching task, tracing *what they both attacked* back to *anti-intellectualism* (and, more broadly, to reason crumbling in their hands) is a bit of a feat, particularly since Miller has not committed himself to the factuality of their having attacked anything (i.e., that they *did* attack anything is not really Given). But I think a convention of academic writing (i.e., a formal scheme) can be used by readers here that we might call 'Grain of Truth Extraction': we are given a Common Opinion followed by reasons why that Opinion cannot be exactly right, but then we extract what was right in the Common Opinion (which finally then can be classed as an Oversimplification). And I think Miller implicitly invokes this convention in treating 'their having in fact attacked something' as Given.

Before examining the Givenness with *it*-clefts in the samples, we take note of an observation of Ellen Prince's: because the constraint on the Givenness of the *that*-clause is rather loose, there is a tendency, especially in formal written discourse, to put New information in the *that*-clause and to put a brief summary of Given, even Topical, material in the 'focus' slot, thus reversing the 'official' pattern and returning to the more ordinary Given–New order. One effect of doing this is to treat what is actually New information as if it were Known, though, of course, not previously mentioned. These she calls 'informative presupposition' clefts, observing that "Their function, or at least one of their functions, is TO MARK A PIECE OF INFORMATION AS FACT, known to some people although not yet known to the intended hearer."[22] Here is one of her examples:

> "It is for this reason that HALLE'S ARGUMENT AGAINST AUTONOMOUS (*Halle, 1959*) IS OF SUCH IMPORTANCE: it demonstrates that. . . ."

We might say that the backgrounding force of the *it*-cleft is sufficient to color the material in the *that*-clause as Known, but not strong enough to suggest that it was already in consciousness (i.e., Given).

There are two (pairs) of *it*-clefts in the prose samples, and, as it happens, they both illustrate the nonstandard pattern just referred to. The first of these begins the second paragraph of the Johnson passage:

It is from this wide extension of design that so much instruction is derived. It is this which fills the plays of Shakespeare with practical axioms and domestic wisdom.

The ostensibly New information *this wide extension of design* is tagged for anaphoricity by *this* and in fact summarizes the topic of the preceding paragraph (that Shakespeare's characters are universal and general rather than particular). The ostensibly Given *so much instruction is derived* has not been mentioned, but here is 'presupposed' as a piece of common knowledge (i.e., treated as Known, but not Given). Sometimes the redescription or summary portion of a cleft is sufficiently novel as to be informative in its own right. In these cases, rather than say the 'official' pattern is reversed, we should probably say that the distinction between Given and New cannot be made in a straightforward fashion. Consider, for example, the following passage from the second Macaulay passage:

> That critical discernment is not sufficient to make men poets, is generally allowed. Why it could keep them from becoming poets, is not perhaps equally evident: but the fact is, that poetry requires not an examining but a believing frame of mind. Those feel it most, and write it best, who forget that it is a work of art; to whom its imitations, like the realities from which they are taken, are subjects not for connoisseurship, but for tears and laughter, resentment and affection; who are too much under the influence of the illusion to admire the genius which has produced it; who are too much frightened for Ulysses in the cave of Polyphemus to care whether the pun about Outis be good or bad; who forget that such a person as Shakespeare ever existed, while they weep and curse with Lear. It is by giving faith to the creations of the imagination that a man becomes a poet. It is by treating those creations as deceptions, and by resolving them, as nearly as possible, into their elements, that he becomes a critic. In the moment in which the skill of the artist is perceived, the spell of the art is broken. (Macaulay, II, 3)

Taking the first cleft first, the nominally New *by giving faith to the creations of the imagination* harks back to *a believing frame of mind* by fairly immediate synonym-matching; *become a poet*, strictly speaking, has not directly been spoken of, though the first sentence touches on what is NOT sufficient to make men poets, and so 'getting to be a poet' is implicit enough in the passage and for Macaulay's purposes blurs the difference between reading as a poet and being one. The parallelism of the two *it*-clefts, which appear to summarize each of the two opposing stances described in the paragraph, directs the reader to match *by treating them as deceptions and resolving them into their elements* with *critical discernment / examining . . . frame of mind,* although the 'deceptions' business goes a bit beyond previous description of the critical attitude. Here, as with the paragraph from George Miller, our perception of Given and New and the interpretive matching required is governed by the larger structural pattern of contrast that is also our guide in the thicket of *not x but y, y not x* oppositions that require integrative alignment as follows:

not examining	but believing
	who forget it is a work of art
	to whom its imitations . . . are subjects
not for connoisseurship	but for tears and laughter . . .
	who are too much under the influence of the illusion
to admire the genius which produced it	
	who are too much frightened for Ulysses
to care whether the pun about Outis be good or bad	
	who forget that such a person . . .
	It is by giving faith . . . poet
It is by treating . . . critic	
the skill of the artist is perceived	the spell of the art is broken

Here is parallelism in the service of antithesis with a vengeance, and part of the passage's persuasive power arises from the sheer integrative effort the reader must put forth: struggling to get the 'good' things on one side and the 'bad' things on the other, the reader finds it hard to think critically about the passage—it is much easier to accept a number of questionable equations in order to get the paragraph together!

To use a cleft, then, commits you to redescription; it sets up stereoscopic opportunities of major proportions and allows the importation of quantities of New information while directing attention away from its novelty. The effect is to enrich or reshape the background as one points to a new foreground.

There is a standard account of subordinate adverbial and relative clauses that is quite comparable to this one about the Givenness of material in the *that*-clause of a cleft and the *what*-clause of the pseudo-cleft. One finds the statement that the material in (restrictive) relative clauses is Known; this follows from the usual definition of a restrictive clause as one that helps identify the noun it modifies: presumably one would want to use material already known to the hearer / reader in order to identify. (This argument cannot be extended, and indeed must not be, to nonrestrictive relative clauses.) The second paragraph of the second Macaulay sample, however, is largely made up of restrictive relative clauses that purport to rehearse what is unquestionably true, and yet the paragraph is in fact arguing the point and setting up Macaulay's entire argument. Similarly, *since*-clauses are said to strongly indicate their material as Known, perhaps even Given. It may be that all these constructions have the 'have you stopped beating your wife' capacity to induce readers to accept as Known what is in fact new to them, to draw readers into the writer's world of assumptions and facts. A simple example of this effect occurs in one of the student's self-classifications and was discussed in chapter two. It begins *Since I come from a large family.* . . . Written on the first day of class, this information was totally new to me and gave me the impression that the student assumed I would be interested in his family background if it were relevant. To put it another way, these constructions impose a perspective on the context and project an implied reader who shares a similar knowledge and sense of what is novel and worth highlighting. The effect is to say, paraphrasing Hamlet, 'assume an address if you have it not,' and 'let's pretend you know this; all my best readers do.' The pleasure for readers, if they choose to play, is of learning to be insiders or intimates by learning what insiders treat as Known. There is a danger, however, that readers will balk at too much material being treated as Known that they do not know. But at least the writer is not watching us, and we can, if we wish, pretend.

I will leave it to the reader to decide how to respond to the offer of intimacy in the following paragraph from a freshman essay:

> In the areas of altered consciousness, both guitar and drum playing can be very rewarding and productive. If you ever explore altered states, play your instrument! You may or may not play better—that's not the point. Being stoned tends to get you out of the physical ruts that the hands and fingers get stuck in from practice— you will forget the musical cliches and riffs that you normally use. Therefore the product of your playing is fresh and newly inspired. As far as alcohol goes—skip it. Marijuana is not so great for rhythmic function but makes guitar a lot of fun. Hashish is especially good for guitar playing, and is my favorite music drug. You will find yourself thinking out the notes and chords way before you play them, and new ideas will fall like rain. LSD can be good for both drumming and guitar playing, depending on your mood and providing you get past marvelling at the shape of the guitar pick. Psilocybin mushrooms are the drummer's treasure, especially right after you take them and are just coming on. The physical energy that comes with the first rushes can be harnessed for a most productive rhythmic session.

Did you know about the physical energy that comes with the first rushes?

Perhaps the most useful way of thinking about this creation of intimacy, however, is to think about it as getting someone to face the same way you do and to walk a stretch of road together, thus getting her or him to most closely approximate your perspective and point of view. What is then central, or salient, will appear the same, and what is peripheral, and what is behind you, and the relation of things to each other, the foreground and depth, will be alike. The visual metaphor implicit in *perspective* also embraces the stereoscopic effect of seeing an object in slightly different ways as the angle on it changes. The essential direction of this chapter is thus away from the initial, one-dimensional metaphor of inflowing information toward the three-dimensional metaphor of perspective, which does, after all, seem a more appropriate one for the experience of human subjects.

If it is true that the experience of texts cannot be adequately accounted for in linear terms, then we are left with a major question about how the effects of consciousness described in this chapter are related to memory. It is, of course, possible that they are not directly recorded in memory at all, or reflected only via the sorts of recall differences that are adduced in evidence of the memory model. There is no reason to expect that memory would provide an exact record of all that transpired in consciousness—it is notoriously (or famously) selective in other regards. What then, one might ask, is the use of these manipulations of perspective and attention? And as soon as one asks that question, the appeal of the memory model stands exposed as a utilitarian grounding of what may well be an aesthetic dimension of text construction. On the other hand, the management of perspective may have effects in the interpretations of passages constructed by readers that we currently have no way of determining.

If we want to describe the function of Topic progressions, inversions, and clefts psychologically, we will have to avoid the tendency of most treatments to collapse distinctions into a single dichotomy like Given / New. The terms developed in this chapter go together in the following fashion: *Known* material is in memory or derivable from the material that is; *Given* material is that portion of Known material that is 'up' in consciousness, among which some element is in the foreground of consciousness; the *Topic* (of a sentence) usually links to a piece of material already in consciousness (Given) and often, in the two 'liaison' progressions, it links to the foregrounded element, but it may also be relatively novel or faded from consciousness—the function of inversions and initial adverbs is often to signal a shift in the Topic progression to a new sub-Topic. The *focused* element in a cleft is (momentarily) the center of attention, and the function of clefting is not so much to prominently introduce New material as to draw attention to the element, which then may or may not become the Topic in the next sentence. The *backgrounding* associated with clefts essentially involves marking the material in the *that* or *what* clause as Given (especially with *wh*-clefts) or Known (with *it*-clefts). In the next chapter, we will use these terms and extend this model to account for the function of subordination.

CHAPTER SIX

Subordination

There is a proper frame of mind in which to read statements like the following, which can be found in virtually every composition handbook:

> Subordination, the placing of certain elements in modifying roles, is a fundamental principle of writing. Adjectives and adverbs, phrases of all types, and subordinate clauses all serve to specify or qualify words that convey primary meaning. There are, to be sure, ways of making a technically subordinate element more prominent than anything else in its sentence, but in general, subordination is the main device for indicating the difference between core statements and elements of support or elaboration.[1]

> *Subordination.* A device that allows the writer to indicate distinctions between the weight, the intensity, and the relevancy of ideas is **subordination.** The most obvious form of subordination in sentences involves the use of the dependent clause. In a great variety of ways, the dependent clause allows the writer to choose the appropriate logical relationships between parts of a sentence.[2]

One should not approach these in a critical or analytic fashion; rather, one should take them as metaphorical prompts to stylistic intuitions. Our concern is not with their pedagogical usefulness (though the suspicion arises that any student who can interpret this advice probably already knows how to subordinate) but with their import for a theory of text construction: how is the sort of foreground / backgrounding suggested by these statements related to the other kinds discussed in the last chapter? What, in other words, is the theoretical context for such remarks?

As before, it will be useful to approach this question by considering these statements in their practical or pedagogical context. It is clear from the examples cited, for one thing, that 'subordination' is recommended as an alternative or 'cure' for strings of coordinated clauses—nominal clauses (*that* clauses, gerundives, and infinitives) are mostly ignored in these sections—so the statements do not characterize syntactic embedding or subordination as such; they center on the kinds of consolidations that can be achieved via adverbial, relative, and participial clauses, but also include examples of reduction of these clauses down to phrases. So again Crews and Good and Minnick:

Some writers, anxious to avoid a string of brief, abrupt sentences, loop independent clauses together with coordinating conjunctions. But the resulting *compound sentences* aren't much of an improvement:
x The right to secede is very dubious, *and* perhaps it shouldn't be considered a right at all, *for* it threatens the existing order, *and* that order denies the right in the first place.
Subordinate clauses or phrases can tighten the loose joints:
. Perhaps the right to secede, *dubious at best,* shouldn't be considered a right at all. Can the existing order grant a right *that threatens its own existence?*
One difficult sentence has become two clear ones, thanks largely to the use of subordination. (Crews, pp. 137–38)

Properly used, subordination adds interest to a sentence by relieving the monotony that sometimes accompanies a string of coordinate statements. Unrelieved coordination tends to cause choppy sentences and undeveloped ideas, so the art of subordination is crucial to varied, interesting, and emphatic writing.
FAULTY: I went to the movies, and I saw *Casablanca,* and it was old-fashioned, and I did not like it.
REVISED: I saw *Casablanca* when I went to the movies, but I did not like it because its style was old-fashioned.
FAULTY: The art teacher ordered supplies, invited a model to pose for the class, fell down a flight of stairs, was hospitalized briefly, attended a conference on pigments, and met her students for most of the semester.
REVISED: The art teacher ordered supplies, invited a model to pose for the class, and was able to meet her students for most of the semester, although she was hospitalized briefly after a fall down a flight of stairs and had to be out of town once to attend a conference on pigments.

Faulty coordination in the example about the art teacher tends to flatten the distinctions between such routine events as ordering supplies and attending class, on the one hand, and, on the other, the surprising and potentially tragic event of a fall down a flight of stairs. The revised version sets these events into a balanced statement that explains, through subordination, the effect that the accident had on the other events of the teacher's semester. (Good and Minnick, pp. 80–81)

There is something of a snippet problem with the examples, and, indeed, with most of the sentences used by psycholinguists to study the processing of subordinate clauses: plainly, what one wants to emphasize or highlight is determined by one's larger purposes and interests; the matter does not intrinsically dictate its own best organization—a point Good and Minnick seem to acknowledge in appending their paragraph explaining the improvement in their last example, which on first reading doesn't seem overwhelmingly better than their faulty version.

It is widely recognized that strings of coordinate sentences are characteristic of immature writers; Kellogg Hunt's famous study, and subsequent ones by Frank O'Hare and others, have substantiated this point, which has become the basis for the 'sentence embedding' techniques used in colleges chiefly for remediation.[3] Hunt did not find increases in the use of all forms of subordination: the most dramatic increases were in the proportion of relative clauses and gerunds and in the variety of adverbial clauses, which suggested to Hunt, correctly I believe, that these are features of the written language, and that is certainly the case with some of the absolute and participial consolidations advocated in the handbooks. So we have to do with description and inculcation of features of written language.

There is a danger, also widely recognized, that this pedagogic thrust will carry writers too far into excess subordination. E. D. Hirsch points this out with a 'contrived example' (*Philosophy,* p. 133). This is considered to be one of the dangers of too intensive a devotion to sentence-embedding. Crews gives an unusual amount of space to a final caution:

> x Although he was reluctant to accuse Patsy of sabotage, Paul wondered why his toy freight train had exploded, because he hadn't been playing "munitions shipment" at the time, although he did have some gunpowder in the basement.
>
> Here there is one main clause, *Paul wondered why his freight train had exploded.* If the sentence ended after *exploded* there would be no problem; the structure would be *Although a, b.* What we actually have is *Although a, b, because c, although d.* This is too much twisting and turning for a reader to bear without discomfort. Once you have launched a subordinate clause in the direction of an *although,* a *because,* an *unless,* etc., you have committed the whole sentence to a basic movement of thought; *although a, b; because a, b; unless a, b.* When you then begin qualifying *b* (the main clause), you are hacking away at the effectiveness of your own statement. Take care of the extra qualifications in a new sentence:
>
> > . Although he was reluctant to accuse Patsy of sabotage, Paul wondered why his toy freight train had exploded. It is true that he had some gunpowder in the basement, but he hadn't been playing "munitions shipment" at the time. (Crews, pp. 140–41)

Though the example is shaky and loses a certain charming touch of interior monologue in the revision, Crews's description is a wonderfully rich barrage of metaphors: how can such observations be accounted for within the present framework? The discussion will be divided into three parts, the first dealing with the kind of backgrounding said to accompany subordination, the second dealing with the related issue of placement of adverbial clauses, and the third with the reduction of subordinate clauses.

1. *How do subordinate clauses subordinate?*

There are at least five different approaches to the backgrounding effect of subordination. The first will get fairly short shrift: some have suggested that only the main clause is asserted, material in the subordinate clause being presupposed.[4] This idea is rather like the suggestion that in saying that someone is a bachelor, you would be taken as saying more he is unmarried than that he is male, adult, human, and so on. Likewise, when you say he is not a bachelor, you most likely are denying his singleness, not his adulthood or humanness: the 'presupposed' material (adult, human) cannot be negated because it is not part of the assertion. However, material in subordinate clauses can be negated by *not* in the main clause (if the subordinate clause follows the main clause), so strictly logical presupposition is not present; further, on almost all accounts of *assertion,* modifying elements (such as subordinate clauses) must be counted as part of the assertion. The only way to make this approach work is to stipulate a special meaning for assertion, and then the problem is simply shifted to another term.

The second approach makes use of the Given/New distinction (or rather Known/New, consciousness not being at issue here), suggesting that subordinate clauses contain largely Known information, which explains why the communicative focus is not on them. As noted in the previous chapter, this makes sense in that relative clauses and adverbials are often used to identify individuals or locate events in time or place or provide a reason for an action or event, and such identifications and explanations would presumably be in terms that are familiar to the reader. Still, this cannot be correct for all cases, because explanation, description, and so on are not always given in terms of Known information. Moreover, this explanation would not hold for concessive or conditional clauses, though perhaps Knownness is less associated with them anyway. In fact, the degree of commitment to Knownness of subordinate material might vary from clause-type to type, or even from subordinator to subordinator, as suggested by Ilene Lanin for *since / because.*[5] It would seem that determining the strength of the commitment to Knownness would be a simple empirical question: look at texts and see whether the material in the clauses is in fact Known. But we run into 'treating as Known' again. Do relative clauses and adverbials have such a power? That is, when we turn to our samples and find material in these clauses that is not strictly in memory or common knowledge, does that refute the claim that subordinate clauses contain Known information? How do we know whether something is being treated as Known? It turns out that this question is easier to answer for our extended texts than for the short examples in the handbooks because it is easier to grasp our writers' communicative purposes.

There is no question about the Knownness of some of the subordinate clauses in the samples, because they clearly involve redescription. The first clause of the Miller sample is redescriptive, referring to work described in the preceding paragraphs. The sentence, in fact, is a bridging transition to Sherrington's work. Here is another example from later in the sample:

> Pavlov's interest in experimental neurosis increased as he grew older; he devoted the last decade of his life largely to psychiatric problems. When at last be began to think seriously about human behavior Pavlov recognized that the enormous complexities introduced by language required new explanations. (Miller, 4)

Here Miller is using the adverbial clause of time for redescription to point out the shift from animal behavior to human behavior. The next example is a discourse-referential participial from Arnold:

> The critical power is of lower rank than the creative. True; but in assenting to this proposition, one or two things are to be kept in mind. (Arnold, 2)

In assenting to this proposition clearly refers to the act of assent in "True." Redescriptive relative clauses are a feature of Miller's and Hamilton's styles: consider the beginning of Hamilton's second paragraph (redescriptive clauses italicized):

> The causes responsible for this achievement, however, are not so generally understood. Rather is it the fashion nowadays to speak of the Greek miracle, to consider the radiant bloom of Greek genius as having no root in any soil *that we can give an account of.* The anthropologists are busy, indeed, and ready to transport us back into the savage forest where all human things, the Greek things, too, had their beginnings; but the seed never explains the flower. Between those strange rites *they point us to* through the dim vistas of far-away ages, and a Greek tragedy, there lies a gap *they cannot help us over.*

(I class these clauses as redescriptive though the initial descriptions are somewhat implicit.) The second one may help the recognition that *strange rites* are part of *savage forest* (if the demonstrative *those* is not sufficient). Another, shorter example occurs in the third paragraph of the sample (*the spirit of the East that never changes*).

The longer passage just cited also contains a relative clause (*the savage forest where all human things, the Greek things, too, had their beginnings*), the Knownness of which might be said to arise from some general knowledge of Cambridge cultural anthropology. There are numerous subordinate clauses that draw on various kinds of 'common knowledge and experience,' (e.g., "every calamity which is incident to our nature," Macaulay, I, 3; "that asperity which is produced by pride struggling with misery," Macaulay, I, 2), though in some cases the knowledge isn't exactly common and we begin to shade into the 'treat as Known' area. Consider first some of the other relative clause examples:

> Many things there pointed back to the old world and away to the East, and with the emperors *who were gods and fed a brutalized people full of horrors as their dearest form of amusement,* the ancient and the Oriental state has a true revival. Not that the spirit of Rome was of the Eastern stamp. Common-sense men of affairs were its product *to whom the cogitations of Eastern sages ever seemed the idlest nonsense.* (Hamilton, 4)

The contents of the relative clauses here might be classed as common assessments and lore about the Classical world. Compare some of the relative clauses from the Johnson sample:

> The irregular combinations of fanciful invention may delight awhile by that novelty *of which the common satiety of life sends us all in quest;* (Johnson, 1)

> His persons act and speak by the influence of these general passions and principles *by which all minds are agitated and the whole system of life is continued in motion.* (Johnson, 2)

These clauses draw on that body of Universal Truths so central to the Augustan mentality; perhaps the 'treating as Known' effect is most noticeable here because those concepts are so far from common knowledge today. Other writers treat other areas of experience and knowledge as Known: Macaulay, for example, assumes familiarity with the details of Milton's life and with the experience of poetry—reasonable assumptions, to be sure, considering the intended or imagined audiences for his writing.

Examples with *since* (or *as*) are even more striking because this subordinator has been said to strongly mark its clause as Known. Consider the last sentence of the Carson sample:

> Since none of the present evidence is conclusive, however, we simply do not know how the canyons came into being, and their mystery remains. (Carson, 10)

Carson has not actually said that the evidence was inconclusive, though she did observe that it would not support the theory she seems to lean to, so there is a little leap forward in thought in the adverbial clause, though one we are not prepared to object to. The last sentence in the first paragraph of the Miller sample also makes a little leap:

> Since experimental psychologists, inspired in no small measure by Pavlov's success, have pursued the objective description and analysis of behavior, Pavlov's work has had its major effect on behavioristic psychology, rather than on physiology.

Treating the *since* clause as Known is to assume some familiarity with the basic tenets and procedures of experimental psychology (which Miller quickly reminds us is, in his view, equivalent to behavioristic psychology). The last sample has the power to boggle many a modern reader:

> But love is only one of many passions; and as it has no great influence upon the sum of life, it has little operation in the dramas of a poet who caught his ideas from the living world and exhibited only what he saw before him. (Johnson, 5)

Today it is the rare reader indeed who will accept the contents of the *as*-clause as Known! These examples, along with the relative clauses cited above, strongly suggest that subordinate clauses do provide a way of inobtrusively enriching the background of ideas and assumptions in the fashion described at the end of the last chapter, and I think more extended analysis of what writers put in their subordinate clauses would yield some interesting insights into the kinds of common grounds they establish with the reader. This then is another point where the imagination or postulation of an audience enters into text construction—not just with the inferences they are prepared to make, and the schemata they will apply, but what they are prepared to accept as Known.

Something would be missed, however, if we simply equate the

backgrounding of subordinate clauses with Knownness, and this brings us to the third approach. A clue to what this is can be found in discussions by Teun van Dijk and, more extendedly, Richard Smaby. Both writers suggest that main clause material should be more closely connected to the theme (or 'topic') of the passage.[6] Smaby puts it in terms of main clause material having more anaphoric ties to preceding and following sentences. This seems reasonable as far as it goes, which isn't very, but Smaby further suggests that subordinate clauses do not have the power to foreground entities and, I would add, do not contribute to Topic liaisons and shifts. This generalization accounts for several facts: Smaby contrives examples illustrating the point that adverbial and relative clauses do not introduce entities that become the antecedents of following pronouns. Similarly, Halliday and Hasan note that material in the predicate of a restrictive relative or adverbial clause is weak as a controller ('antecedent') of subsequent ellipsed elements:

> The policeman paid no attention to the girl who was driving the car.—Was she?
> I shall stay in the city when I retire this year.—Do you?

Note that this is true of straight anaphora as well:

> The policeman paid no attention to the girl who was driving with gloves. They were grey.

This is not true of predicates in nonrestrictive relative and loosely attached subordinate clauses:

> The policeman paid no attention to Mrs. Jones, who was driving the car.—Was she?
> I shall stay in the city, even though I retire this year.—Do you?

They attribute this difference to a difference in the degree of integration or subordination of material into the main clause: restrictive modifiers are more integrated and less able to serve as antecedents.[7] Another, apparently unrelated, fact is that subordinate clauses do not usually take the inversions discussed in the last chapter that serve to manipulate Topic and perspective (e.g., no 'When Algebra you pass with an A, I'll give you a Ferrari'). Various explanations have been offered for this fact, including a putative Grammatical Universal,[8] but it seems worth considering that inversions don't occur in subordinate clauses because they have no business to do there. This carries us a bit further than simply saying 'peripheral material goes into subordinate clauses'; the subordination or subjection of material in such clauses prevents it from getting into the foreground, competing with what is there. This may be the explanation we have been seeking for the uncluttering effect of subordination. That is, subordination is said to establish a hierarchy or ranking of importance of ideas ("weight, intensity, and relevancy," as Good and Minnick have it); what we can now say is that it does so by marking some material as not in the Topic progression but ancillary to it.

Some of these facts were noted by Thomas Bever and David Townsend in an article offering a fourth approach, what we might call a processing version of backgrounding, to wit, that subordinate clauses are held in verbatim memory and only processed after the main clause has been processed. The evidence they offer is very scanty and open to several objections; further, their whole discussion is based on the idea that because subordinate clauses contain less important or Known information, subjects would naturally put off processing them until they had the main story straight.[9] Perhaps subjects could be induced to act in this way in certain experimental situations, but (as usual) it is by no means clear what if anything this tells us about reading. As long as we remain in the dark about the exact function of Topic progressions in processing, we will not have much to say about how the separation of material in subordinate clauses affects its processing.

2. Placement of adverbial clauses

One of the most venerable and entrenched notions in grammar is that placement of adverbial clauses initially or later in the sentence is optional and does not affect meaning (hence transformational grammar has an 'adverbial preposing transformation'). Moreover, if our observation that the material in an adverbial clause does not enter into the Topical progression is correct, one ought to be free to place them first or last, perhaps choosing first position if the clause has strong anaphoric links to the preceding sentence (like the transitional example from Miller), or to leave the prominence of end position to the main clause. In that case, we would have a genuine 'stylistic' option. We could note that an initial subordinating conjunction is proleptic and suspensive in that it signals that the complete integration and interpretation of initial clause will depend on reaching the main clause: this apparently is what Crews means by commitments and launching in, though I don't agree that the commitment extends so far as that the main clause will end the sentence. Using initial adverbials would then be a way of raising the 'periodicity' or suspensiveness of your prose, whether for emphasis or for playing a guessing game with the reader (Although X . . .), or what have you. We could even recommend them as a way of getting some variety in your sentence openings. Finally, we might note a general tendency with temporal adverbials to shadow the order of events in the order of clauses; thus if event A occurred on Tuesday and B the next day, we find:

> A, then B.
> After A, B.
> A, before B.

rather than:

> B, after A.
> Before B, A.

This preference is well known in children's language, and it is distinct in Kellogg Hunt's data as well (p. 83).[10] One might suggest that if you reverse the pattern, you should have a good reason for doing so. Observations and advice like this have been offered and they are certainly part of the story, but they are all based on the assumption that positional alternatives do not affect meaning—and that is wrong.

One of Dwight Bolinger's main theses in "Pronouns and Repeated Nouns" is that initial and final position are not equivalent semantically: initial position, with temporal adverbs, suggests more than a contingent, temporal relationship in the direction of a setting, anticipation, or cause-and-effect relationship.[11] Ilene Lanin similarly observes that initial placement of *because* clauses stresses the logical consequence relation. This placement does not give us the 'speaker's reason for saying' sense of *because*:

> John must be home, because his lights are on.
> ?Because his lights are on, John must be home.

The notion of setting is particularly interesting, because it links up with a general point about sentence interpretation stressed by Teun van Dijk, namely that initial material often gives access to the relevant portions of the possible world projected in the text in which the rest of the sentence has value. This is an unfamiliar notion, and in some ways a complex one, but it is fairly easy to grasp by examples, of which there are many in the samples. Here first are cause-and-effect illustrations:

> As the petroleum reserves left on continental areas by ancient seas
> become depleted, petroleum geologists look more and more to the
> oil that may lie, as yet unmapped and unexploited, under these bor-
> dering lands of the sea. (Carson, 1)

(The *as*-clause gives the conditions that stimulate the search for oil
undersea—it is not a coincidence.)

> The canyons have now been found in so many parts of the world
> that when soundings have been taken in presently unexplored areas
> we shall probably find that they are of world-wide occurrence. (Car-
> son, 8)

(The *when*-clause is both a logical and a temporal condition for the
probable finding. In addition, the soundings are the basis of the
finding.)

> Ordinarily the nervous system can establish an equilibrium between
> them, but when the sources of excitation and inhibition get very close
> together, the equilibrium breaks down and a generally excited or
> inhibited state appears. (Miller, 2)

(The stimuli's occurring close together *causes* the equilibrium to
break down.)

    Another example of cause-and-effect interpretation is from
Johnson:

> The theatre, when it is under any other direction, is peopled by such
> characters as were never seen, conversing in a language which was
> never heard, upon topics which will never arise in the commerce of
> mankind. (Johnson, 4)

To be sure, there are anaphoric ties in the *when*-clause (*any other
direction*) that could be said to attract it to initial position, but the
special shading of its being first (nearly) is that it gives the circumstances or conditions under which the rest of the sentence holds.
The next two examples illustrate a more literal sense of setting
(though one is a phrase–plus–modifying clause, the other a participial):

> every one can see that a poet, for instance, ought to know life and
> the world before dealing with them in poetry; and life and the world
> being in modern times very complex things, the creation of a mod-
> ern poet, to be worth much, implies a great critical effort behind it;
> (Arnold, 4)

Again, despite the anaphoric links (*life and the world*), the participial could be placed at the end; the effect of its position as written, however, is to stress that it is this circumstance of the modern poet which creates the need for great critical effort. The last example is the final sentence in the Hamilton passage:

> In a world where the irrational had played the chief role, they came forward as the protagonists of the mind.

This sentence is a truly artful recapitulation of the preceding two paragraphs, which are about the differentiation and emergence of the uniquely Greek genius: this is 'setting' in the most literal sense.

Bolinger notes that initial adverbials, while they establish the setting or portion of the world crucial for the interpretation of the main clause, are not integrated into the predicate as modifiers as tightly as those in end position. He suggests, however, that adverbials may occur in end position if separated from the main clause by a comma (or other disjunction), and in that position no longer function as settings determining the relevant world but are "to some extent parenthetical and afterthoughtive" (p. 30). He contrasts the pair

> As the night fell the wind rose.
> The wind rose, as the night fell.

which have a setting or circumstance sense for the adverbial, with

> The wind rose as the night fell.
> The night fell as the wind rose.

which truly predicate simultaneity of two events, and he points out the oddity of both members of the pair

> As the wind rose the night fell.
> The night fell, as the wind rose.

concluding that the offset final adverbial more resembles an initial one than a nonoffset final one. Hence we should think more of an adverbial *postposing* transformation, which would shift initial adverbials to end position and set them off with a comma. The comma, like initial position, prevents the 'capture' of the adverbial clause by the predicate and thus signals that it is not to be taken as a specifier or modifier of the predicate. Consider the following example, where the *when*-clause has the force of 'when and only when'—i.e., it is a condition for the occurrence of the main clause, not a temporal modifier:

> The grand work of literary genius is a work of synthesis and exposi-
> tion, not of analysis and discovery; its gift lies in the faculty of being
> happily inspired by a certain intellectual and spiritual atmosphere, by
> a certain order of ideas, when it finds itself in them; (Arnold, 1)

Bolinger here touches on one of the standard pieces of handbook
advice on punctuation, which is to set off final adverbial clauses that
are 'loosely related' or 'inessential to the meaning of' the main
clause. Handbooks give examples like the following:

> You will not pass the examination unless you study carefully.

versus

> You did not pass the examination, although I am sure you studied
> carefully.[12]
> An Hispano student who is told to apologize cannot do it, because
> the word does not exist in Spanish.[13]

which we might contrast with

> An Hispano student who is told to apologize cannot do it because his
> macho code forbids it.

Moreover, as Bolinger shows, since the very same sequence of words
can have a different interpretation depending on whether a comma
is present or not, we must conclude that both position and punctuation are pointers affecting the interpretation of the text and are not
completely predictable in terms of grammatical units or relations (at
least as presently understood).

The Bolinger–van Dijk account of initial material seems to me to
capture something about the (my) experience of reading these texts
and other texts as well. If indeed it is an account of language processing, then the Bever-Townsend notion of holding initial adverbial
clauses suspended until the main clause is processed cannot be the
right model for these experiences. For one thing, setting adverbials
would fall together with afterthoughtive and restrictively modifying
ones, and, for another, it makes no distinction between the latter two
types. Certainly it seems an odd strategy to apply to all initial subordinate clauses, considering that some of them are heavily anaphoric
and tend to contain information that should be more readily assimilable than that in the main clause. As noted earlier, the evidence for
this 'delay' strategy, even under experimental conditions, is fairly
shaky, and it seems to me that the view of processing implicit in van

Dijk's and Bolinger's observations is as or more plausible, at least for the reading of these texts.

Recently Bever and Townsend have modified their earlier sketch of delayed processing in three ways so that it now more resembles the van Dijk/Bolinger model.[14] First, they have abandoned the explanation for delay phenomena in terms of Known/New information; second, they have established a scale of subordinators in the order *if, since, when, while*, and *though* in terms of increasing tendency to trigger delayed processing in initial position. The new explanation is that when the initial clause introduces a causal (or causelike) basis for the interpretation of the main clause (most often signaled by *if* and *since*), the reader/hearer is more likely to interpret it first; when the subordinator is concessive (*though*), the interpretation of the initial clause depends more on the material in the main clause and so the initial *though* clause is more likely to be held (delayed) until the main clause has been processed. This rather loose notion of cause is very close to what van Dijk and Bolinger mean by setting. Third, Bever and Townsend's discussion of their new position gives much greater recognition to the constructive acts of hearers and readers: "the underlying factor affecting performance is not the structural or presuppositional properties of the clauses but, instead, is the meaning of the conjunctions and the kinds of organizing strategies they elicit" (p. 195).

3. *To reduce or not*

Just as the handbooks give little advice on the placement of subordinate clauses, so they also say little about whether a clause should be reduced or not, or what difference there is between reduced and unreduced forms. There are two points worth making, however, about this stylistic option, one having to do with the clause material's integration into or dependence on the main clause, the other with the scribal nature of reduced clauses.

When one reduces a full subordinate clause, whether adverbial or adjectival (relative) in nature, what is omitted is the subordinator (the relative pronoun or subordinating conjunction) and/or the tense (and aspect) marker, so that the relation of the material to the main sentence is not as explicitly indicated as it is in unreduced form. Quirk et al. speak of the "semantic versatility" of these clauses, which is filled in by the context, e.g.,

> Cleared, this site will be very valuable. (When it is cleared . . .)
> Cleared, this site would be very valuable. (If it were cleared . . .)[15]

However, in another way these clauses are less versatile, since they usually contain less material than a full finite subordinate clause. Further, as Quirk et al. note, the relation with a reduced clause tends to be tighter in the direction of cause and effect than in nonreduced clauses. So there is an almost paradoxical combination of inexplicitness in surface marking and tightness of semantic dependence: essentially, reduction makes the material even more dependent on the main clause, even less capable of making a comment or adding New information than the unreduced clause. We have, then, a scale of dependence from main to finite nonrestrictive to finite modifying to reduced participial clauses (or phrases). The point here about dependence is very much like that made in chapter three about connection; the reduced form signals a close and immediate link—this is perhaps what underlies the metaphor of 'tightness' employed, for example, by Crews in his comment on the revision cited earlier.

Clause reduction seems to be a practice especially cultivated in written discourse and markedly more present in formal and 'mature' prose than in personal letters or grade school compositions. It is essentially a product of editing in the direction of concision (more a virtue of writing than of speech, because limitations of channel and distraction are less pressing) and presupposes command both of certain forms obscure in speech (the -ing and -ed participles) and of conventions of 'attachment' that are widely disregarded in speech when reduced forms do occur ("Thinking it over, it is clear what you were trying to get at"). It is a little hard to understand the extreme indignation that unattached ('dangling') participles often meet with, and the ferocity of penalties levied by some composition teachers, since they do not stigmatize the user as lower class or crude in the way that, say, *he don't* or *hisself* do. Perhaps it is just because the convention is a scribal one that the guardians of convention feel a no-quarter stand is necessary.

Reduced constructions are among the last syntactic constructions to appear in the writing of children. This may be due to a tendency not to omit optional elements, which Dan Slobin proposed as a universal principle of child acquisition of language.[16] The evidence for Slobin's generalization came largely from the spoken language, but there is much support for it in the study by Roy O'Donnell, William Griffin, and Raymond Norris, which shows comparable preference for the longer forms in writing as well as speech.[17] One can see the difference between connected and subordinated (but not ellipsed) discourse and a more literary rendering by comparing the story of "The Ant and the Dove" as told by a third-grader (after seeing an eight-minute movie with the sound turned off) and the standard

Aesop's version, which takes pride in using as few sentences as possible.

Once upon a time there lived an ant, One day when he was walking along he found an apple and rolled it over close to his bed. Then he got a ride on a locust. When they got up in the air the ant fell off onto a long peace of grass that was hanging across a river, then he fell into the river and stayed for about five minutes. A Dove saw him almost drowning. The Dove got a leaf and dropped it into the river and the ant got on and reaching the shore safely. Then the ant got another apple and broke it into peaces and put it where he put the first one. When the ant got up out of the hole he saw great big feet on the other side of the bushes, he watched the man and saw him aim the gun at the Dove. So he got some tweasers and just as the man was about to shoot the Dove the ant climed up the man's leg and peanched the man, the man droped the gun, the Dove woke up and that's all I can remember.

A thirsty ant went to a spring for a drink of water.

(a) While climbing down a blade of grass to reach the spring he fell in. The ant might very well have drowned had it not been for a dove who happened to be perched in a nearby tree. (b) Seeing the ant's danger the dove quickly plucked off a leaf and let it drop into the water near the struggling insect. The ant climbed upon the leaf and presently was wafted safely ashore.

Just at that time a hunter was spreading his net in the hope of snaring the dove. The gratified ant, (c) perceiving the hunter's plan, bit him in the heel. Startled, the huntsman dropped his net, and the dove flew away to safety.[18]

Apparently the movie seen by the boy lost no chance to inculcate a bit of ethological lore, and there are other differences in the two accounts, but the two tellings are comparable enough to make the point dramatically: at (a), (b), and (c), material in two sentences in the first account is condensed into a participial in the 'Aesop's' version, in each case with a cause-and-effect relation being stressed.

Two incidental points are worth noting. The boy's version is not perfect in its handling of description and later mention. Although he observes the basic convention of introduction via an indefinite and later mention with a definite (*a/the ant, a/the river*), he does first mention the gun with a definite (perhaps in his view guns go with hunters just like big feet do). Also, he repeats noun phrases where we would use pronouns, particularly with *the man*. A marked

difference between the versions is the number of adjectives modifying the nouns in the Aesop's version (*thirsty, struggling, gratified*).
These do not perform the function described in chapter four of cutting or narrowing the set of individuals denoted— there being only
one on hand; rather, they refer to temporary attributes that explain
why he does what he does ("gratified") or remind us, in the case of
struggling, of what is obvious (note the shift from *ant* to *insect,* also
hunter / huntsman). This use of adjectives is part of the heavy didacti-
cism of the Fables, which appears also in the interpretive third
sentence—the boy's story is fine without it—and in *startled,* the remains of a reduced clause, which clarifies the point that the man was
scarcely intimidated or greatly injured. Certainly if one wants to
comment on this sort of thing, it is best to tuck it away after the
fashion of Aesop and not give it the equal rank that the boy's syntax
would probably require: . . . The man was startled, so he dropped
his gun. . . .

   As a recapitulation and application of the notions discussed in this
chapter, let us consider two brief, heavily subordinated passages.
The first is from the Johnson sample:

> Characters thus ample and general were not easily discriminated
> and preserved, yet perhaps no poet ever kept his personages more
> distinct from each other. I will not say with Pope that every speech
> may be assigned to the proper speaker, because many speeches there
> are which have nothing characteristical; but, perhaps, though some
> may be equally adapted to every person, it will be difficult to find any
> that can be properly transferred from the present possessor to an-
> other claimant. The choice is right, when there is reason for choice.
> (Johnson, 6)

The final *when*-clause is a prime example of an 'afterthoughtive'
qualification—its sense is that of 'when it happens that,' not 'when
and only when' or 'just when.' Note also that the *because*-clause is a
rare counterexample to the generalization that subordinate clauses
don't have inversions, and that the inversion of *many speeches* does
Topicalize *speeches* so that it can be the antecedent for *some* and *any*.
So the *because* clause here is simply being treated as a main clause
with a 'main clause' inversion. Main clause treatment is more often
given to 'afterthoughtive' clauses than to the other subordinate ones,
above all with good old nonrestrictive '. . . , *which* . . . ' sometimes
frowned on in handbooks but regularly used by many skilled writers.
   This paragraph is not the easiest reading in the world—Johnson,
it seems, has not gone about things in the most direct manner—and

I come out of the final sentence with a distinct sense of relief that I have finally gotten the point. The difficulty, though, may have as much to do with the fluid variation in terms for the same entity (*characters, personage, speaker, person, possessor*) as with the thicket of *yet* and *but* reversals with subordinate clauses interspersed. The labor of thought here brings to mind Crews's comment on his example of excessive subordination that "There is too much twisting and turning for the reader to bear without discomfort." This passage from Johnson is only one of countless examples that could be cited to remind us that the reader who takes on Johnson is going to have to put up with some discomfort, presumably in return for some higher gain. Actually, I think Crews's experience is one of distaste (a source, I suppose, of discomfort) at the rambling, unplanned sprawl of his example, so characteristic of relaxed conversation and so indecorous for the essay. The grounds of Crews's objection, I am suggesting, are esthetic, not practical. This passage from Johnson is much 'harder to process' than his, but we may perhaps value it as evoking a struggle to extract from Pope's observation what is correct without committing Pope's excess.

The second example, cited earlier in chapter three in the discussion of periodicity, is from the first Macaulay passage:

> Such as it was when, on the eve of great events, he returned from his travels, in the prime of health and manly beauty, loaded with literary distinctions, and glowing with patriotic hopes, such it continued to be when, after having experienced every calamity which is incident to our nature, old, poor, sightless and disgraced, he retired to his hovel to die. (Macaulay, I, 3)

Most of the material is contained within two *when*-clauses, each of which contains two participial or verbless 'clauses' with an extra relative clause attached to *every calamity*. The embedding goes down four levels, packing in material all of which is essentially circumstantial. But Macaulay is not merely loading in biographical details after the fashion of some historians: the circumstances are those one would expect to alter Milton's 'temper' (toward ebullience on the one hand and dejection on the other), but they did not—this is Macaulay's point. So the tight integration, or dependency, associated with reduced clauses yields a cause-and-(non)effect relation.

The question posed at the outset of the chapter was what account of the stylistic impressions of the handbooks we could give within the theory of text construction. There does seem to be a correlation between the notion of importance of information and its relation to Knownness and Topicality, and between the sense of looseness /

tightness and the practice of clause reduction. Treatment of these topics has always involved a good bit of lumping into broad categories like subordinate/main, restrictive/nonrestrictive, though there seem to be significant differences between clause types, in clause position and fullness, between individual subordinators, and perhaps in the handling of these matters by individual writers. The figurative language of the handbook accounts (choppy, looped, loose, uncluttered, tight) accommodates itself to this diversity by suggesting a mode of thinking built around tendencies and possible distinctions rather than sharply defined categories, and if we had to choose between these traditional metaphors and the precise categories of syntax and semantics (embedded sentences, restrictive modifiers, cause), the traditional terms might well be the better choice.

CHAPTER SEVEN

Words

With words, we at last reach the 'bottom' in this survey of text structures. In no area is bottom-to-top thinking more entrenched than with words, both in pedagogy and in linguistic semantics. Pedagogically, students are told to look up words they don't know, to select the appropriate sense, and to plug that sense into the text at the appropriate place. 'Vocabulary' is treated as an elementary skill, with words being fitted into sentences containing slots or being used in a sentence of the student's composing. Semantics is firmly committed to the principle of compositionality of sentence meaning, which is that the meaning (or 'reading') of whole sentences is some sort of compositional function of the meanings of the words. There is some question, however, of whether this theoretically posited 'reading' has any psychological reality. Writing at the very beginning of the current surge of interest in semantics, Uriel Weinreich described certain phenomena that a compositional theory could not handle, among which is the difference in the way *eat soup,* and *eat bread* are understood—different motions, different instruments, and so on.[1] Yet these differences cannot be attributed to the sense of *soup* or *meat*, or to two different senses of *eat,* without an explosive increase in the numbers of senses and specification of senses of words. So we have a situation where the whole is greater than the sum of the parts, and compositional theories cannot account for this: constructing the reading for a passage must involve more than the recognition and recall of word senses, and it will be the task of this chapter to specify what some of these constructive processes are. For the *eat bread / soup* case, the notion of instantiation or particularization touched on in the fourth chapter seems applicable: one builds a scene by adding 'knowledge of the world,' in this case what one knows of or thinks of as typical or canonical events of bread-eating and soup-eating. In more complex cases, of course, the construction will be guided by the context; the aptness or salience of portions of a word's meaning is shaped by the concerns that are in mind when the word arises. Even a tiny little context like a contrasting phrase can render certain attributes salient and others irrelevant, as in a

sentence like *We are men, not machines,* in which the aspects of men
that contrast with women, for example, are irrelevant to the meaning of *men.* Much is unknown about this interaction of word and
context, but it does at least seem clear that it involves networks of
meanings and latent imagery, the sort of things approached in terms
of etymology and connotation in traditional discussions of word lore
and left completely out of account in contemporary linguistic
semantics.

Approached in this fashion, figurative word senses appear as special cases of these more general constructive processes, and we are
less likely to exaggerate the 'differentness' or the 'poetry' of figurative language, some of which is quite mundane, when we see that
imagination and interpretation are equally involved in many so-
called literal uses. Sensitivity to imagery and nuance is not confined
to figurative language; in fact, it is essentially variable: words can be
'vivified' to various degrees. There are times when any one of several
words will do the job (the words are effectively or functionally syn-
onymous) and metaphors are transparent, other times when one
word or image must be sought and happily found. It is futile and
preposterous to claim that each word must be chosen with maximum
deliberation and care, but it is equally wide of the mark to suggest
that the word choice is good if you have avoided using any in
nonstandard ways. Word choice can be relatively rich and resonant
or spare and utilitarian; words can be interanimated (as I. A.
Richards would say) or inert.

1. Building meanings

Leaving aside for a moment the question of whether the senses of
words given in dictionaries are psychologically real, let us try to formulate the relation of dictionary sense to the way a word is understood in context. It is important to recognize that dictionary senses
are abstractions of uses: dozens or hundreds of short citations of the
word's use are gathered by the lexicographer and sorted into piles,
each pile representing uses that seem to cluster around a single notion. The lexicographer then tries to characterize this common notion in other words, often indicating a common contextual element
as well, as when the domain of learned discourse is noted (as *astron.,*
music, etc.), or, more subtly, by using defining words that also occur
in the same contexts (that *collocate* with the word, as British linguists
say). The sense thus represents or marks out an *area* of meaning, as
far as meanings can be determined from the relatively short citations

used. The focus is not on characterizing the particular colorings or nuances of the words in the individual contexts; so, if we think of particular meanings as built up out of senses like those in dictionaries, we would certainly want to include some particularizing or detail-filling or specifying process. We might think of the word senses as rough-cut materials out of which meanings are constructed. Richard Anderson and Andrew Ortony conclude from their psycholinguistic investigation of meanings that "sentence comprehension and memory involve constructing particularized representations whose sense cannot be reliably predicted from the dictionary readings of the constituent words (see also Anderson and McGaw, 1973). In our view, the most plausible explanation for the results is that words loosely and flexibly constrain the building of a representation. . . ."[2]

The question of the psychological reality of word senses is, moreover, a thorny one: there are both linguistic and psycholinguistic reasons to question it. It has been suggested that the word senses given in most current desk-top dictionaries are *excessively* specified as characterizations of what is contributed by the word itself; rather, the 'senses' in dictionaries are already particularized to various degrees with details from contexts. One hundred fifteen senses and subsenses for *turn*, Weinreich suggested years ago, are too many;[3] David Bennett has similarly argued that dictionaries err in giving separate temporal and spatial senses for many prepositions: the difference can be worked out in terms of contextual cues specifying a more abstract unitary sense as involving either relations in time or space. For example, *in* in the following two sentences,

> Brighton is in Sussex.
> Some people have their main meal . . . in the evening.

should not be regarded as having two senses, 'position or enclosure within a particular place, area or object . . . ' and 'a period of time . . . within which something takes place,' but a single sense of something being at the interior of something else.[4] Similar doubts have been voiced by Alfonso Caramazza and Ellen Grober and by George Miller and Phillip Johnson-Laird.[5] All these writers suggest that if we regard the sense of the word as only the unique material that cannot be inferred from the word's context, then much more abstract word senses could be coded in memory. Consequently, dictionary senses are already on the way to interpreted meanings. Regardless of the psychological reality of dictionary senses, however, all parties agree that the meanings that are constructed as one reads (or listens) are specialized and particularized beyond what is given in the dictionary, and it is this process that requires further investigation.[6]

Let us begin this investigation with an illustration from the first sentence of the Johnson sample, asking how we construct a meaning for the key phrase *just representations of general nature.* Suppose we attempt to 'plug in' dictionary senses; the *American Heritage Dictionary* lists three plausible ones for *just:*

> 5. Suitable; fitting. 6. Sound: well-founded: *a just appraisal.*
> 7. Exact; accurate: *a just measure.*

These correspond roughly to the three subdivisions of sense 1 in *Webster's Eighth Collegiate:*

> 1a: having a basis in or conforming sometimes rigidly to fact or reason: REASONABLE <a ~ but not a generous decision> < ~ anger> b *archaic:* faithful to an original c: conforming to a standard of correctness: PROPER < ~ proportions>

It is curious that one likely candidate for our sentence is marked *archaic* in *Webster's* though the corresponding one in *American Heritage* is not—or do they in fact correspond exactly? Is *Webster's* thinking of special qualities in old-fashioned uses? What sort of weight or centering to give to *just* here depends in part on how *representations* (of general nature) is meant: does it have a strongly visual orientation, or more the sense of a construct? This in turn depends on how we think about *general nature:* is this something that is readily visible and accessible, in the writer's view, or is it also the product of abstractive, analytic thought? Already we are beyond the question of sense selection and into the area of the particular context of thought in which this phrase takes on its particular meaning. I do not think we can answer these questions at this point; the meaning of the phrase must remain indeterminate until further clues to the context of thought appear. They are quick in coming, for Johnson recognizes that the phrase is dense and somewhat cryptic: "Particular manners can be known to few; and therefore few only can judge how nearly they are copied." *Particular manners* helps to stabilize and specify the meaning of *general nature* in the direction of 'personality types' (provided, that is, the reader is familiar with the archaic sense of *manners* used here—otherwise the specification only works for *particular*). Even more helpful are the words *judge* and *copied:* these point to a fairly visual meaning for *representations* and an 'accuracy' meaning for *just.* The second sentence thus creates a context for the first that enables us to specify its meaning—the construction of meaning apparently does not stop when the word is first read, or even the sentence containing it. Some uncertainty may remain about how committed Johnson is to this 'copy' view of art (drama, in the present instance), which is to say how much he will invoke it and stay within its confines, but it is clear that he intends us to entertain it for his purposes at this point. The whole passage, in fact, works in this way to establish its own specifying network of terms: the very dense phrase *the irregular combinations of fanciful invention,* for example, contrasts to *just representations,* near copies, and *the stability of truth* and is narrowed and specified by these contrasts rather than, say, by direct definition or example. Another example of contrastive specification occurs in the second Macaulay sample in the clause *he who can resolve will be able to combine* — the clause suggests an opposition that would steer the reader away from the 'act of will' and 'solution' senses of *resolve* toward 'analyze into elements,' and this contrast is reinforced by the context. But contrastiveness is only the most obvious, pointed, and citable of the many ways contexts specify and enrich meanings. Continuing with the Johnson excerpt, for example, we can see how the concern with the permanent and true provides the context that brings to life the word *accidents* in the next paragraph (*the accidents of transient fashions or temporary opinions*), not merely by steering us away from the 'unfortunate event' sense but by invoking the contrast to *essence* that lies at the heart of the Greek and scholastic tradition. We might call this kind of invocation an aura; it is not essential (pardon!) to the plain sense of things (the propositional content), but rather leads or links into larger conceptual frameworks in which the current concern has significance of bearings—*meaning,* in a sense that extends far beyond truth conditions.

Another resource that the reader can learn to draw on in reading Johnson is his or her knowledge of etymology, for Johnson is fond of slanting his meanings in a way that awakens awareness of their roots, as in his use of *approximate (Shakespeare approximates the remote and familiarizes the wonderful)* and *aggravated (Other dramatists can only gain attention by hyperbolical or aggravated characters).* This is a notable and pedantic feature of Johnson's style, but as a general possibility, it is a resource drawn on by many writers. The etymology of a word lies latent behind it and can be one of the ways its particular meaning is specified. Meanings can be specified not only by contrast, parallelism, and looser networks of association but also by the past history of the word, if the reader can be sensitized to it. Etymology is a mode of understanding that shapes word use even when it is erroneous. That is, people construct supposed histories and origins for usages that bear with them certain implicit cues to their appropriate use. For example, one gets more violent connotations for *strike* (= 'work stoppage') if one relates it to blows instead of the somewhat limited, possibly archaic, sense of cessation (strike camp, flag, sail, scene) and this connotation will shape the way one chooses to apply the term to new situations. Similarly, the word *fan* is a textbook sample of a shortened form (from *fanatic*), but this origin jars with the generally positive view of fanhood prevalent today, and recently Dik Browne, the cartoonist who draws *Hi and Lois,* had Hi explain it to his child as derived from *fancier.* If the etymology does not account for the usage, change the etymology![7]

Some of the examples of specification shade into the second major process of meaning building, which is the highlighting of some aspect of a word's general sense or connotation. Perhaps the most obvious way of calling attention to the exact weight of a particular word is to italicize to it:

> . . . the elements with which the creative power works are ideas: the best ideas, on every matter which literature touches, current at the time. At any rate we may lay it down as certain that in modern literature no manifestation of the creative power not working with these can be very important or fruitful. And I say *current* at the time, not merely accessible at the time; (Arnold, 2)

Here, of course, Arnold, having focused on the word, also sharpens it by contrast. The word *current* used the first time might bear relatively little weight, but he insists that it is to be attended to with full sensitivity; there are no synonyms in this instance. Here is a second example, this time from Thoreau:

> Thus the state never intentionally confronts a man's sense, intellectual or moral. . . . I will breathe after my own fashion. Let us see who is the strongest. What force has a multitude? They only can force me who obey a higher law than I. They force me to become like themselves. I do not hear of *men* being *forced* to live this way or that by masses of men. What sort of life were that to live?[8]

Thoreau uses italics to indicate that *men* suddenly is to be taken in a different, richer way than the merely generic way it is used in surrounding sentences, and similarly *forced* is suddenly focused on in a way that makes us distinguish it from, say, *pressured.* These passages illustrate one way of creating what Gustav Stern and William Empson call a pregnancy, adopting a term from Gestalt psychology.[9] One type of this heightening is what Stern called specialization, which involves focusing on particular attributes of the thing: in the Arnold citation, the 'in the air' quality of currentness is specialized on. Stern was concerned with change of meaning, but he recognized that for the center of a word's sense to shift in the language generally, this sort of specialization must constantly be at work.

Another way that pregnancy or highlighting can be achieved is through the establishment of associative sets. Rachel Carson does this rather overtly, linking *alien, abyss, stark / starkness, mystery, press / pressure,* and *pulse* with the sea beyond the continental shelves in a way that makes the description resonate with suggestions of the unconscious. Each of these words, of course, could be used by itself in other contexts to evoke other suggestions. We associate this sort of evocative use of language with poetry—or, at least, we study it primarily in 'literature' classes—but it is an aspect of word meaning that runs throughout all writing; often it is the source of interest or a sense of 'relevance.' Such employment of words chiefly to evoke their connotations probably should not be called figurative, since the imagery or alternative domain stays latent or submerged, though it clearly tends in that direction and may lay the groundwork for more explicit simile or metaphor.

The work of integrating particular statements with, or establishing their connection to, the overall argument may highlight certain aspects of a thing. Consider in this regard the last sentence of the Johnson sample, which is clearly a summary:

> This, therefore, is the praise of Shakespeare, that his drama is the mirror of life; that he who has mazed his imagination in following the phantoms which other writers raise up before him, may here be cured of his delirious ecstasies by reading human sentiments in human language, by scenes from which a hermit may estimate the transactions of the world and a confessor predict the progress of the passions.

The words *hermit* and *confessor* repay attention, though the content, I suppose, gets through without it. To take the last clauses as advocating the inclusion of Shakespeare in the education of the religious would be flat-footed: the property of hermits that is relevant here derives from their withdrawal from the world, from which we may infer lack of experience with life in the social world (this, of course, is not always the case with hermits, some of whom presumably have acquired an exact and detailed knowledge of these matters in choosing to abandon the world)—it is, however, the way hermits are to be viewed in order to interpret the sentence as maximally summarizing what has gone before. Similarly, the properties of confessors that they usually work in confessionals, set penance, and offer absolution are quite irrelevant; even the fact that they hear confessions is only a starting point. The property of confessors that is highlighted here is that the confessor (in contrast to the hermit) has the maximum access to the secrets and passions of men's hearts (*men* understood generically), and yet even *he* can learn from Shakespeare's wisdom. Hence we might say he who knows the least can acquire all the knowledge that experience of life would give, and he who knows the most can still learn more. Readers do not, and perhaps need not, always carry interpretation this far—attention is not always repaid—but students should be shown that such attention can be obtained from readers if it is cultivated. A writer may simply be trying to get some information down on the page and will happily grab a convenient word to 'lexicalize' a chunk of meaning, or he may reach for more ambitious effects, letting the words take the lead, interlacing the verbal surface more intricately, and allowing, even seeding, undercurrents of imagery and association—what Peter Elbow calls cooking an idea by playing it against its expressions in words. Sloppy or insipid choice of words is pernicious because it desensitizes readers, signaling that little attention has gone into the writing and little should be expended on it.

The example with *confessor,* by the way, makes it quite clear that the resources drawn on in this specializing mode of meaning construction extend well beyond the sense of the word as it would appear in a dictionary: it draws on the knowledge or body of opinions that we hold, or can infer, about the things referred to. The process cannot therefore be regarded as simply narrowing or selecting a portion of the word's *sense.*

The processes of specifying and highlighting a word's sense are of course subject to certain conventions and constraints. The principal one is that the specifications wrought by context must be consistent. Disregard of this convention seems to be one of the problems with the following passage describing the writer's teen-age sister:

> Except for her clumsiness, she is a very fashionable person. She spends alot of time and money on her hair, make-up, and clothes. She orders all types of jewelry and perfumes to look in style. She is very sensitive, also. Her sensitivity is not very noticeable unless you know her very well. She will go in her room and cry for hours if a sensitive nerve is struck.

Fashionable is specified in three ways here: by contrast to *clumsy* (pushing it in the direction of "smart" or stylish), by example (pushing it in the direction of femme-y), and by pairing with *sensitive* as two traits belonging in the same paragraph. It is not immediately obvious what specification this pairing suggests, since *sensitive* can range from an honorific attribute to a negative one ("touchy"). This negative meaning is especially likely in spoken English—"She's so sensitive"—though it is also the one that applies in talking of injuries. It is the application to a person that is colloquial. The ensuing illustration suggests this negative meaning is in fact the intended one, and so the question arises as to how it pairs with *fashionable* (touchy and fashionable?). It seems that the word *fashionable* is being pulled in incompatible directions in this paragraph, or that there is some progression of thought that is masked by the word. Considering the overall situation—the writer is describing his sister—one might propose that the meaning of *fashionable* that will unify the paragraph is "excessively concerned with appearance," a judgment the writer avoids as too critical. *Fashionable* then is partly a euphemism and reflects the same impulse that *sensitive* for "touchy" does. We may now feel we have a grasp of the writer's possible meaning, but we may also object that we have had to engage in unusual and inordinate interpretive maneuvers and end up with only a plausible conjecture. As noted above, we may wonder whether we are not expending too much ingenuity on this paragraph, given the general looseness of phrasing (perfume to look in style, strike a sensitive nerve, etc.). I have spelled this all out just to elucidate the basis for the mark WW (wrong word) that many teachers would place next to *fashionable*. I am not sure how much of this the student needs to know, though I think it is probably more than she or he is usually told.

Another way of highlighting a portion of a word is to use a so-called periphrastic form. In the case of a verb, the periphrastic form is made up of a verb of general meaning plus some Direct Object or other modifier. So, for example, the language provides us options like the following:

give assistance to/assist	take away/remove
give, pay attention to/attend to	get better/improve
give thought to/consider	get larger/increase
make an attempt/attempt	get well/recover
make a comment/comment	

Composition handbooks usually urge students to choose the more concise form to avoid wordiness, and it is certainly true that the shorter forms give more of an impression of formality than the more conversational periphrastic ones. Futher, it is true that periphrastic constructions do sometimes result in verbal tangles, as in the following examples from Mina Shaughnessy's *Errors and Expectations*:

After junkies have asorved a great quantity of liquor it causes a depression on their will power. (cf. their will power diminishes)

It hurts their moral and makes them feel ugly. (cf. demoralizes them)

As children grow older meaning adults . . . (mature)[10]

These illustrations also point up a final defect of periphrastics, which is that they suggest an impoverished vocabulary, as if the writer were limited to an effective vocabulary of about one thousand words.

Nonetheless, there are some things to be said for periphrastics. For one, the longer form allows the content of the verb or noun to be spread out, with that of the verb often placed in end position, where it can have more prominence (if that is desired). Also, by spreading out the concept over several words, the possibility of modification arises, often in ways that cannot be rendered adverbially. So parallel to *take a quick shower* we have *shower quickly,* but there is no parallel adverbial modifier for *take a cold shower;* parallel to *give someone a loud kiss* is *kiss someone loudly,* but what is a parallel to *give someone a tiny kiss*? The general point is that concision is not an absolute virtue: 'making every word count' can conflict with the needs for highlighting and emphasis and can result in an excessively dense style if carried to the extreme. As with so many writing maxims, this one is perhaps useful as a corrective to a rambling, casual style but does not capture an unqualified excellence of writing.

The fundamental limitation of traditional word lore is the view of words as bearing meanings and connotations. From this view springs the implication that one can determine whether a word is the 'right' word or not by checking its meaning in the dictionary. At most, however, one can only determine that it is not the wrong word. Rather than thinking of a dictionary entry as giving a positive specification of a word's meaning, we should think of it as outlining a range and suggesting certain potentials for meaning that might be actualized or built upon in particular uses. 'Vocabulary' accordingly should be taught by examining words in fairly large contexts and discussing the way the word plus the networks of meaning surrounding it contribute to the construction of meanings that are greater, more particular, or more salient than the sum of the senses of the individual words.

2. *Figurative language*

One of the conventions of the expository essay discussed in chapter two is that which says that figurative language, broadly construed to include metaphor, simile, and analogy, plays a more limited and ancillary role in essays than in some other types of writing. In part, this is so because the expository essay has little use for expressive language generally (e.g., to evoke moods and atmospheres or convey impressions). Further, figurative language is not expected to carry the communicative weight that it does in poetry. Handbooks recommend it for vividness, freshness, and clarity, but it is still held to be inessential to stating the line of argument or developing the essay. Indeed, the treatment in some handbooks suggests the very old-fashioned attitude that it is an 'ornament' or grace of expression — an applique, as it were. Until recently, few explicit accounts of comprehension of metaphor and figurative language had been constructed, though much has been written about how figurative language differs structurally from literal (or nonfigurative) uses, whether simile and metaphor are essentially similar or not, how they are related to analogy, and so on. Fortunately, it is not crucial for our purposes to solve all these problems of definition, for figurative language is usually fairly easy to recognize in expository prose, at least in the samples. We will take the defining characteristic of figurative language to be language usually applied in one class of domains being used to make a point in another, namely the domain of the matter under discussion. Our concern will be with the how and the why of this process.

Concentrating first on the *how*, we can begin with the observation that not all of the properties of the figure are to be carried over into the primary domain. So when Shakespeare writes,

> They that have power to hurt and will do none,
> That do not do the thing they most do show,
> Who, moving others, are themselves as stone,
> Unmoved, cold, and to temptation slow

the question to be answered is 'what does it mean for the personality type being described to be as stone?' and we may begin to think of attributes of stone that may carry over, with some interpretation, into the domain of personal characteristics. Stone is often thought of as being hard, impenetrable, and stable (as opposed to sand), and these properties have psychological analogues that may apply, but an attribute like indestructibility (as opposed to wood) may be less applicable. Essentially, this process of selection is a kind of specialization, and, like the other kinds of specialization discussed in the last section, requires an interpretive act on the reader's part that is shaped by context and the reader's larger sense of what the writer is

getting at. It is widely recognized that we cannot expect to find all or
even most of these relevant properties in the sense of the word as
recorded in the dictionary (*stone:* a concretion of earthy or mineral
matter—*Webster's Eighth Collegiate*); rather, beliefs about the thing,
attitudes commonly associated with it, the various schemata in which
it participates—all may be relevant. The essence of figurative language is thinking of one thing in terms of another, with the figurative domain furnishing a kind of overlay or doubling of statement.
The more points of possible relevance one can find, the richer and
more appropriate a particular figure will be felt to be.

   Normally, the immediately preceding or following context guides
the reader in the selection/interpretation process. The last line in the
citation from Shakespeare's Sonnet 94, for example, seems to spell
out some of the stoney properties meant. An even more explicit
example of spelling out occurs in Bacon's essay "Of Studies":

> Some books are to be tasted, others to be swallowed, and some few to
> be chewed and digested; that is, some books are to be read only in
> parts; others to be read, but not curiously; and some few to be read
> wholly and with diligence and attention.[11]

In this case, Bacon suggests that his metaphors are not to be taken as
especially rich. Their function is certainly not to express the inexpressible; rather, they seem to be a challenge to the wit of the reader
on the order of a riddle. It is well to remember that Donne was
Bacon's contemporary, and that the famous compass analogy is
spelled out in this fashion. More common in expository prose, however, is the use of figurative language to comment on a point already
introduced. The lead material in this case makes the figurative expressions fairly easy to interpret. Andrew Ortony, Diane L. Schallert,
Ralph E. Reynolds, and Stephen J. Antos found that figurative
sentences were comprehended almost as quickly as literal ones when
they came at the end of a 'priming' context of which the figure was a
kind of summary, as for example:

> Lucy and Phil needed a marriage councelor [sic]. They had once
> been very happy but after several years of marriage they had become
> discontented with one another. Little habits which had at first been
> endearing were now irritating and caused many senseless and heated
> arguments. The fabric had begun to fray.[12]

With this amount of attention given to 'the relationship' and its constituent parts, the selection of attributes from *fabric* and *fray* (or
rather, 'fabric fraying') is easily made. Comprehension time for the

line was twice as long when it was placed immediately after the first sentence without the intervening context. It would be interesting to see whether a roughly comparable line such as *The petals had begun to droop* would be as successfully primed by this context. I would suppose not, which is to say that the fraying fabric is more tightly integrated, more appropriate, than the drooping petals. Suppose, similarly, that the sentence about little habits were replaced by one like

> Fundamental conflicts and antagonisms long securely repressed began to appear in irritability and withdrawal.

Then one might expect a conclusion like

> Deep in the dungeon, the prisoners were rattling their chains.

This sort of use of a figure to summarize and effectively tie off a point is common in literate prose; there are several instances in the samples. Johnson uses the 'old story' of the brick to underline the point he has just stated abstractly:

> Yet his real power is not shown in the splendour of particular passages, but by the progress of his fable and the tenor of his dialogue; and he that tries to recommend him by select quotations will succeed like the pedant in Hierocles, who, when he offered his house to sale, carried a brick in his pocket as a specimen. (Johnson, 3)

A somewhat richer and more subtle use occurs in the last paragraph of the Macaulay passage where the simile of Milton's poetry to Alpine scenery is announced and then expanded into particular points of similarity. The simile is not thereby interpreted or explained in the fashion of Bacon's metaphors, however: it remains for the reader to pick out the aspects of the scene that correspond to aspects of Milton's poetry. The rugged and gigantic elevations suggest sublimity; the avalanche, however, suggests something more in the context of the passage: the properties of disaster and destruction seem to link up with the events of Milton's life, so that the simile is not of qualities inherent in the poetry, but of the relation of the poetry to his life; that is, the application here spreads beyond the portion of the literal domain explicitly indicated. This example is also a salutary reminder of the potential open-endedness of figurative language: one can carry the comparison as far as one wishes. The convention of Text narrowly construed, however, is that figures should not be open-ended in this sense, or at least that the openness should not be essential to the development of the argument.

When we turn our attention from the how to the why of figurative language, we come directly to statements about vividness, freshness, clarity, and so on. Here, as with so many other handbook generalizations, we encounter the difficulty of making a single statement about a diverse group of functions and purposes. There is simply a vast difference between figures of convenience, like Edith Hamilton's bloom-root-seed-flower, gap-bridge–way across and the more elaborated and abstruse figures that Macaulay uses to argue the unanalyzability of poetry. Hamilton's metaphors are low voltage, mundane, moribund if not dead, and she is not greatly concerned with reviving them, nor does she lean heavily on the organic metaphor for cultural development. Discussions of the importance or utility of figurative language usually have more elaborate uses like Macaulay's in mind.[13]

One such discussion is Andrew Ortony's "Why Metaphors Are Necessary and Not Just Nice." In this attempt to get beyond the purely decorative view of figurative language, Ortony argues, as others have,[14] that metaphor is a mode of knowledge: by it, we come to understand the unknown in terms of the known. This would explain the impression of vividness. It is certainly true that most figurative language deals with familiar, common, and concrete experience, but it is also true that in order to interpret a metaphor, we need to understand what is being explained in the literal domain well enough to separate the parts that do carry over from the figurative domain from those that do not. If this separation is faulty, one can actually be misled by the figure, and it is this possibility that underlies Bacon's and the Royal Society's distrust of figurative language as a medium of science. Ortony explains,

> Whereas metaphor can be used to supplement knowledge about some already quite well understood topic, it can also be used to describe very unfamiliar topics. The potential problem here is that the person who uses the metaphor needs to know how much he can assume about his addressee's knowledge of the topic in advance. If he makes an incorrect judgement in this respect a situation may arise in which his addressee cannot construct an appropriate distinctive set of characteristics because he doesn't know enough about the topic to eliminate tension-reducing ones. There can be two consequences. He may simply fail to grasp the metaphor and recognise his failure, or, worse, he may attribute inappropriate characteristics to the topic and go away misled.[15]

There is at least the appearance of a paradox in all of this: one cannot judge that some attribute is to be carried over to the literal domain without already knowing the matter in the literal domain.

Something is being missed in this account, and I suspect it has to
do with treating the knowledge or understanding promoted by
metaphor in terms of a set of attributes. It is a little surprising to see
Ortony adopting this mode of expression, though it is very common
among linguists, because he is quite familiar with the notion of
schemata and the view of understanding that is more than an aggre-
gation of properties; it is a whole, a gestalt, a structured configuration of parts, so that thinking of one thing in terms of another
may yield a useful sense of structural or functional properties—
with, to be sure, some haziness about exact details that can be
worked out later. For every case like Whorf's famous example of
spun limestone (thought by some workers to present no fire hazard
because it was 'stone'), there are several like the analogy of electricity
to water, which provides an extremely handy way of grasping several
properties of electricity at once. There is a second consideration as
well, which we have touched on repeatedly in this work, namely that
understanding is far more than the intake of content: it involves the
integration of that content into one's knowledge base, and we might
say that we feel we understand something better as we establish
more connections to the rest of what we know. We are quite prepared to acknowledge that, as the old saying has it, a simile always
limps on one foot, but we may experience intellectual delight in the
reduction of strangeness that figurative language allows. This is not
to deny that we may become limited by a metaphor that was initially
helpful as a way of organizing our thinking about an unfamiliar
matter—indeed, that was precisely the point of the objections to the
memory model in chapter five—nor to deny that writers may use
figurative language to imply more than they can actually prove, as is
the case, I think, with Macaulay's contrasts of taking machines apart
and dissecting organic forms, or Pavlov's use of physiological language to describe psychological processes (in Miller's account). The
dangers, as well as the attractions, of figurative language are at a
maximum when dealing with abstract topics, for the unfamiliar ideas
less obviously dictate where the simile limps, but their very strangeness makes an analogy to the more familiar welcome.

Despite our primary focus on the cognitive function of metaphor,
we should not overlook the rhetorical impact of figurative language.
Inasmuch as figures presuppose familiarity with the common experience, they sketch in a background of knowledge, treating it as
Known (indeed, as well known), and hence projecting an implied or
'model' reader. And, as noted in previous chapters, the fit between
real and implied reader may involve some pretending and tension.
Johnson's simile to the pedant from Hierocles is not likely to be

familiar to the modern reader, but nothing is lost if we merely pretend such a knowledge. Such a use also projects an implied author,
of course, and may establish his credentials, culture, or amiability.
One of my students once observed of Strunk and White that they
treat their reader as a sensible, virile country gentleman, not the
least through their homely similes to gardening and working with
tools. And, of course, they may establish credibility and appeal by
banishing the image of effete intellectual snobs. On the other hand,
a writer who likens writing and revision to acts of chopping,
sharpening, cutting, and pruning too exclusively may convey an ag-
gressive attitude toward writing and project an unpleasantly hostile
personality.

   The basic thesis of this chapter, that 'literal' meanings as much as
figurative ones are constructed out of the words of the text, and are
not inherent in them, was set forth some years ago by Peter Elbow:

> We can let ourselves talk about words "having meaning" and even
> "carrying meaning from one head to another" as long as we now
> realize these phrases denote something complex: the words don't
> transport the contents of my head into yours, they give you a set of
> directions for building your own meaning. If we are both good at
> writing directions and following directions for building meaning, we
> end up with similar things in our heads—that is, we communicate.
> Otherwise, we experience each other's words as "not having any
> meaning in them," or "having the wrong meaning in them."
>   The question is then how these meaning-building rules operate in
> ordinary language. Meaning in ordinary language—English, for
> example, is midway on a continuum between meaning in dreams and
> meaning in mathematics.[16]

Elbow rightly points out that the application of these meaning-
building rules varies with the type of language assumed to be operating: the language of dreams allows anything to mean anything; the
language of mathematics explicitly defines the rules for interpreting
the symbols. Ordinary language (and, we might add, the language of
the essay) manifests a tug-of-war between these principles. The resulting picture of how words come to have meanings is beautifully
phrased:

> This model implies that meaning in ordinary language consists of
> delicate, flexible transactions among people in overlapping speech
> communities—peculiar transactions governed by unspoken agree-
> ments to abide by unspecified, constantly changing rules as to what
> meanings to build into what words and phrases. All the parties
> merely keep on making these transactions and assuming that all the
> other parties abide by the same rules and agreements. Thus, though

words are capable of extreme precision among good players, they
nevertheless float and drift all the time. (P. 156)

This view of how words mean is both a charter of freedom for the
writer and a challenge: word meanings are not reliable, predictable
chunks that pop up in the reader's mind when the writer presses the
appropriate word-lever, but, correspondingly, what does pop up is
not so simply and directly controlled; rather, shaping that meaning-
construction requires cunning management. This point probably so
often escapes our notice because we do not probe the reader's response much beyond determining whether actual misunderstanding
or nonrecognition has occurred. When the signs of misunderstanding are not evident, we tend to assume 'understanding' has occurred
and do not look too closely at what goes on behind the closed doors
of other peoples' crania. The crucial practical weakness of the 'words
as counters' view is that it trivializes wording for the writer down to
avoiding clichés, eccentric usages, inappropriate informalities, and
jargon; in short, making sure you have the right counters. But the
traditional corrective for the resulting flatness of diction and imagery, namely to expatiate upon the wonderful life and subtle envelope
of connotations surrounding each word and metaphor is equally
limiting and artificial, and students are wise to cling to their commonsense feeling that most of the time words ain't all that magical
(or pregnant)—though they may feel a twinge of shame for being
such insensitive clods. The real solution is a sort of compromise,
which concedes that words and figures are not always precise and
richly resonant but focuses on some cases where they are and
analyzes the way that this richness is obtained by writer and reader.
Again we are left with more mysteries and uncertainties about
processing than we started with. It seems clear that the meaning-
building rules must operate on something; one can learn the meaning of a word, and without that knowledge, the rules are powerless.
And it seems clear that this question reaches far beyond the matter
of generality/particularity of the senses coded; at times words can
evoke their histories, latent imagery, and other associations. But it is
equally clear that words do not always do this, which is to say that the
readers' and writers' verbal attentiveness is flexible and selective in
ways psycholinguists have scarcely begun to explore.

CONCLUSION

⟨⟨⟩⟩⟨⟨⟩⟩

Limitations and Prospects

The overarching thesis of this work is that current models of language processing do not adequately characterize the experience of reading; they are reductionist, and the attempt to base a theory of prose composition on them can only produce significant omissions and distortions. The general design of the attempt is seductive, both because it offers composition the support and guidance of 'empirical science' and because it fits neatly into certain traditional attitudes and stances. The equation of good prose with efficient prose, for example, has a robustly practical ring to it: composition teachers and English departments can more easily defend a university-wide requirement in composition if they claim to teach practical skills and save their esthetic tastes and interests for literature classes. It also sells better to many students if we abjure all estheticism and elitism of taste and sensibility. And as long as the instructor's notion of efficiency includes being interesting and the definition of clarity includes some gracefulness, little seems to be lost in this pact with the practical devil. It is only when, under the stimulation of work in psycholinguistics, one begins to specify more narrowly what is meant by efficiency and the experience of texts that the distortions and omissions begin.

Perhaps the crucial narrowing occurs when we take memory to provide an accurate and complete record of the experience of reading, or at least the repository of all of its significant results. Under certain experimental conditions, subjects behave as if they have extracted content from its verbal form: they will report passive sentences in active form, substitute synonyms for the original words, and so on.[1] From this it is concluded that the verbal surface is significant only as it facilitates or impedes intake of content. It is as if one were to rate paintings of landscapes in terms of the number of objects remembered. This is an extraordinary conclusion to come to, and one must admire E. D. Hirsch's courage in spelling it out, while at the same time wondering that it did not strike him as the *absurdam* of the whole reduction of reading to the intake of content.

The intake-of-content model makes three major oversim-

162

plifications. First, treating content as a list of propositions (or 'gist units') is atomistic: we need to test for what sort of altered understanding a text has brought about, not just what facts have been recorded. Second, not all content is information for a human subject; even if we could quantify the content of a text in terms of its propositions after the fashion of Walter Kintsch and others,[2] it would be hard to quantify or predict the amount or nature of information it will contain for a human reader. We cannot talk about efficiency of transmission unless we can specify ahead of time what is to be transmitted. Third, not all the information is meaningful for the reader: under many conditions, readers are guided in the texts they construct by their interests. We might even propose as a general principle that readers read for meaning, just as writers write to convey meaning, though in some cases what is meaningful is primarily the information they obtain. And they construct this meaning by assimilating the text into their body of knowledge and conviction — otherwise they have acquired but a bunch of meaningless information. If this finding and expression of meaning involves constructive activity by human subjects as outlined in these chapters, then quantifying the content and measuring the efficiency of its transmission by various sentence forms becomes an impossible and futile undertaking. In short, for all the talk about subjects in the reports of experiments, the intake model really has no place for the human subject in it.

In place of the intake-of-content model of reading, which regards the rules of good writing as strategies for meeting the channel limitations of readers, I have tried to sketch a theory of reading that makes little or no use of biological limitations. The conventions of the expository essay are viewed as constraints and guides to text construction; they are to various degrees special to written prose and the essay and are subject to adaptation and modification by individual writers. Paragraphing, parallelism, and punctuation, for example, indicate units and relations of some sort; they and other conventions constitute a loose and flexible framework within which writers and readers of essays work. The 'needy reader' turns out, at least for the texts we have considered, to be a naïve fiction. We have replaced this entity with the model (or implied) reader of current literary and semiotic theory[3] and have traced the ways various constructions project or presuppose a reader to whom certain information is familiar, or one who is willing to pretend it is familiar, one who shares a common background and orientation. The process of imagining a reader is accordingly not an attempt to approximate the knowledge and viewpoint of actual persons who might peruse the

text but of projecting a self that readers will try on and find agree-
able.[4] To a limited degree, the projections of reader and writer made
by a text can be modelled by listing the pieces of information
presupposed or treated as Known by the sentences and connections
of sentences.[5] What such an approach fails to capture, however, is
that readers encounter projected writers (and vice versa) in an
essentially personal way; personal knowledge, rather than propositional knowledge, is primary here, and, while it can be proposi-
tionalized at least to some degree, personal knowledge is of a different order of experience, based, as it is, on perceiving writing as a
human action embodying a human voice, however impersonal it may
strive to sound. How we will take what we read—the meaning and
significance we find in it, the value we place upon it, whether we
assent to it or even continue to read it with attention and sympathy,
or at all—will largely be determined by considerations that are most
difficult to represent or quantify. A theory of discourse that views it
as human action and interaction is one that will be very hard to formalize and impossible to formalize in a system that focuses on
transmission of content. The 'conduit metaphor' of language, as
Michael Reddy calls it, is simply an inappropriate basis for a theory
of discourse[6]—as inappropriate, I have argued, for the expository
essay as for any other type of discourse. The 'cognitive' obsession of
current discourse processing needs to be supplemented with much
more investigation of the process of 'hearing voices.'[7]

So, too, the teaching of composition should concentrate on writing
as a mode of interaction, not as transmission of facts or presentation
of material. The writer's fundamental need is the ability to project
the experience of readers so that she or he can judge how much to
say and how to say it, when to reintroduce an item, when to use a
demonstrative or personal pronoun, what can (or should) be treated
as Known, how to influence and specify the interpretation of words
and figures, and so on. And this need to know is not in order to
meet readers' needs but to shape their experience of the text. It follows that in order to teach writing, we need extensive discussion of
experiences of reading, with analysis of how language and contexts
can shape them. I say *can* and not *does*, because no unit—word, construction, connective, or what have you—controls or predicts response; that is always guided from the top as an orchestration of the
whole. Whenever possible, correction or comment on student writing should be linked to the real experience of real readers. Most
teachers know that a nonstandard punctuation or modifier placement teaches best when it occasions actual uncertainty or misunderstanding on the part of some reader, especially a classmate. Student

writers need as much feedback about other people's experiences of reading their writing as they can get, but it should be at least as much positive as negative. To discover that a reader has achieved a precise and detailed understanding of what they were trying to say is extremely exciting and gratifying to student writers; they do not expect to be read very closely and often do not read their own writing with full attention.

All of this is part of the general pedagogical point that good teaching of a practical activity like writing is a matter of showing, not telling, and learning is a matter of discovery, not obedience. Handbooks tell too much—'put your most important ideas in main sentences,' 'put the most important words last in the sentence,' and so on. I would be greatly disappointed if the points made in this book were used merely to tell students better what the function of inversions is, for example, or subordination, or figurative language. There is a place for this sort of consciousness and reflection about writing, but it is in a course in stylistics or possibly a small portion of Advanced Expository Writing. A theory can give teachers a needed perspective on their work and relate writing essays to other meaningful human actions; it can release us from some of the mind-forged manacles of traditional lore and the new technology; but it can only indirectly point to the one thing needful: how to convey to students the joy and challenge of writing.

Samuel Johnson

From "The Preface to Shakespeare." Cited from *The Norton Anthology of English Literature,* edited by J. B. Trapp, John Hollander, Frank Kermode, and Martin Price, vol. I, pp. 2107–2109. New York: Norton, 1973.

1   Nothing can please many, and please long, but just representations of general nature. Particular manners can be known to few; and therefore few only can judge how nearly they are copied. The irregular combinations of fanciful invention may delight awhile by that novelty of which the common satiety of life sends us all in quest; but the pleasures of sudden wonder are soon exhausted, and the mind can only repose on the stability of truth.

2   Shakespeare is, above all writers, at least above all modern writers, the poet of nature, the poet that holds up to his readers a faithful mirror of manners and of life. His characters are not modified by the customs of particular places, unpractised by the rest of the world; by the peculiarities of studies or professions which can operate but upon small numbers; or by the accidents of transient fashions or temporary opinions: they are the genuine progeny of common humanity, such as the world will always supply, and observation will always find. His persons act and speak by the influence of those general passions and principles by which all minds are agitated and the whole system of life is continued in motion. In the writings of other poets a character is too often an individual; in those of Shakespeare it is commonly a species.

3   It is from this wide extension of design that so much instruction is derived. It is this which fills the plays of Shakespeare with practical axioms and domestic wisdom. It was said of Euripides that every verse was a precept; and it may be said of Shakespeare that from his works may be collected a system of civil and economical prudence. Yet his real power is not shown in the splendour of particular passages, but by the progress of his fable and the tenor of his dialogue; and he that tries to recommend him by select quotations will succeed like the pedant in Hierocles, who, when he offered his house to sale, carried a brick in his pocket as a specimen.

4   It will not easily be imagined how much Shakespeare excels in accommodating his sentiments to real life but by comparing him with other authors. It was observed of the ancient schools of declamation that the more diligently they were frequented, the more was the student disqualified for the world, because he found nothing there which he should ever meet in any other place. The same remark may be applied to every stage but that of Shake-

speare. The theatre, when it is under any other direction, is peopled by such characters as were never seen, conversing in a language which was never heard, upon topics which will never arise in the commerce of mankind. But the dialogue of this author is often so evidently determined by the incident which produces it, and is pursued with so much ease and simplicity, that it seems scarcely to claim the merit of fiction, but to have been gleaned by diligent selection out of common conversation and common occurrences.

5   Upon every other stage the universal agent is love, by whose power all good and evil is distributed and every action quickened or retarded. To bring a lover, a lady, and a rival into the fable; to entangle them in contradictory obligations, perplex them with oppositions of interest, and harass them with violence of desires inconsistent with each other; to make them meet in rapture and part in agony, to fill their mouths with hyperbolical joy and outrageous sorrow, to distress them as nothing human ever was distressed, to deliver them as nothing human ever was delivered, is the business of a modern dramatist. For this, probability is violated, life is misrepresented, and language is depraved. But love is only one of many passions; and as it has no great influence upon the sum of life, it has little operation in the dramas of a poet who caught his ideas from the living world and exhibited only what he saw before him. He knew that any other passion, as it was regular or exorbitant, was a cause of happiness or calamity.

6   Characters thus ample and general were not easily discriminated and preserved, yet perhaps no poet ever kept his personages more distinct from each other. I will not say with Pope that every speech may be assigned to the proper speaker, because many speeches there are which have nothing characteristical; but, perhaps, though some may be equally adapted to every person, it will be difficult to find any that can be properly transferred from the present possessor to another claimant. The choice is right, when there is reason for choice.

7   Other dramatists can only gain attention by hyperbolical or aggravated characters, by fabulous and unexampled excellence or depravity, as the writers of barbarous romances invigorated the reader by a giant and a dwarf; and he that should form his expectations of human affairs from the play, or from the tale, would be equally deceived. Shakespeare has no heroes; his scenes are occupied only by men, who act and speak as the reader thinks that he should himself have spoken or acted on the same occasion. Even where the agency is supernatural, the dialogue is level with life. Other writers disguise the most natural passions and most frequent incidents; so that he who contemplates them in the book will not know them in the world. Shakespeare approximates

the remote and familiarizes the wonderful; the event which he represents will not happen, but, if it were possible, its effects would probably be such as he has assigned; and it may be said that he has not only shown human nature as it acts in real exigences, but as it would be found in trials to which it cannot be exposed.

8   This, therefore, is the praise of Shakespeare, that his drama is the mirror of life; that he who has mazed his imagination in following the phantoms which other writers raise up before him, may here be cured of his delirious ecstasies by reading human sentiments in human language, by scenes from which a hermit may estimate the transactions of the world and a confessor predict the progress of the passions.

Thomas Babington, Lord Macaulay (I)

From "Milton." In *The Critical, Historical and Miscellaneous Essays* by Lord Macaulay, vol. I, pp. 229–32. New York: Hurd and Houghton; Cambridge: The Riverside Press, 1977.

1   To return for a moment to the parallel which we have been attempting to draw between Milton and Dante, we would add that the poetry of these great men has in a considerable degree taken its character from their moral qualities. They are not egotists. They rarely obtrude their idiosyncrasies on their readers. They have nothing in common with those modern beggars for fame, who extort a pittance from the compassion of the inexperienced by exposing the nakedness and sores of their minds. Yet it would be difficult to name two writers whose works have been more completely, though undesignedly, coloured by their personal feelings.

2   The character of Milton was peculiarly distinguished by loftiness of spirit; that of Dante by intensity of feelings. In every line of the Divine Comedy we discern the asperity which is produced by pride struggling with misery. There is perhaps no work in the world so deeply and uniformly sorrowful. The melancholy of Dante was no fantastic caprice. It was not, as far as at this distance of time can be judged, the effect of external circumstances. It was from within. Neither love nor glory, neither the conflicts of earth nor the hope of heaven could dispel it. It turned every consolation and every pleasure into its own nature. It resembled that noxious Sardinian soil of which the intense bitterness is said to have been perceptible even in its honey. His mind was, in the noble language of the Hebrew poet, "a land of darkness, as

darkness itself, and where the light was as darkness." The gloom of his character discolours all the passions of men, and all the face of nature, and tinges with its own livid hue the flowers of Paradise and the glories of the eternal throne. All the portraits of him are singularly characteristic. No person can look on the features, noble even to ruggedness, the dark furrows of the cheek, the haggard and woful stare of the eye, the sullen and contemptuous curve of the lip, and doubt that they belong to a man too proud and too sensitive to be happy.

3   Milton was, like Dante, a statesman and a lover; and, like Dante, he had been unfortunate in ambition and in love. He had survived his health and his sight, the comforts of his home, and the prosperity of his party. Of the great men by whom he had been distinguished at his entrance into life, some had been taken away from the evil to come; some had carried into foreign climates their unconquerable hatred of oppression; some were pining in dungeons; and some had poured forth their bloods on scaffolds. Venal and licentious scribblers, with just sufficient talent to clothe the thoughts of a pandar in the style of a bellman, were now the favourite writers of the Sovereign and of the public. It was a loathsome herd, which could be compared to nothing so fitly as to the rabble of Comus, grotesque monsters, half bestial half human, dropping with wine, bloated with gluttony, and reeling in obscene dances. Amidst these that fair Muse was placed, like the chaste lady of the Masque, lofty, spotless, and serene, to be chattered at, and pointed at, and grinned at, by the whole rout of Satyrs and Goblins. If ever despondency and asperity could be excused in any man, they might have been excused in Milton. But the strength of his mind overcame every calamity. Neither blindness, nor gout, nor age, nor penury, nor domestic afflictions, nor political disappointments, nor abuse, nor proscription, nor neglect, had power to disturb his sedate and majestic patience. His spirits do not seem to have been high, but they were singularly equable. His temper was serious, perhaps stern; but it was a temper which no sufferings could render sullen or fretful. Such as it was when, on the eve of great events, he returned from his travels, in the prime of health and manly beauty, loaded with literary distinctions, and glowing with patriotic hopes, such it continued to be when, after having experienced every calamity which is incident to our nature, old, poor, sightless and disgraced, he retired to his hovel to die.

4   Hence it was that, though he wrote the Paradise Lost at a time of life when images of beauty and tenderness are in general beginning to fade, even from those minds in which they have not been effaced by anxiety and disappointment, he adorned it with all that is most lovely and delightful in the physical and in the

moral world. Neither Theocritus nor Ariosto had a finer or more healthful sense of the pleasantness of external objects, or loved better to luxuriate amidst sunbeams and flowers, the songs of nightingales, the juice of summer fruits, and the coolness of shady fountains. His conception of love unites all the voluptuousness of the Oriental harem, and all the gallantry of the chivalric tournament, with all the pure and quiet affection of an English fireside. His poetry reminds us of the miracles of Alpine scenery. Nooks and dells, beautiful as fairy land, are embosomed in its most rugged and gigantic elevations. The roses and myrtles bloom unchilled on the verge of the avalanche.

Thomas Babington, Lord Macaulay (II)

From "On Dryden." *Essays,* vol. I, pp. 325–28.

1   The ages in which the master-pieces of imagination have been produced have by no means been those in which taste has been most correct. It seems that the creative faculty, and the critical faculty, cannot exist together in their highest perfection. The causes of this phenomenon it is not difficult to assign.

2   It is true that the man who is best able to take a machine to pieces, and who most clearly comprehends the manner in which all its wheels and springs conduce to its general effect, will be the man most competent to form another machine of similar power. In all the branches of physical and moral sciences which admit of perfect analysis, he who can resolve will be able to combine. But the analysis which criticism can effect of poetry is necessarily imperfect. One element must for ever elude its researches; and that is the very element by which poetry is poetry. In the description of nature, for example, a judicious reader will easily detect an incongruous image. But he will find it impossible to explain in what consists the art of a writer who, in a few words, brings some spot before him so vividly that he shall know it as if he had lived there from childhood; while another, employing the same materials, the same verdure, the same water, and the same flowers, committing no inaccuracy, introducing nothing which can be positively pronounced superfluous, omitting nothing which can be positively pronounced necessary, shall produce no more effect than an advertisement of a capital residence and a desirable pleasure-ground. To take another example: the great features of the character of Hotspur are obvious to the most superficial reader. We at once perceive that his courage is splendid, his thirst of glory intense, his animal spirits high, his temper careless, arbi-

trary, and petulant; that he indulges his own humour without caring whose feelings he may wound, or whose emnity he may provoke, by his levity. Thus far criticism will go. But something is still wanting. A man might have all those qualities, and every other quality which the most minute examiner can introduce into his catalogue of the virtues and faults of Hotspur, and yet he would not be Hotspur. Almost everything that we have said of him applies equally to Falconbridge. Yet in the mouth of Falconbridge most of his speeches would seem out of place. In real life this perpetually occurs. We are sensible of wide differences between men whom, if we were required to describe them, we should describe in almost the same terms. If we were attempting to draw elaborate characters of them, we should scarcely be able to point out any strong distinction; yet we approach them with feelings altogether dissimilar. We cannot conceive of them as using the expressions or the gestures of each other. Let us suppose that a zoologist should attempt to give an account of some animal, a porcupine for instance, to people who had never seen it. The porcupine, he might say, is of the genus mammalia, and the order glires. There are whiskers on its face; it is two feet long; it has four toes before, five behind, two fore teeth, and eight grinders. Its body is covered with hair and quills. And, when all this had been said, would any one of the auditors have formed a just idea of a porcupine? Would any two of them have formed the same idea? There might exist innumerable races of animals, possessing all the characteristics which have been mentioned, yet altogether unlike to each other. What the description of our naturalist is to a real porcupine, the remarks of criticism are to the images of poetry. What it so imperfectly decomposes it cannot perfectly re-construct. It is evidently as impossible to produce an Othello or a Macbeth by reversing an analytical process so defective, as it would be for an anatomist to form a living man out of the fragments of his dissecting-room. In both cases the vital principle eludes the finest instruments, and vanishes in the very instant in which its seat is touched. Hence those who, trusting to their critical skill, attempt to write poems give us, not images of things, but catalogues of qualities. Their characters are allegories; not good men and bad men, but cardinal virtues and deadly sins. We seem to have fallen among the acquaintances of our old friend Christian: sometimes we meet Mistrust and Timorous; sometimes Mr. Hate-good and Mr. Love-lust; and then again Prudence, Piety, and Charity.

3   That critical discernment is not sufficient to make men poets, is generally allowed. Why it should keep them from becoming poets, is not perhaps equally evident: but the fact is, that poetry requires not an examining but a believing frame of mind. Those

feel it most, and write it best, who forget that it is a work of art;
to whom its imitations, like the realities from which they are
taken, are subjects, not for connoisseurship, but for tears and
laughter, resentment and affection; who are too much under the
influence of the illusion to admire the genius which has produced
it; who are too much frightened for Ulysses in the cave of
Polyphemus to care whether the pun about Outis be good or
bad; who forget that such a person as Shakespeare ever existed,
while they weep and curse with Lear. It is by giving faith to the
creations of the imagination that a man becomes a poet. It is by
treating those creations as deceptions, and by resolving them, as
nearly as possible, into their elements, that he becomes a critic. In
the moment in which the skill of the artist is perceived, the spell
of the art is broken.

4   These considerations account for the absurdities into which the
greatest writers have fallen, when they have attempted to give
general rules for composition, or to pronounce judgement on the
works of others. They are unaccustomed to analyse what they
feel; they, therefore, perpetually refer their emotions to causes
which have not in the slightest degree tended to produce them.
They feel pleasure in reading a book. They never consider that
this pleasure may be the effect of ideas which some unmeaning
expression, striking on the first link of a chain of associations,
may have called up in their own minds—that they have themselves furnished to the author the beauties which they admire.

Matthew Arnold

From "The Function of Criticism at the Present Time." Cited from
The Norton Anthology of English Literature, edited by Harold Bloom,
Lionel Trilling, Frank Kermode, and John Hollander, vol. II, pp.
1002–1004. New York: Norton, 1973.

1   It is almost too much to expect of poor human nature, that a
man capable of producing some effect in one line of literature,
should, for the greater good of society, voluntarily doom himself
to impotence and obscurity in another. Still less is this to be expected from men addicted to the composition of the 'false or
malicious criticism' of which Wordsworth speaks. However,
everybody would admit that a false or malicious criticism had better never have been written. Everybody, too, would be willing to
admit, as a general proposition, that the critical faculty is lower
than the inventive. But is it true that criticism is really, in itself, a
baneful and injurious employment; is it true that all time given to

writing critiques on the works of others would be much better employed if it were given to original composition, of whatever kind this may be? Is it true that Johnson had better have gone on producing more *Irenes* instead of writing his *Lives of the Poets;* nay, is it certain that Wordsworth himself was better employed in making his Ecclesiastical Sonnets than when he made his celebrated Preface, so full of criticism, and criticism of the works of others? Wordsworth was himself a great critic, and it is to be sincerely regretted that he has not left us more criticism; Goethe was one of the greatest of critics, and we may sincerely congratulate ourselves that he has left us so much criticism. Without wasting time over the exaggeration which Wordsworth's judgment on criticism clearly contains, or over an attempt to trace the causes,—not difficult, I think, to be traced,—which may have led Wordsworth to this exaggeration, a critic may with advantage seize an occasion for trying his own conscience, and for asking himself of what real service at any given moment the practice of criticism either is or may be made to his own mind and spirit, and to the minds and spirits of others.

2   The critical power is of lower rank than the creative. True; but in assenting to this proposition, one or two things are to be kept in mind. It is undeniable that the exercise of a creative power, that a free creative activity, is the highest function of man; it is proved to be so by man's finding in it his true happiness. But it is undeniable, also, that men may have the sense of exercising this free creative activity in other ways than in producing great works of literature or art; if it were not so, all but a very few men would be shut out from the true happiness of all men. They may have it in well-doing, they may have it in learning, they may have it even in criticising. This is one thing to be kept in mind. Another is, that the exercise of the creative power in the production of great works of literature or art, however high this exercise of it may rank, is not at all epochs and under all conditions possible; and that therefore labour may be vainly spent in attempting it, which might with more fruit be used in preparing for it, in rendering it possible. This creative power works with elements, with materials; what if it has not those materials, those elements, ready for its use? In that case it must surely wait till they are ready. Now, in literature,—I will limit myself to literature, for it is about literature that the question arises,—the elements with which the creative power works are ideas; the best ideas, on every matter which literature touches, current at the time. At any rate we may lay it down as certain that in modern literature no manifestation of the creative power not working with these can be very important or fruitful. And I say *current* at the time, not merely accessible at the time; for creative literary genius does not principally

show itself in discovering new ideas, that is rather the business of the philosopher. The grand work of literary genius is a work of synthesis and exposition, not of analysis and discovery; its gift lies in the faculty of being happily inspired by a certain intellectual and spiritual atmosphere, by a certain order of ideas, when it finds itself in them; of dealing divinely with these ideas, presenting them in the most effective and attractive combinations,— making beautiful works with them, in short. But it must have the atmosphere, it must find itself amidst the order of ideas, in order to work freely; and these it is not so easy to command. This is why great creative epochs in literature are so rare, this is why there is so much that is unsatisfactory in the productions of many men of real genius; because for the creation of a master-work of literature two powers must concur, the power of the man and the power of the moment, and the man is not enough without the moment; the creative power has, for its happy exercise, appointed elements, and those elements are not in its own control.

3   Nay, they are more within the control of the critical power. It is the business of the critical power, as I said in the words already quoted, 'in all branches of knowledge, theology, philosophy, history, art, science, to see the object as in itself it really is.' Thus it tends, at last, to make an intellectual situation of which the creative power can profitably avail itself. It tends to establish an order of ideas, if not absolutely true, yet true by comparison with that which it displaces, to make the best ideas prevail. Presently these new ideas reach society, the touch of truth is the touch of life, and there is a stir and growth everywhere; out of this stir and growth come the creative epochs of literature.

4   Or, to narrow our range, and quit these considerations of the general march of genius and society,—considerations which are apt to become too abstract and impalpable,—every one can see that a poet, for instance, ought to know life and the world before dealing with them in poetry; and life and the world being in modern times very complex things, the creation of a modern poet, to be worth much, implies a great critical effort behind it; else it must be a comparatively poor, barren, and short-lived affair. This is why Byron's poetry had so little endurance in it, and Goethe's so much; both Byron and Goethe had a great productive power, but Goethe's was nourished by a great critical effort providing the true materials for it, and Byron's was not; Goethe knew life and the world, the poet's necessary subjects, much more comprehensively and thoroughly than Byron. He knew a great deal more of them, and he knew them much more as they really are.

Edith Hamilton

1   Of all that the Greeks did only a very small part has come
down to us and we have no means of knowing if we have their
best. It would be strange if we had. In the convulsions of that
world of long ago there was no law that guaranteed to art the
survival of the fittest. But this little remnant preserved by the
haphazard of chance shows the high-water mark reached in
every region of thought and beauty the Greeks entered. No
sculpture comparable to theirs; no buildings ever more beautiful;
no writings superior. Prose, always late of development, they had
time only to touch upon, but they left masterpieces. History has
yet to find a greater exponent than Thucydides; outside of the
Bible there is no poetical prose that can touch Plato. In poetry
they are all but supreme; no epic is to be mentioned with Homer;
no odes to be set beside Pindar; of the four masters of the tragic
stage three are Greek. Little is left of all this wealth of great art;
the sculptures, defaced and broken into bits, have crumbled
away; the buildings are fallen; the paintings have gone forever;
of the writings, all lost but a very few. We have only the ruin of
what was; the world has had no more than that for well on to two
thousand years; yet these few remains of the mighty structure
have been a challenge and an incitement to men ever since and
they are among our possessions to-day which we value as most
precious. There is no danger now that the world will not give
Greek genius full recognition. Greek achievement is a fact universally acknowledged.

2   The causes responsible for this achievement, however, are not
so generally understood. Rather is it the fashion nowadays to
speak of the Greek miracle, to consider the radiant bloom of
Greek genius as having no root in any soil that we can give an
account of. The anthropologists are busy, indeed, and ready to
transport us back into the savage forest where all human things,
the Greek things, too, had their beginnings; but the seed never
explains the flower. Between those strange rites they point us to
through the dim vistas of far-away ages, and a Greek tragedy,
there lies a gap they cannot help us over. The easy way out is to
refuse to bridge it and dismiss the need to explain by calling the
tragedy a miracle, but in truth the way across is not impassable;
some reasons appear for the mental and spiritual activity which
made those few years in Athens productive as no other age in
history has been.

3   By universal consent the Greeks belong to the ancient world.

Wherever the line is drawn by this or that historian between the old and the new the Greeks' unquestioned position is in the old. But they are in it as a matter of centuries only; they have not the hallmarks that give title to a place there. The ancient world, in so far as we can reconstruct it, bears everywhere the same stamp. In Egypt, in Crete, in Mesopotamia, wherever we can read bits of the story, we find the same conditions: a despot enthroned, whose whims and passions are the determining factor in the state; a wretched, subjugated populace; a great priestly organization to which is handed over the domain of the intellect. This is what we know as the Oriental state to-day. It has persisted down from the ancient world through thousands of years, never changing in any essential. Only in the last hundred years—less than that—it has shown a semblance of change, made a gesture of outward conformity with the demands of the modern world. But the spirit that informs it is the spirit of the East that never changes. It has remained the same through all the ages down from the antique world, forever aloof from all that is modern. This state and this spirit were alien to the Greeks. None of the great civilizations that preceded them and surrounded them served them as model. With them something completely new came into the world. They were the first Westerners; the spirit of the West, the modern spirit, is a Greek discovery and the place of the Greeks is in the modern world.

4   The same cannot be said of Rome. Many things there pointed back to the old world and away to the East, and with the emperors who were gods and fed a brutalized people full of horrors as their dearest form of amusement, the ancient and the Oriental state had a true revival. Not that the spirit of Rome was of the Eastern stamp. Common-sense men of affairs were its product to whom the cogitations of Eastern sages ever seemed the idlest nonsense. "What is truth?" said Pilate scornfully. But it was equally far removed from the Greek spirit. Greek thought, science, mathematics, philosophy, and eager investigation into the nature of the world and the ways of the world which was the distinguishing mark of Greece, came to an end for many a century when the leadership passed from Greece to Rome. The classical world is a myth in so far as it is conceived of as marked by the same characteristics. Athens and Rome had little in common. That which distinguishes the modern world from the ancient, and that which divides the West from the East, is the supremacy of mind in the affairs of men, and this came to birth in Greece and lived in Greece alone of all the ancient world. The Greeks were the first intellectualists. In a world where the irrational had played the chief role, they came forward as the protagonists of the mind.

Rachel Carson

1   Of all parts of the sea, the continental shelves are perhaps most directly important to man as a source of material things. The great fisheries of the world, with only a few exceptions, are confined to the relatively shallow waters over the continental shelves. Seaweeds are gathered from their submerged plains to make scores of substances used in foods, drugs, and articles of commerce. As the petroleum reserves left on continental areas by ancient seas become depleted, petroleum geologists look more and more to the oil that may lie, as yet unmapped and un-exploited, under these bordering lands of the sea.

2   The shelves begin at the tidelines and extend seaward as gently sloping plains. The 100-fathom contour used to be taken as the boundary between the continental shelf and the slope; now it is customary to place the division wherever the gentle declivity of the shelf changes abruptly to a steeper descent toward abyssal depths. The world over, the average depth at which this change occurs is about 72 fathoms; the greatest depth of any shelf is probably 200 to 300 fathoms.

3   Nowhere off the Pacific coast of the United States is the conti-nental shelf much more than 20 miles wide—a narrowness char-acteristic of coasts bordered by young mountains perhaps still in the process of formation. On the American east coast, however, north of Cape Hatteras the shelf is as much as 150 miles wide. But at Hatteras and off southern Florida it is merely the nar-rowest of thresholds to the sea. Here its scant development seems to be related to the press of that great and rapidly flowing river-in-the-sea, the Gulf Stream, which at these places swings close inshore.

4   The widest shelves in all the world are those bordering the Arctic. The Barents Sea shelf is 750 miles across. It is also rela-tively deep, lying for the most part 100 to 200 fathoms below the surface, as though its floor had sagged and been downwarped under the load of glacial ice. It is scored by deep troughs between which banks and islands rise—further evidence of the work of the ice. The deepest shelves surround the Antarctic continent, where soundings in many areas show depths of several hundred fathoms near the coast and continuing out across the shelf.

5   Once beyond the edge of the shelf, as we visualize the steeper declivities of the continental slope, we begin to feel the mystery and the alien quality of the deep sea—the gathering darkness, the growing pressure, the starkness of a seascape in which all

plant life has been left behind and there are only the unrelieved contours of rock and clay, of mud and sand.

6   Biologically the world of the continental slope, like that of the abyss, is a world of animals—a world of carnivores where each creature preys upon another. For no plants live here, and the only ones that drift down from above are the dead husks of the flora of the sunlit waters. Most of the slopes are below the zone of surface wave action, yet the moving water masses of the ocean currents press against them in their coastwise passage; the pulse of the tide beats against them; they feel the surge of the deep, internal waves.

7   Geographically, the slopes are the most imposing features of all the surface of the earth. They are the walls of the deep-sea basins. They are the farthermost bounds of the continents, the true place of beginning of the sea. The slopes are the longest and highest escarpments found anywhere on the earth; their average height is 12,000 feet, but in some places they reach the immense height of 30,000 feet. No continental mountain range has so great a difference of elevation between its foothills and its peaks.

8   Nor is the grandeur of slope topography confined to steepness and height. The slopes are the site of one of the most mysterious features of the sea. These are the submarine canyons with their steep cliffs and winding valleys cutting back into the walls of the continents. The canyons have now been found in so many parts of the world that when soundings have been taken in presently unexplored areas we shall probably find that they are of worldwide occurrence. Geologists say that some of the canyons were formed well within the most recent division of geologic time, the Cenozoic, most of them probably within the Pleistocene, a million years ago, or less. But how and by what they were carved, no one can say. Their origin is one of the most hotly disputed problems of the ocean.

9   Only the fact that the canyons are deeply hidden in the darkness of the sea (many extending a mile or more below present sea level) prevents them from being classed with the world's most spectacular scenery. The comparison with the Grand Canyon of the Colorado is irresistible. Like river-cut land canyons, sea canyons are deep and winding valleys, V-shaped in cross section, their walls sloping down at a steep angle to a narrow floor. The location of many of the largest ones suggests a past connection with some of the great rivers of the earth of our time. Hudson Canyon, one of the largest of the Atlantic coast, is separated by only a shallow sill from a long valley that wanders for more than a hundred miles across the continental shelf, originating at the entrance of New York Harbor and the estuary of the Hudson River. There are large canyons off the Congo, the Indus, the

Ganges, the Columbia, the São Francisco, and the Mississippi, according to Francis Shepard, one of the principal students of the canyon problem. Monterey Canyon in California, Professor Shepard points out, is located off an old mouth of the Salinas River; the Cape Breton Canyon in France appears to have no relation to an existing river but actually lies off an old fifteenth-century mouth of the Adour River.

10 Their shape and apparent relation to existing rivers have led Shepard to suggest that the submarine canyons were cut by rivers at some time when their gorges were above sea level. The relative youth of the canyons seems to relate them to some happenings in the world of the Ice Age. It is generally agreed that sea level was lowered during the existence of the great glaciers, for water was withdrawn from the sea and frozen in the ice sheet. But most geologists say that the sea was lowered only a few hundred feet—not the mile that would be necessary to account for the canyons. According to one theory, there were heavy submarine mud flows during the times when the glaciers were advancing and sea level fell the lowest; mud stirred up by waves poured down the continental slopes and scoured out the canyons. Since none of the present evidence is conclusive, however, we simply do not know how the canyons came into being, and their mystery remains.

George A. Miller

Excerpt from pp. 189–92 in *Psychology: The Science of Mental Life* by George A. Miller. Copyright © 1962 by George A. Miller. Reprinted by permission of Harper & Row, Publishers, Inc.

1 Just prior to the time Pavlov began his research on the higher nervous centers in the brain, interest in the activity of the lower nervous centers in the spinal cord had developed independently in England. C. S. Sherrington and his school carried out a brilliant analysis of the interactions among the various spinal reflexes; their results are today a generally accepted part of physiological knowledge. It is interesting historically that Pavlov's work, similar in purpose and equally brilliant, has had almost no influence upon other branches of physiology. Pavlov's principal impact has been felt in psychology. The fact is a bit ironic, considering his low opinion of psychology as a science, but the reason is not difficult to find. Pavlov did not make any direct observations of the processes going on in the brain. He based his opinion of them entirely upon inferences from what the animals

did in his experiments. What he looked at directly was not the animal's brain, but the animal's behavior. Consequently, all his statements about waves of excitation and inhibition that irradiate over the surface of the brain are little more than plausible fictions; if you opened up the skull you would not know how or where to look for them. His description of the animal's behavior in the conditioning experiment, however, is wonderfully acute. Since experimental psychologists, inspired in no small measure by Pavlov's success, have pursued the objective description and analysis of behavior, Pavlov's work has had its major effect on behavioristic psychology, rather than on physiology.

2   From a psychological point of view one of his most interesting discoveries was experimental neurosis. If a dog is forced to learn a very difficult discrimination between two stimuli, it may become extremely disturbed. The first systematic observations of this emotional reaction were made in 1914. A dog was trained to salivate when it saw a circle. Then an ellipse was presented without any reinforcement by food; the discrimination was easily established. On subsequent days the difference between the ellipse and the circle was reduced progressively. Finally the two were so much alike that discrimination failed. After three weeks of unsuccessful training the whole behavior of the dog changed abruptly:

> The hitherto quiet dog began to squeal in its stand, kept wriggling about, tore off with its teeth the apparatus for mechanical stimulation of the skin, and bit through the tubes connecting the animal's room with the observer, a behavior which never happened before. On being taken into the experimental room the dog now barked violently, which was also contrary to its usual custom; in short it presented all the symptoms of a condition of acute neurosis.

Pavlov explained these symptoms as a conflict between the excitatory and inhibitory processes. Ordinarily the nervous system can establish an equilibrium between them, but when the sources of excitation and inhibition get very close together, the equilibrium breaks down and a generally excited or inhibited state appears.

3   The explanation is ingenious but somewhat unreal. Considering the amount of frustration normally involved in a conditioning experiment—the restraint in the test frame, the monotonous repetition of particular stimuli—the addition of a difficult discrimination seems but a small part of the animal's discomfort. If Pavlov's excitation and inhibition had been less metaphorical, it would have been easier to test his theory directly. But it is not a physiological theory at all; it is a psychological theory disguised in physiological language.

4   Pavlov's interest in experimental neurosis increased as he grew older; he devoted the last decade of his life largely to psychiatric problems. When at last he began to think seriously about human behavior Pavlov recognized that the enormous complexities introduced by language required new explanations. To his earlier distinction between inborn and conditional reflexes, therefore, he added verbal symbols. The conditional reflexes that he had so long studied in animals comprised a "first signaling system." Men, he said, have evolved another, a "second signaling system" of verbal symbols. Although he was not able to develop this proposal himself, it has stimulated considerable speculation and research by subsequent generations of Russian psychologists.

5   Pavlov's contributions to science are everywhere known and admired, but their implications for social policy and their effects upon our conception of human nature are often deplored. Many people have been frightened by grim visions of a brave, new world where machines will condition every child into submissive uniformity. Such fears are fed by ignorance, but some fairly able spokesmen have given voice to them. George Bernard Shaw once called Pavlov a scoundrel and his teaching a crackle of blazing nonsense from beginning to end. Similar appreciations have been expressed by many other humanists.

6   Pavlov has often been classed with Freud as a major source of anti-intellectualism in the twentieth century. In their hands Sovereign Reason, benevolent ruler of the eighteenth-century mind, crumbled into unconscious reflexes and instincts, automatic processes that are the very antithesis of ratiocinative thought. Reason seemed to refute itself. Yet both men, Pavlov and Freud, were true children of the Enlightenment; both believed that the search for knowledge must never stop, that only knowledge allows reason to function, that only reason can make men free. Both were loyal to the highest values of their positivistic education. What they both attacked was not sovereign reason, but foolish optimism about the inevitability of human progress. To dismiss them as anti-intellectuals is a dangerous oversimplification.

7   No doubt Pavlov himself would prefer to be classed with his hero Darwin, with the famous biologist rather than the famous psychologist. And there is reason to respect his wish. Where Darwin showed how living organisms can adapt to their environments by changing slowly from one generation to the next, Pavlov showed how a living organism can adapt by changing rapidly during its own lifetime. And, like Darwin, Pavlov angered the nonscientists whose preconceived notions were threatened by his discoveries. But such anger is the way we pay our greatest men. It is a special tribute reserved for those whose work is truly significant.

꧁꧂

Notes

Introduction

1. James Britton, "The Composing Processes and the Functions of Writing," in *Research in Composition: Points of Departure*, ed. Charles R. Cooper and Lee Odell (Urbana, Ill.: NCTE, 1978), pp. 13–28; Janet Emig, *The Composing Processes of Twelfth Graders* (Urbana, Ill.: NCTE, 1971).

2. Richard Ohmann, "Use Definite, Specific, Concrete Language," *College English* 41 (1979): 390–97.

3. I was delighted to see Miller's style praised by E. D. Hirsch, Jr., in *The Philosophy of Composition* (Chicago: University of Chicago Press, 1977), p. 96. And Hirsch is not his only fan: recently Yale University conferred on him the honorary degree of Doctor of Social Science, addressing him as "Scholar of communication and writer of graceful prose."

4. Francis Christensen, *Notes Toward a New Rhetoric* (New York: Harper and Row, 1967); Kellogg W. Hunt, *Grammatical Structures Written at Three Grade Levels* (Champaign, Ill.: NCTE, 1965); Richard Braddock, "The Frequency and Placement of Topic Sentences in Expository Prose," *Research in the Teaching of English*, 8 (1974), 287–302.

Chapter One: Biology and Convention

1. E. D. Hirsch, Jr., *The Philosophy of Composition* (Chicago: University of Chicago Press, 1977); Joseph Williams, "Defining Complexity," *College English* 40 (1979): 595–609; Patricia A. Carpenter and Marcel Adam Just, "Integrative Processes in Comprehension," in *Basic Processes in Reading*, ed. David LaBerge and S. Jay Samuels (Hillsdale, N.J.: Lawrence Erlbaum Associates, 1977), pp. 217–42.

2. Intonation provides comparable clues in speech, but only roughly so — intonational clues function in terms of information units, which may or may not correspond to syntactic units. See M. A. K. Halliday and Ruqaiya Hasan, *Cohesion in English* (London: Longman, 1976), p. 325.

3. The useful survey in Eleanor Gibson and Harry Levin, *The Psychology of Reading* (Cambridge, Mass.: MIT Press, 1975), pp. 351–56, is updated in Patricia Carpenter and Marcel Adam Just, "Reading Comprehension as Eyes See It," in *Cognitive Processes in Comprehension*, ed. Carpenter and Just (Hillsdale, N.J.: Lawrence Erlbaum Associates, 1977), pp. 109–16. Beyond that, one should examine the articles in *Eye Movements and Psychological Processes*, ed. R. A. Monty and J. W. Senders (Hillsdale, N.J.: Lawrence Erlbaum Associates, 1976); also *Processing of Visible Language*, ed. P. A. Kolers, M. Wrolstad, and H. Bouma (New York: Plenum Press, 1979).

4. Hirsch, *Philosophy*, p. 94. Flesch scores do not correlate very well with other measures of ease/difficulty of reading. See the discussion in Gibson and Levin, pp. 413–17; Walter Kintsch and Doug Vipond, "Reading Com-

prehension and Readability in Educational Practice and Psychological Theory," in *Perspectives on Memory Research*, ed. L. G. Nilsson (Hillsdale, N.J.: Lawrence Erlbaum Associates, 1979). Sticht found that his subjects comprehended (or remembered) less from texts written at grade level 14 than at 7.5 (Flesch grading) whether they were heard or read. Similar discussions may be found in Diane L. Schallert, G. M. Kleiman, and Ann D. Rubin, "Analysis of Differences between Written and Oral Language," ERIC doc. number ED 144038 (1977).

5. Thomas G. Sticht, "Comprehending Reading at Work," in *Cognitive Processes in Comprehension*, ed. Just and Carpenter, p. 245.

6. See, for example, the remarks of Rand J. Spiro cited and discussed by Roger Schank and Robert Abelson in *Scripts, Plans, Goals, and Understanding* (Hillsdale, N.J.: Lawrence Erlbaum Associates, 1977), p. 6; also the work of Graesser et al. discussed and cited in chapter three.

7. See, for example, Robert Zoellner, "Talk-Write: A Behavioral Pedagogy for Composition," *College English* 30 (1969): 267–302; Terry Radcliffe, "Talk-Write Composition: A Theoretical Model Proposing the Use of Speech to Improve Writing," *Research in the Teaching of English* 6 (1972): 187–99; Wilson Currin Snipes, "Oral Composing as an Approach to Writing," *College Composition and Communication* 24 (1973): 200–205; and Joseph Colligon, "Why Leroy Can't Write," *College English* 39 (1977–78):852–59. It should be noted, however, that most of these proposals are based on pedagogical or behavioral considerations rather than the cognitive model I have associated with them.

8. Elaine Chaika, "Who Can Be Taught?" *College English* 35 (1974): 575–83; Mina P. Shaughnessy, *Errors and Expectations* (New York: Oxford University Press, 1977), p. 79; Roger L. Cayer and Renee K. Sachs, "Oral and Written Discourse of Basic Writers: Similarities and Differences," *Research in the Teaching of English* 13 (1979): 121–28.

9. David LaBerge, "Beyond Auditory Coding," in *Language by Ear and by Eye*, ed. James F. Kavanagh and Ignatius G. Mattingly (Cambridge, Mass.: MIT Press, 1972), p. 242. For a further discussion of a model like this, see Walter Kintsch and Ely Kozminski, "Summarizing Stories After Reading and Listening," *Journal of Educational Psychology* 69 (1977): 491–99.

10. See Donald Shankweiler and Isabelle Y. Liberman, "Exploring the Relation Between Reading and Speech," in *Neuropsychology of Learning Disorders: Theoretical Approaches*, ed. Robert M. Knight and Dirk J. Bakker (Baltimore: University Park Press, 1976), pp. 297–314, and Betty Ann Levy, "Speech Processing During Reading," in *Cognitive Psychology and Instruction*, ed. Alan M. Lesgold, James W. Pellegrino, Lipke D. Fokkema, and Robert Glaser (New York: Plenum Press, 1978), pp. 123–49.

11. James Moffett, *Teaching the Universe of Discourse* (Boston: Houghton Mifflin Company, 1968), pp. 4–5.

12. Francis Christensen, *Notes Toward a New Rhetoric* (New York: Harper and Row, 1967), especially "A Generative Rhetoric of the Sentence." Joseph Williams, "Defining Complexity," pp. 600–604. In his recent book *Style* (Glencoe, Ill.: Scott, Foresman, 1981), however, Williams explicitly subordinates concern for sentence clarity to the fit of the sentence into its context (p. 108).

13. Walker Gibson, *Tough, Sweet, and Stuffy* (Bloomington: Indiana University Press, 1966); Roger Shuy and Don Larkin, "Linguistic Considerations in the Simplification/Clarification of Insurance Policy Language," *Discourse Processes* 1 (1978), pp. 305–21; Richard Lanham, *Revising Prose* (New York: Charles Scribner's Sons, 1979). Note also Donald C. Freeman, "Non-Linguistic Linguistics and the Teaching of Style," in *Linguistics, Stylistics, and*

The Teaching of Composition, ed. Donald McQuade (Department of English, University of Akron, 1979), pp. 24–40, and the discussions of nominalization in Roger Fowler, Bob Hodge, Gunther Kress, and Tony Trew, *Language and Control* (London: Routledge and Kegan Paul, 1979).

14. J. R. Bormuth, "New Developments in Readability Research," *Elementary English* 44 (1967): 844.

15. Shuy and Larkin, "Linguistic Considerations," p. 308.

16. The section in Brooks and Warren's *Modern Rhetoric* on "Tone as a Qualification of Content" is excellent and detailed. Their summary statement is quite right: "Tone, indeed, represents a kind of final integration of all the elements that go into a piece of writing. Writing that is toneless or confused in tone is usually bad writing" (p. 478).

17. Wallace L. Chafe, "Creativity in Verbalization and Its Implications for the Nature of Stored Knowledge," in *Discourse Production and Comprehension,* ed. Roy O. Freedle (Norwoou, N.J.: Ablex Publishing Corporation, 1977), p. 51.

18. Peter Elbow, *Writing Without Teachers* (New York: Oxford University Press, 1973), pp. 51–53.

19. Here are two accounts of the writing process:

> We focus upon the end in view, shaping the utterance as we write; and when the seam is "played out" or we are interrupted, we get started again by reading what we have written, running along the track we have laid down. . . .
>
> A more prosaic way of referring to "shaping at the point of utterance" is perhaps to say that a writer develops an inner voice capable of dictating to him or to her in the forms of the written language. (James Britton, "The Composing Processes and Functions of Writing," in *Research in Composition: Points of Departure,* ed. Charles R. Cooper and Lee Odell [Urbana, Ill.: NCTE, 1978], p. 24.)

> There is not much linking, or not good linking, in the spontaneous expression of the mind when it gropes toward a meaning. For one does not usually think in full sentences or in single words, but in clumps of half-formed ideas that correspond very imperfectly to one's intention. The intention itself changes and grows as one talks or writes. (Jacques Barzun, *Simple and Direct* [New York: Harper and Row, 1975], p. 46.)

20. See, for example, Richard Eastman, *Style* (New York: Oxford University Press, 1970), p. 224; Donald Hall, *Writing Well,* 3d ed., pp. 202, 212.

21. William Irmscher, *Teaching Expository Writing* (New York: Holt, Rinehart and Winston, 1979), pp. 45–47.

22. Lanham, *Revising Prose.* His remarks on wordiness reflect this view: "Prose, then, unlike beefsteak, does not become more choice when marbled with fat. Because fat in prose, as in our bodies, affects the shape more immediately than the meaning, a feeling for shape and emphasis constitutes our best weapon against wordiness" (p. 12).

Chapter Two: The Conventions of Text

1. Crews has perhaps the best treatment of the conventions of essay. By way of contrast, the headnote added to the *Harper Handbook*'s fourth edition (George S. Wykoff and Harry Shaw) defining "The Theme" is preposterously funny: "The word *theme* has, in one of its various uses, a unique and peculiar meaning. In this meaning it is the word applied to work done in English classes during the freshman year in college and sometimes to written work done in English classes in high school. . . . As a type of writing, the word *theme* has no other use" (p. 2).

2. Basil Bernstein, "Aspects of Language and Learning in the Genesis of the Social Process," in *Language in Culture and Society,* ed. Dell Hymes (New York: Harper & Row, 1964), pp. 251–64; "A Sociolinguistic Approach to Socialization: With Some Reference to Educatability," in *Directions in Sociolinguistics,* ed. John J. Gumperz and Dell Hymes (New York: Holt, Rinehart and Winston, 1972), pp. 465–97; "Social Class, Language, and Socialization," in *Language and Social Context,* ed. Pier Paolo Giglioli (New York: Penguin Books, 1972), pp. 157–79. David R. Olson, "From Utterance to Text: The Bias of Language in Speech and Writing," *Harvard Educational Review* 47 (1977): 257–81.

3. This corresponds to James Kinneavy's 'exploratory' version of referential discourse in *A Theory of Discourse,* (Englewood Cliffs, N.J.: Prentice-Hall, 1971).

4. Peter Elbow, *Writing Without Teachers* (New York and Oxford: Oxford University Press, 1973), p. 127.

5. Donald Murray also addresses this issue squarely, though his concern is with teaching composition in high school (largely)—*A Writer Teaches Writing* (Boston: Houghton Mifflin Company, 1968), pp. 16, 42.

6. This and the subsequent citation are cited from the third edition of Brooks and Warren, *Modern Rhetoric,* p. 374.

7. Robert L. Brown, Jr., and Martin Steinmann, Jr., "Native Readers of Fiction: A Speech-Act and Genre-Rule Approach to Defining Literature," in *What is Literature?* ed. Paul Hernadi (Bloomington: Indiana University Press, 1978), pp. 141–60.

8. David Siff, "Teaching Freshman Composition to New York Cops," in *Ideas for Teaching English 101,* ed. Richard Ohmann and W. B. Coley (Urbana: NCTE, 1975), pp. 64–71.

9. It is this convention, of course, that prevents a collapse into total and radical explicitness, which, E. D. Hirsch observes, would paralyze communication (*Philosophy,* p. 27). See also Joseph Williams's remarks in his *Style* (Glencoe, Ill.: Scott, Foresman, 1981), pp. 117–18.

10. Nancy Marshall and Marvin Glock, "Comprehension of Connected Discourse: A Study into the Relationships between the Structure of Text and Information Recalled," *Reading Research Quarterly* 14 (1978/79): 10–57.

11. Elizabeth Traugott, *A History of English Syntax* (New York: Holt, Rinehart and Winston, 1972), p. 184.

12. Charles A. Ferguson, "Diglossa," *Word* 15 (1959): 325–40.

13. See, for example, the articles in *The State of the Language,* ed. Leonard Michaels and Christopher Ricks (Berkeley and Los Angeles: University of California Press, 1980). The conservative position sketched by Ferguson is vividly represented by John Simon. Stephen Judy argues in *The ABCs of Literacy* (New York: Oxford University Press, 1980) that we have had a 'literacy crisis' each time colleges have broadened their base and admitted a new, less 'groomed' segment of the population.

14. Strunk and White, *The Elements of Style,* p. 56.

15. The most detailed, practical, and intelligent presentation of this notion is, again, Crews, where the matter is discussed in its proper place— first.

16. Martin Joos, *The Five Clocks* (New York: Harcourt, Brace & World, 1961), pp. 21–22. On the general question of the relation of the units of speech to those of writing, see Wallace L. Chafe, "The Deployment of Consciousness in the Production of a Narrative," in *The Pear Stories,* ed. Wallace L. Chafe (Norwood, N.J.: Ablex Publishing Corporation, 1980), pp. 9–50; Gunther Kress, "The Social Values of Speech and Writing," in *Language and Control,* ed. Roger Fowler et al. (London: Routledge and Kegan Paul, 1979), pp. 46–62; and Elinor Ochs, "Planned and Unplanned Discourse," in *Syntax*

and Semantics, Vol. 12, ed. Talmy Givón (New York: Academic Press, 1979) pp. 51-80.

17. Roger Sale, *On Writing* (New York: Random House, 1970), p. 130.

18. Adrienne Lehrer, "The Development and Use of Scientific Language," unpublished ms., University of Arizona.

19. James Britton, "The Composing Processes and the Functions of Writing," in *Research in Composition: Points of Departure,* ed. Charles R. Cooper and Lee Odell (Urbana: NCTE, 1978).

20. Walker Gibson, *Tough, Sweet, and Stuffy* (Bloomington: Indiana University Press, 1966), p. 12.

21. C. D. Hardyck and L. F. Petrinovich, "Subvocal Speech and Comprehension Levels as a Function of the Difficulty Level of Reading Materials," *Journal of Verbal Learning and Verbal Behavior* 9 (1970): 647-52; see also Betty Ann Levy, "Speech Processing During Reading," in *Cognitive Psychology and Instruction,* ed. Alan M. Lesgold, James W. Pellegrino, Lipke D. Fokkema, and Robert Glaser (New York: Plenum Press, 1978), pp. 123-49.

22. Hirsch, *Philosophy,* p. 66; Richard C. Lanham, *Analyzing Prose* (unpublished ms., UCLA). Lanham backdates the revolution to St. Jerome.

23. Ignatius G. Mattingly, "Reading, the Linguistic Process, and Linguistic Awareness," in *Language by Ear and by Eye,* ed. Ignatius G. Mattingly and James F. Kavanagh (Cambridge, Mass.: MIT Press, 1972), pp. 133-48, and R. Conrad, "Speech and Reading," in the same volume, pp. 205-40.

24. The term *expressive writing,* however, is sometimes used for conventionally elaborated nondiscursive writing—i.e., defined in opposition to Expository Essay (as by Irmscher, *Holt Guide,* pp. 73-75)—though Kinneavy treats it as the fourth major aim of discourse, citing the Declaration of Independence as a prototype. So the term is really up for grabs.

25. Donald Murray is a good example (*A Writer Teaches Writing,* p. 167), though again the high school context must be borne in mind.

26. See Wolfgang Iser, *The Act of Reading* (Baltimore: Johns Hopkins Press, 1978), esp. pp. 109 ff., and Umberto Eco, *The Role of the Reader* (Bloomington: Indiana University Press, 1979), esp. chapter one.

27. Joos, *The Five Clocks;* the place of rereading is a dramatic indicator, insisted upon by Joos and Eco and eliminated by Hirsch's 'principle of linearity.'

Chapter Three: Ideas of Order

1. William Irmscher, *Teaching English Composition* (New York: Holt, Rinehart and Winston, 1979), pp. 45-47.

2. Frank D'Angelo, *A Conceptual Theory of Rhetoric* (Cambridge, Mass.: Winthrop Publishing Co., 1975).

3. A survey of opinions on 'invention' can be found in the bibliographical essays by Richard Young and Richard L. Larson in *Teaching Composition: Ten Bibliographic Essays,* ed. Gary Tate (Fort Worth, Texas: Texas Christian University Press, 1976).

4. Roger Schank and Robert Abelson distinguish scripts, plans, goals, and themes in their study *Scripts, Plans, Goals, and Understanding* (Hillsdale, New Jersey: Lawrence Erlbaum Associates, 1977).

5. Charlotte Linde and William Labov, "Spatial Networks as a Site for the Study of Language and Thought," *Language* 51 (1975): 924-39.

6. Wallace L. Chafe, "Creativity in Verbalization and Its Implications for the Nature of Stored Knowledge," in *Discourse Production and Comprehension,* ed. Roy O. Freedle (Norwood, N.J.: Ablex Publishing Corporation, 1977), pp. 41-56.

7. David E. Rumelhart, "Understanding and Summarizing Brief

Stories," in *Basic Processes in Reading*, ed. David LaBerge and S. Jay Samuels (Hillsdale, N.J.: Lawrence Erlbaum Associates, 1977), p. 268.

8. Richard Hofstadter, *Anti-Intellectualism in American Life*, cited from Susan Wittig, Franklin Holcomb, and Anne Dunn, *The Participating Reader* (Englewood Cliffs, N.J., 1978), pp. 277–78.

9. Robert P. Stockwell, *Foundations of Syntactic Theory* (Englewood Cliffs, N.J.: Prentice-Hall, Inc., 1977), pp. 116, 118.

10. Tom Wolfe, "O Rotten Gotham: Sliding Down the Behavioral Sink," cited from Randall E. Decker, *Patterns of Exposition 6* (Boston: Little, Brown and Company, 1978), p. 117.

11. See James Moffett, *Teaching the Universe of Discourse* (Boston: Houghton Mifflin Company, 1968) and *A Student-Centered Language Arts Curriculum, Grades K–13: A Handbook for Teachers* (Boston: Houghton Mifflin Company, 1968).

12. Arthur C. Graesser, Michael W. Higginbotham, Scott P. Robertson, and William R. Smith, "A Natural Inquiry into the *National Enquirer:* Self-induced versus Task-Induced Reading Comprehension," *Discourse Processes* 1 (1978): 355–72.

13. Richard C. Omanson, William H. Warren, and Tom Trabasso, "Goals, Inferential Comprehension, and Recall of Stories by Children," *Discourse Processes* 1 (1978): 337.

14. Schank and Abelson, *Scripts, Plans*, pp. 17–19.

15. Bonnie J. F. Meyer, "Organizational Patterns in Prose and Their Use in Reading" (unpublished ms., Arizona State University, 1978).

16. P. Clements, "The Effects of Staging on Recall from Prose," in *New Directions in Discourse Processing*, ed. Roy O. Freedle (Norwood, N.J.: Ablex Publishing Corporation, 1979), pp. 328–29.

17. Francis Christensen, "A Generative Rhetoric of the Sentence," in *Notes Toward a New Rhetoric* (New York: Harper and Row, 1967), pp. 23–44.

18. See, for example, Eugene A. Nida, *Componential Analysis of Meaning* (The Hague: Mouton, 1975), pp. 60–61; David R. Olson, "Language and Thought: Aspects of a Cognitive Theory of Semantics," *Psychological Review* 77 (1970): 257–73.

19. Richard Lanham, *Style: An Anti-textbook* (New Haven, Conn.: Yale University Press, 1974).

20. John Locke, *An Essay Concerning Human Understanding*, ed. Alexander Campbell Fraser (New York: Dover Publications, Inc., 1959), II, pp. 98–99.

21. Patricia Carpenter and Marcel Adam Just, "Integrative Processes in Comprehension," in LaBerge and Samuels, *Basic Processes in Reading*, p. 235.

22. There are discussions in Schank and Abelson, by Teun A. van Dijk in *Text and Context* (London: Longman, 1975) and in "Relevance Assignment in Discourse Comprehension," *Discourse Processes* 2 (1979): 113–26; by Edward J. Crothers in *Paragraph Structure Inference* (Norwood, N.J.: Ablex Publishing Corporation, 1979)—though Crothers treats the connective link as established if it is spelled out with a connective word; and by William H. Warren, David W. Nicholas, and Tom Trabasso, "Event Chains and Inferences in Understanding Narrative," in Freedle, *New Directions in Discourse Processing*, pp. 23–52.

23. See the discussion in M. A. K. Halliday and Ruqaiya Hasan, *Cohesion in English* (London: Longman, 1976), pp. 244–46, 250–53.

24. See Teun van Dijk's comments on *but* in *Text and Context*, pp. 139–40.

25. When a passage is markedly disordered, subjects remember that it was disordered, though they don't remember the disordered format exactly.

This effect has been reported by Robert de Beaugrande, *Text, Discourse and Process* (Norwood, N.J.: Ablex Publishing Corporation, 1980), and by Gordon H. Bower, John B. Black, and Terrence J. Turner, "Scripts in Memory for Text," *Cognitive Psychology* 11 (1979): 177–220.

26. Perry Thorndyke, "Knowledge Acquisition from Newspaper Stories," *Discourse Processes* 2 (1979): 95–112.

27. Thorndyke also noted, however, that some stories, by their nature, were more suited to one format or another (in terms of making their content memorable, that is).

Chapter Four: Specificity and Reference

1. See Roger Brown's famous essay "How Shall a Thing Be Called?" in the *Psychological Review* 65 (1958): 14–21, and Eleanor Rosch, C. B. Mervis, W. Gray, D. Johnson, and P. Boyes-Braem, "Basic Objects in Natural Categories," *Cognitive Psychology* 8 (1976): 382–439.

2. D. A. Cruse deals with some of these secondary implicatures of excess or deficient specificity in his article "The Pragmatics of Lexical Specificity," *Journal of Linguistics* 13 (1977): 153–64.

3. Richard C. Anderson, James W. Pichert, Ernest T. Goetz, Diana Schallert, Kathleen V. Stevens, and Stanley R. Trillip, "Instantiation of General Terms," *Journal of Verbal Learning and Verbal Behavior* 15 (1976): 667–80.

4. See, for example, the account of modification given in Robert P. Stockwell, *Foundations of Syntactic Theory* (Englewood Cliffs, N.J.: Prentice-Hall, Inc., 1977), pp. 88–94; the deficiencies of this model as an account of all modification are noted in chapter four of my *Introduction to Contemporary Linguistic Semantics* (Englewood Cliffs, N.J.: Prentice-Hall, 1977).

5. It might be well to note that the discriminations involved should be understood to take place between sets in the domain of interpretation; the assumption of the standard accounts is that this domain is 'our familiar world' and not some specialized, limited world (e.g., one in which all bugs were brown). It is by virtue of this link to the commonsense world that the 'instantiation' enrichment discussed by Richard Anderson et al. can be carried out. There is, of course, a text-internal dimension to the establishment of sets and subsets, namely, the text may evolve its own divisions and subdivisions (causes of the revolution: immediate/long standing, economic/political, and so on), and whichever sets get established first determine the order of subsets. This is just one further point of difference between physical world models and the problems of description arising in more abstract texts.

6. Some would say ungrammaticality, but there is a strong trend these days away from incorporating the principles of clear antecedence in the rules of grammar.

7. Wallace L. Chafe, "Discourse Structure and Human Knowledge," in *Language Comprehension and the Acquisition of Knowledge,* ed. John B. Carroll and Roy O. Freedle (Washington, D.C.: V. H. Winston and Sons, 1972), pp. 41–69; Dwight Bolinger, "Pronouns and Repeated Nouns," distributed by the Indiana University Linguistics Club, Bloomington, Indiana, 1977. And see also Charlotte Linde, "Focus of Attention and the Choice of Pronouns in Discourse," in *Syntax and Semantics, Vol. 12* ed. Talmy Givón (New York: Academic Press, 1979), pp. 337–54.

8. Joseph Grimes calls this 'forestalling intonation,' with the sense "the interpretation of this element is not what I think you expect it to be" (*The Thread of Discourse* [The Hague: Mouton, 1975], p. 291), but this seems a

little too specific; the sense might perhaps better be phrased, "pay particular attention to the reference of this pronoun."

9. Henry David Thoreau, "On the Duty of Civil Disobedience" in *The Works of Thoreau*, ed. Henry Seidel Canby (Cambridge, Mass.: Riverside Press, 1946), p. 801.

10. Stephen Isard, "Changing the Context," in *Formal Semantics of Natural Language*, ed. Edward L. Keenan (Cambridge: Cambridge University Press, 1975), pp. 287–96.

11. M. A. K. Halliday and Ruqaiya Hasan, *Cohesion in English* (London: Longman, 1976), p. 69.

12. Robert Kantor, "Discourse Connection and Demonstratives," paper delivered at the Winter 1976 LSA Meeting, Philadelphia.

13. Charles E. Osgood, "Where Do Sentences Come From?" in *Semantics, An Interdisciplinary Reader in Philosophy, Linguistics, and Psychology*, ed. D. D. Steinberg and L. A. Jakobovits (Cambridge: Cambridge University Press, 1971), pp. 497–529.

14. Bolinger, "Pronouns," pp. 6, 24.

15. Cited in Patricia Carpenter and Marcel Adam Just, "Integrative Processes in Comprehension," in *Basic Processes in Reading*, ed. David LaBerge and S. Jay Samuels (Hillsdale, N.J.: Lawrence Erlbaum Associates, 1977), p. 238.

16. Simon Garrod and Anthony Sanford, "Interpreting Anaphoric Relations: The Integration of Semantic Information While Reading," *Journal of Verbal Learning and Verbal Behavior* 16 (1977): 77–90.

17. Roger Shuy and Don Larkin, "Linguistic Considerations in the Simplification/Clarification of Insurance Policy Language," *Discourse Processes* 1 (1978): 305–21.

18. E. D. Hirsch, Jr., *The Aims of Interpretation* (Chicago: The University of Chicago Press, 1976), p. 55.

19. Henry Fowler, *Modern English Usage*, 2d ed. (Oxford: Oxford University Press, 1968), s.v. Elegant Variation.

20. Patricia Carpenter and Marcel Just, "Reading Comprehension as the Eyes See It," in *Cognitive Processes in Comprehension*, ed. Patricia Carpenter and Marcel Just (Hillsdale, N.J.: Lawrence Erlbaum Associates, 1977), pp 109–40.

Chapter Five: Focus, Emphasis, and Flow of Information

1. Susan E. Haviland and Herbert H. Clark, "What's New? Acquiring New Information as a Process of Comprehension," *Journal of Verbal Learning and Verbal Behavior* 13 (1974): 512–21; Herbert H. Clark and Susan E. Haviland, "Comprehension and the Given-New Contract," in *Discourse Production and Comprehension*, ed. Roy O. Freedle (Norwood, N.J.: Ablex Publishing Corporation, 1977), pp. 1–40; Herbert H. Clark, "Inferences in Comprehension," in *Basic Processes in Reading*, ed. David LaBerge and S. Jay Samuels (Hillsdale, N.J.: Lawrence Erlbaum Associates, 1977), pp. 243–64.

2. Patricia A. Carpenter and Marcel Adam Just, "Integrative Processes in Comprehension," in LaBerge and Samuels, *Basic Processes*, pp. 217–42. See also Teun A. van Dijk, *Text and Context* (London: Longman, 1977), p. 118.

3. Charles A. Perfetti and Alan M. Lesgold, "Discourse Comprehension and Sources of Individual Difference," in *Cognitive Processes in Comprehension*, ed. Marcel Adam Just and Patricia A. Carpenter (Hillsdale, N.J.: Lawrence Erlbaum Associates, 1977), pp. 141–84; here p. 164.

4. Recall, e.g., the work of Marshall and Glock discussed in the second chapter.

5. Wallace L. Chafe, "Language and Consciousness," *Language* 50 (1974): 11–33.

6. František Daneš, "Functional Sentence Perspective and the Organization of the Text," in *Papers on Functional Sentence Perspective,* ed. Daneš (Prague: Academica; The Hague: Mouton, 1974), pp. 106–28.

7. The definition of sentence that we need for this discussion departs slightly from the simple typographic one of 'stretch extending from Period-plus-Capitalization to Period-plus-Capitalization' because each main (independent) clause may be thought of as having a Topic-Comment structure. Subordinate clauses do not have their own Topics, a matter that will be taken up in the following chapter. The basic unit for this analysis then is the main clause plus any subordinate satellites it may have (what Kellogg Hunt calls a Minimal Terminal Unit or T-Unit in quite a different connection). Thus main clauses linked by a semicolon count as distinct sentences, as do main clauses linked by commas in a series (as, for example, in the Arnold sample: *They may have it in well-doing, they may have it in learning, they may have it even in criticising*=three sentences). One should remember, however, that joining sentences with semicolons or commas indicates that they are more closely related 'in thought' than if periods were used, and one common type of relatedness is having a common Topic.

8. Richard Eastman, *Style* (New York: Oxford University Press, 1970), p. 226.

9. Carpenter and Just, "Integrative Processes," p. 233.

10. Richard Smaby, "Subordinate Clauses and Asymmetry in English," *Journal of Linguistics* 10 (1974), pp. 249–50.

11. Hedrick Smith, (*New York Times,* 17 Feb. 1974, Sec. 4, p. 1, col. 8).

12. Rodney Huddleston, *The Sentence in Written English* (Cambridge: Cambridge University Press, 1971), p. 315.

13. Otto Jespersen, *A Modern English Grammar on Historical Principles;* cited from Wallace L. Chafe, "Givenness, Contrastiveness, Definiteness, Subjects, and Topics," in *Subject and Topic,* ed. Charles N. Li (New York: Academic Press, 1976), p. 37.

14. Randolph Quirk, Sidney Greenbaum, Geoffrey Leech, and Jan Svartvik, *A Grammar of Contemporary English* (London: Longman, 1972), p. 951.

15. Otto Jespersen, *Analytic Syntax* (New York: Holt, Rinehart, and Winston, 1969), pp. 75–76.

16. Robert P. Stockwell, *Foundations of Syntactic Theory* (Englewood Cliffs, N.J.: Prentice-Hall, Inc., 1977), p. 157.

17. For the record, Stockwell ascribes contrastive force to the foregrounding of Topicalization but not to the foregrounding of clefts. Note we have accumulated two new visual metaphors, prominence and highlighting.

18. Carpenter and Just, "Reading Comprehension as Eyes See It," in Carpenter and Just, *Cognitive Processes in Comprehension,* pp. 117–19.

19. Wallace Chafe, "Givenness," p. 42; cited in part in Ellen Prince, "A Comparison of *wh*-clefts and *it*-clefts in Discourse," *Language* 54 (1978): 883–906.

20. Studs Terkel, *Working* (New York: Avon Books, 1975), p. 409.

21. Possibly *wh*-clefts are more tightly constrained in the Given portion because, unlike *it*-clefts, they are essentially reversible ("Just the covers are what is rotten")—one would expect this *wh*-clause–last form only if it were relatively less Given. Prince's account of the differing constraints on Givenness in *wh*-clefts and *it*-clefts is based on her own intuitions of acceptability

and occurrence in her corpus of texts. Peter Hornby, working with matching of pictures and sentences, found that a mismatch between material in picture and sentence was more likely to go unnoticed if the sentence material was in the Given portion of a cleft of either type than in a simple declarative sentence and more likely to be unnoticed if it occurred in the Given portion of a *wh*-cleft than of an *it*-cleft ("Surface Structure and Presupposition," *Journal of Verbal Learning and Verbal Behavior* 13 [1974]: 330–38). That is, the hearer of these sentences picks out the information marked as New to verify against the picture and appears not to devote much attention to checking the appropriateness of the material marked as Given. Hornby concludes that some sentence-forms mark New information more strongly than others, but Clark and Haviland object that on any specific interpretation, "one portion of the content is Given and one portion is New, and there is no gradient possible in this dichotomy ("Contract," p. 26). This may be true as a purely structural apportionment, but, as we have seen, the range of options and degree of integration of the material structurally marked as Given is much broader for *it*-clefts than *wh*-clefts. In effect, since the ostensibly Given portion of the *it*-cleft does occasionally contain New information, it is not unreasonable to suppose that hearers and readers would be more likely to check it for truthfulness than the Given portion of a *wh*-cleft. Earlier in their article, Clark and Haviland do mention 'restructuring' as a way of turning an apparently inappropriate *it*-cleft around to make it appropriate. They say that an utterance "must convey as part of its new information material from which the listener can build the restructured given information. These cases should be relatively rare" ("Contract," p. 8). Why they think they should be rare I do not know, but they do not appear to be at all rare in formal written English, if our samples are any indication. It may be, of course, that written texts are freer to elaborate on these patterns because readers may intake texts in the more leisurely fashion described in earlier chapters, skipping ahead or back if something seems to have slipped by them.

22. Ellen Prince, "A Comparison of *wh*-clefts and *it*-clefts," pp. 889–900; the subsequent citation of Chomsky also from Prince, p. 900.

Chapter Six: Subordination

1. Frederick Crews, *The Random House Handbook*, 2d ed., p. 135.
2. Donald W. Good and Thomas L. Minnick, *Handbook*, pp. 79–80.
3. Kellogg Hunt, *Grammatical Structures Written at Three Grade Levels* (Champaign, Ill.: NCTE, 1965); John Mellon, *Transformational Sentence-Combining, A Method of Enhancing the Development of Syntactic Fluency in English Composition* (Urbana: NCTE, 1969). Hunt's work has been criticized for lumping together writing on diverse topics; reanalysis shows that student's syntactic proclivities vary with subject matter and audience; see Marion Crowhurst and Gene L. Pick, "Audience and Mode of Discourse Effects on Syntactic Complexity in Writing at Two Grade Levels," *Research in the Teaching of English* 13 (1979): 101–11. These limitations, however, do not diminish the overall import of Hunt's study. Elinor Ochs reports a study of unplanned vs. planned narratives that shows three times as much subordination in the planned narratives. "Planned and Unplanned Discourse," in *Syntax and Semantics, Vol. 12,* ed. Talmy Givón (New York: Academic Press, 1979), pp. 51–80.
4. Randolph Quirk, Sidney Greenbaum, Geoffrey Leech, and Jan Svartvik, *A Grammar of Contemporary English* (London: Longman, 1972), p. 551.

5. Ilene Lanin, "You Can Take the Sentence out of the Discourse but You Can't Take the Discourse out of the Mind of the Speaker," in *Papers from the Thirteenth Regional Meeting of the Chicago Linguistic Society,* ed. Woodford A. Beach, Samuel E. Fox, and Shulamith Philosoph (Chicago: University of Chicago Press, 1977), pp. 288–301.

6. Teun A. van Dijk, *Text and Context* (London: Longman, 1977), pp. 104–105; Richard M. Smaby, "Subordinate Clauses and Asymmetry in English," *Journal of Linguistics* 10 (1974): 235–69.

7. M. A. K. Halliday and Ruqaiya Hasan, *Cohesion in English* (London: Longman, 1976), p. 196.

8. Joan B. Hooper and Sandra A. Thompson, "On the Applicability of Root Transformations," *Linguistic Inquiry* 4 (1973): 465–97; Georgia M. Green, "The Function of Form and the Form of Function," in *Papers from the Tenth Regional Meeting of the Chicago Linguistic Society,* ed. Michael W. La Galy, Robert A. Fox, and Anthony Bruck (Chicago: University of Chicago Press, 1974), pp. 186–97; Thomas G. Bever, "Functional Explanations Require Independently Motivated Functional Theories," in *Papers from the Parasession on Functionalism,* ed. Robin E. Grossman, L. James San, and Timothy J. Vance (Chicago: University of Chicago Linguistic Society, 1975), pp. 580–609.

9. David J. Townsend and Thomas G. Bever, "Main and Subordinate Clauses: A Study in Figure and Ground," distributed by the Indiana University Linguistics Club, 1977.

10. See the summary of research in Lanin, "You Can Take the Sentence out," pp. 288–91.

11. Dwight Bolinger, "Pronouns and Repeated Nouns," distributed by the Indiana University Linguistics Club, 1977, pp. 27–28; see also his revision of this paper, "Pronouns in Discourse," in *Syntax and Semantics, Vol. 12,* pp. 289–309.

12. Glenn A. Leggett, C. David Mead, and William Charvatt, *The Prentice-Hall Handbook for Writers,* 6th ed. p. 120.

13. John C. Hedges and Mary E. Whitten, *Harbrace College Handbook,* 8th ed., p. 110.

14. Thomas G. Bever and David J. Townsend, "Perceptual Mechanisms and Formal Properties of Main and Subordinate Clauses," in *Sentence Processing,* ed. William E. Cooper and Edward C. J. Walker (Hillsdale, N.J.: Lawrence Erlbaum Associates, 1979), pp. 159–226.

15. Quirk et al., *A Grammar of Contemporary English,* p. 729.

16. Dan I. Slobin, "Developmental Psycholinguistics," in *A Survey of Linguistic Science,* ed. William Orr Dingwall (University Park, Maryland: University of Maryland, 1971), pp. 298–411.

17. Roy O'Donnell, William Griffin, and Raymond Norris, *Syntax of Kindergarten and Elementary School Children: A Transformational Analysis* (Champaign, Ill.: NCTE, 1967).

18. Cited from *Aesop's Fables* (New York: Grosset and Dunlap, 1974), p. 36.

Chapter Seven: Words

1. Uriel Weinreich, "Explorations in Semantic Theory," in *Current Trends in Linguistics,* Vol. III, ed. T. A. Sebeok (The Hague: Mouton, 1966), pp. 395–478.

2. Richard C. Anderson and Andrew Ortony, "On Putting Apples into Bottles: A Problem of Polysemy," *Cognitive Psychology* 7 (1975): 167–80; the reference for Anderson and McGaw is "On the Representation of the Mean-

ings of General Terms," *Journal of Experimental Psychology* 101 (1973): 301–306.

3. Uriel Weinreich, "Webster's Third International: A Critique of Its Semantics," *International Journal of American Linguistics* 30 (1964): 405–409.

4. David C. Bennett, *Spatial and Temporal Uses of English Prepositions* (London: Longman, 1975), p. 8.

5. Alfonso Caramazza and Ellen Grober, "Polysemy and the Structure of the Subjective Lexicon," in *Semantics: Theory and Application* (GURT 1976), ed. Clea Rameh (Washington, D.C.: Georgetown University Press, 1976), pp. 181–206; George A. Miller and Philip Johnson-Laird, *Language and Perception* (Cambridge, Mass.: Harvard University Press, 1976), pp. 676–77. Miller and Johnson-Laird speak of 'construal rules,' which help fill in the more abstract, partially specified senses. See also George A. Miller, "Semantic Relations Among Words," in *Linguistic Theory and Psychological Reality*, ed. Morris Halle, Joan Bresnan, and George A. Miller (Cambridge: MIT Press, 1978), pp. 60–118.

6. It would probably clarify matters to keep the terms *sense* and *meaning* distinct, using the latter for the interpreted word in a context. We might even say words only have meanings in contexts.

7. Geoffrey Nunberg observes of slang that the figurative origins speakers construct for the usage will guide them in their use of it—the 'connotations' of slang terms could scarcely be learned by induction from many experiences of use. See his "Slang, Usage-conditions, and l'arbitraire du signe," in *Papers from the Parasession on the Lexicon*, ed. Donka Farkas, Wesley M. Jacobsen, and Karol W. Todrys (Chicago: Chicago Linguistic Society, 1978), pp. 301–11.

8. Henry David Thoreau, *The Works of Thoreau*, ed. Henry Seidel Canby (Cambridge, Mass.: Riverside Press, 1946), p. 801.

9. Gustav Stern, *Meaning and Change of Meaning* (1931; Bloomington: Indiana University Press, 1968); William Empson, *The Structure of Complex Words* (Ann Arbor, Michigan: The University of Michigan Press, 1967).

10. Mina P. Shaughnessy, *Errors and Expectations* (New York: Oxford University Press, 1975), p. 201.

11. Francis Bacon, "Of Studies," in *Francis Bacon, A Selection of his Works*, ed. Sidney Warhaft (Toronto: Macmillan of Canada, 1965), pp. 174–75.

12. Andrew Ortony, Diane L. Schallert, Ralph E. Reynolds, and Stephen J. Antos, "Interpreting Metaphors and Idioms: Some effects of Context on Comprehension," *Journal of Verbal Learning and Verbal Behavior* 17 (1978): 465–77. This passage is cited from Ortony's "Some Psycholinguistic Aspects of Metaphor," Technical Report No. 112 (Champaign, Ill.: Center for the Study of Reading; Cambridge, Mass.: Bolt, Berenek and Newman, 1979), p. 20.

13. Ortony's claim that metaphors should express the inexpressible and do so with more conciseness holds only for more ambitious uses than Hamilton's.

14. For example, Eleanor J. Gibson and Harry Levin, *The Psychology of Reading* (Cambridge, Mass.: MIT Press, 1975), pp. 421–22.

15. Andrew Ortony, "Why Metaphors are Necessary and Not Just Nice," *Educational Theory* 25 (1975): 45–54.

16. Peter Elbow, *Writing Without Teachers* (New York: Oxford University Press, 1973), p. 152.

Conclusion

1. See the summary of research in E. D. Hirsch, Jr., *The Philosophy of Composition*, pp. 86–87, 122–23.

2. Walter Kintsch, *The Representation of Meaning in Memory* (Hillsdale, N.J.: Lawrence Erlbaum Associates, 1974).

3. See, for example, Umberto Eco, *The Role of the Reader* (Bloomington: Indiana University Press, 1979), and Wolfgang Iser, *The Act of Reading* (Baltimore and London: Johns Hopkins University Press, 1978).

4. Walter J. Ong makes this point effectively in "The Writer's Audience Is Always a Fiction," *PMLA* 90 (1975): 9–21.

5. As, for example, is suggested by Terry Winograd, "A Framework for Understanding Discourse," in *Cognitive Processes in Comprehension*, ed. Marcel Adam Just and Patricia A. Carpenter (Hillsdale, N.J.: Lawrence Erlbaum Associates, 1977), pp. 63–88.

6. Michael J. Reddy, "The Conduit Metaphor—A Case of Frame Conflict in Our Language About Language," in *Metaphor and Thought*, ed. Andrew Ortony (Cambridge: Cambridge University Press, 1979), pp. 284–324.

7. A good starting point is the work of Walker Gibson, as in his *Tough, Sweet, and Stuffy* (Bloomington: Indiana University Press, 1966) and *Persona* (New York: Random House, 1969).

Index